SELF-NEGLECT AND HOARDING

of related interest

Safeguarding Adults Under the Care Act 2014
Understanding Good Practice
Edited by Adi Cooper OBE and Emily White
Foreword by Lyn Romeo
ISBN 978 1 78592 094 3
eISBN 978 1 78450 358 1

Care Act 2014
An A–Z of Law and Practice
Michael Mandelstam
ISBN 978 1 84905 559 8
eISBN 978 0 85700 991 3

A Practical Guide to the Mental Capacity Act 2005
Putting the Principles of the Act into Practice
Matthew Graham and Jakki Cowley
ISBN 978 1 84905 520 8
eISBN 978 0 85700 940 1

Recording Skills in Safeguarding Adults
Best Practice and Evidential Requirements
Jacki Pritchard with Simon Leslie
ISBN 978 1 84905 112 5
eISBN 978 0 85700 229 7

Good Practice in Safeguarding Adults
Working Effectively in Adult Protection
Edited by Jacki Pritchard
ISBN 978 1 84310 699 9
eISBN 978 1 84642 825 8

SELF-NEGLECT AND HOARDING

A Guide to Safeguarding and Support

DEBORAH BARNETT

Jessica Kingsley *Publishers*
London and Philadelphia

First published in 2018
by Jessica Kingsley Publishers
73 Collier Street
London N1 9BE, UK
and
400 Market Street, Suite 400
Philadelphia, PA 19106, USA

www.jkp.com

Library of Congress Cataloging in Publication Data
A CIP catalog record for this book is available from the Library of Congress

British Library Cataloguing in Publication Data
A CIP catalogue record for this book is available from the British Library

ISBN 978 1 78592 272 5
eISBN 978 1 78450 569 1

Printed and bound by CPI Group (UK) Ltd, Croydon, CR0 4YY

Contents

Preface – A Word from the Philosophical

Socrates said that wisdom can be shared, but virtues cannot be taught, adding that technical thinking, examples and tools to learn can be given to students by teachers, but that wisdom to use them cannot be. Within this book, I can give you tools, but you must use your own wisdom and judgement in their appropriate use. The danger of a tool is that in human life, there is always the exception to the general rule.

Here are some of the key things that people ask for in training and at conferences and after reading my articles:

- Can you just give me the specific bullet points?

- Can you talk me through the A, B, Cs of this?

- Can you just draw a diagram of what I need to consider?

- Can you give me some examples of this in practice, so that I can relate this to my work?

- Can you just show me what to do?

- This is what the law says, but what do I do with it when I get back to work?

In responding to these requests and trying to help practitioners understand how to interpret the law, procedures, models, methods, research and theories in their practical application, I try to provide as many examples as possible from practice. I try to engage the practitioner in exploring their own understanding of what this means for them, I draw many diagrams, create top tips and identify practical considerations. I supply the audience with anecdotal information from the stories that I have heard, from my own practice experiences and from my personal encounters.

I realise that I could never create enough diverse examples to cover every eventuality in working with the complex and diverse situations that people present. I stress that people must use their own professional judgement and use my examples as a toolkit, where the experienced practitioner selects the appropriate tools for the situations presented. I am offering potential topics for the practitioner to consider, including law, procedures, models, methods, theories, research and anecdotal situations. To ensure that we do not apply a set of criteria to a particular person and make them fit into our models of work we must balance this with the values, ethics and context of the practitioner within their work environment, and the person to whom they are providing a service in the context of their family and community.

The Care Act 2014 is one of the most significant pieces of legislation for health and social care this century and has presented the biggest overhaul of social care statute in more than 30 years. The Act comes from a largely consequentialist perspective exploring the outcomes that an individual would like to achieve. We are also asked to justify a chosen course of action utilising the law, or a theoretical basis. When working with people we cannot specialise in every discipline inexhaustibly and apply expert knowledge to every dimension within a potential situation. In such a complex world, we need to share our knowledge and skills, pool our resources and support each other across agencies. We must seek that specific and specialist knowledge from others. We must work with purpose and reason identifying appropriate, proportionate and compassionate justification for our actions. Defensible decision making is therefore not just based within legislative and theoretical perspectives but also the ethics and values involved in the process and the decision.

Ethics are based on the theory that to know what is good or bad for a person you must know the nature of the person. This is my starting point in working with a person who self-neglects – get to know the person, build a rapport. Begin not with action but with an understanding of the person.

This book comes with a warning: the more specific I make the examples, the more there are likely to be challenges, exceptions and differences, and pure knowledge of a subject matter alone does not translate into practical application. You must learn how to use this virtuously and wisely. You should justify the use of the tool and how and why it applies to the person within their given situation.

In working with people who self-neglect we must consider not just short-term gains, but also the long-term impact of our actions. Achieving this in context with the person will require us to have a clear understanding of not only their history but also the narrative of their history – of the major discussions and events that affected them, the times when things changed for them and how they coped with or managed different situations.

The strengths and solutions that come from a person's own motivation to achieve something, rather than imparted knowledge from someone else, are key in supporting a person to develop a rapport and feel comfortable enough to change their situation.

I consider myself a bit of a pragmatist and a realist; however, I also believe that in working with people, they deserve the best we can offer. The ethical dilemmas and concepts within this book are as ancient as our philosophies of life. How we put them into practice in today's political and economic climate is a different matter. As individuals and organisations you have choices. How much can you achieve and who can fill the gaps in your knowledge, skills and ability to support a person in achieving their goals? Here are some thoughts to ponder in relation to self-neglect and hoarding.

Prevention versus protection

Could earlier intervention and coordinated responses in low-level cases prevent escalation of problems, entrenched behaviours and complexities? Could this prove not only more beneficial for the person we are working with, but also more cost effective? How could this be achieved?

Consider the benefits to the person in gaining care, advice and support when the house is accessible, but issues of self-neglect have been identified. It is so much easier to develop relationships and rapport at this stage, as opposed to the humiliating circumstances that a person may find themselves in, when there is a necessity for intervention and control is taken away from them. The cost of large-scale clear-ups is huge in terms of the emotional impact on the person and only serves to entrench self-neglecting behaviours. For the local authority, large-scale clear-ups and late intervention cause major financial cost with few, if any, positive outcomes. The person hoarding or self-neglecting may feel that power and control have been imposed; they may possibly feel misunderstood, let down by services imposing sanctions and be less willing to engage. The hoarding and self-neglect behaviours will begin again in a different environment, as nothing has changed for the person, they have merely suffered further loss and lack of control and now potentially have a mistrust of services. The work to develop a rapport and to engage may take far longer and many more services may be required as the behaviours escalate.

During a recent training day, this scenario was offered by a practitioner seeking a solution to the problems they were presented with.

I have been working with someone who has severe hoarding problems. The house was filled with bags of goods, newspapers and electrical equipment. I could not get through the front door and could not access most of the rooms. There were rats and flies within the property and neighbours complained repeatedly about the smell coming from the house. Housing services evicted the person and all the goods were disposed of. This was not the first time that the person had been evicted and a clear-up conducted. The person was rehoused and provided with furniture, but they have begun hoarding again.

In the past, this person had maintained contact with health services and the local authority. They have some quite debilitating disabilities. Now they are refusing to accept medical care and treatment. They will not allow services through the door. They always paid their rent and bills, but now they are refusing to make applications for benefits. In the new house, the hoarding is not yet affecting their access to all the rooms, the refusal of medical treatment has not yet impacted on their health and the lack of money is causing debt, although the debt has not as yet accumulated to significant amounts. The local authority has stated that the self-neglect is not significant enough to accept this as a safeguarding matter. What should I do?

This person arguably meets eligibility criteria for safeguarding as they have care and support needs and as a result of those care and support needs cannot prevent neglect. Work to gain the person's trust and develop a rapport will be a long, time-consuming and sensitive process. The debt is accruing, the hoarding is increasing and the person's health will deteriorate. The person is presenting barriers, the coordination of services is not occurring and one individual is left to make things better against all the odds.

Does the practitioner challenge the decision making and spend time trying to get support from other agencies; do they spend time working to develop a rapport with the person; do they spend time finding someone who can dedicate more time to work with the person, in this race against the ticking clock of the person's deteriorating physical and mental wellbeing? How much easier might this intervention have been if services had recognised self-neglect earlier, at a time when the person accepted care and support? How much easier might it have been with the luxury of time to coordinate services with oversight and guidance from the local authority safeguarding procedures to prevent further neglect occurring?

Therapeutic needs assessment versus needs assessment

In assessing someone's needs could we offer more time to conduct this in a therapeutic manner, rather than a purely needs led manner? Is it possible to look not only for the needs and the risks, but also for the strengths and solutions?

Consider the benefits of finding out about what needs are evident, how those needs came about and what triggered the change to create the current needs/risks. Supporting a person to address the underlying cause and become the author of their own solutions means that we can help that person to regain control of their own life and make changes that do not depend so heavily on service intervention in the future. In safeguarding work, do we need to go beyond the surface of observable situations, or locate the causes of the problems that lead to helping strategies (Scourfield 2003)?

Individual social work versus individual, family and community social work

Do we need to consider the person in a context wider than the individual? Is it possible for one agency to manage complex interventions? Are there benefits in earlier multi-agency intervention and creative support arrangements involving the family and the community? Can a person really be understood without understanding the support, or potential support available to them? Is it realistic for assessment to address the whole of the task, engage in ongoing negotiations with a full range of people involved in the situation, support the person to seek solutions, and address the change, care and social control tasks in a manner that goes beyond the individual themselves?

Consider how long it takes a person to change a behaviour. If a person recognises the negative impact a behaviour has, this change can take a long time; however, if a person is unable to see the negative consequences of their behaviours, sensitive work to achieve change with an individual can be a very long-term task. Engaging a professional, family and community support network and coordinating this support can be time consuming initially, but it establishes real connections with people that are sustainable for the individual over a longer period of time (Smale and Tuson 1993).

Personalised safeguarding versus risk management

Is there a difference between managing risks and personalised safeguarding? At what point do we need to intervene and when can we not intervene? Can we ever have personalised intervention without understanding who the decision maker is in each situation? Is it necessary for capacity, consent and information sharing to be central to the safeguarding process?

The answer to all the above questions lies in the correct and appropriate use of the Mental Capacity Act 2005 throughout all interventions. Professionals struggle with how many capacity assessments need to be undertaken, when they need to be undertaken and by whom, particularly if the person we are working with does not engage well with services. When can we overrule a capacitated decision and share information and when must we make sure that capacitated decisions are respected, even when seen to be unwise decisions?

In my experience as a practitioner, manager, educator and trainer, people are wary of capacity assessments – they don't feel comfortable recording judgement decisions and worry about outcomes for individuals. Investing time in all agencies and supporting them to complete capacity assessments, or supporting each other where there are access problems, is difficult to achieve against such anxiety around capacity and consent. It is absolutely necessary in cases of self-neglect, as it is central to our assessment, support planning and intervention. Is the person that we are working with able to make this decision, can we intervene lawfully in this situation, what are our duties and responsibilities, who else can help, what might the impact of our intervention be and who would it benefit? These questions need to be asked as early as possible and reviewed on each intervention. The benefits to the individual are sometimes more important than the risks presented in any given situation. Practitioners feel secure managing risks, but less secure allowing a person to take risks in order that they have a better life. Robust and demonstrative recording of how the practitioner has balanced the actions and ethics is required.

Assessment – how much is enough?

An assessment can be a short, minimal assessment of obvious and identified need, a process to prepare for the task, collect data, weigh up the data collected, make judgements and decide on a course of action (Milner and O'Byrne 2002). Conversely, it can be a complex blend of therapeutic assessment tools to determine significant life events and the impact of those life events on the person, their family and in the context of the community. Therapeutic assessment can also be utilised as a basis for analysing need and identifying outcomes in a complex history with complex dynamics.

There are no quick fixes in working with someone who self-neglects and this poses a challenge for local authorities and partner agencies during times of reduced resources, increasing pressures and austerity measures. For many people who are self-neglecting, the risks continue to increase, with poor mental and physical wellbeing, and as deterioration occurs the risk that the person may die increases. Public bodies have a duty under the Human Rights Act 1998 to do all that they lawfully can to prevent death. To achieve this, resources will be required, but with comprehensive assessment, care and support planning we can be creative about the resources used, identifying family, friends or community resources and the most appropriate person or agency to support the daily practical work.

Most serious case reviews or safeguarding adult reviews in self-neglect in recent years refer to the key topics related above:

- Has information been shared with the right people?

- Have appropriate capacity assessments been undertaken and how comprehensive have those assessments been?

- Did the right people conduct (or support) the capacity assessments and were any best interest decisions made in a manner that was proportionate to the situation?

- Did the assessment process reflect the wishes, views and perspectives of the individual and when making unwise decisions, was the assessment recorded effectively to demonstrate ongoing work and support?

- Were the culture, ethics, values and background of the individual explored by the practitioner?

- Were all of the agencies communicating and supporting each other effectively enough?

- Were family members and carers identified in the assessment process?

- Did all people recognise their roles and responsibilities (including family members and carers)? Was there a key identified lead person throughout the process?

- Did one agency feel isolated, or did they get the support required to prevent abuse or neglect occurring?

Ethics and values

In working with someone who self-neglects, we have to ask ourselves a number of questions about our own ethics and values:

- When a person self-neglecting states, 'This is the way I am, this is just me' are they presenting a true reflection of their identity? Does the person define their identity by the items that they hoard, or is the hoarding a product of their own experiences and beliefs and not really an identity? (Ontological)

- Are we a product of our environment, or do we create our environment? Do we believe that this self-neglect is part of a person's inherent nature, or has this been a by-product of the person's experiences? (Nature versus nurture/determinism versus voluntarism)

- If we ask questions, intervene in the person's life to discover more, and support change, how do we know when the truth has been found, or are we making a value judgement based on our own experiences and beliefs? (Epistemological)

- Have we developed social constructs about what is a clean, tidy and useful home, or is there a tangible structure relating to the purpose and function a home provides? (Nominalism versus realism)

- Are we seeking to describe self-neglect based on preconceived patterns of behaviour and relationships with others? Is there a hypothesis that we assess the person against? Can we ever fully understand behaviour by observing it and applying criteria, as we are filtering the behavioural responses through our own defined criteria and subjective perspectives? (Positivism versus anti-positivism/ideographic versus nomothetic)

- Can we intervene within a person's life without the imposition of our values, or do our personal values and ethical perspectives affect the work that we undertake with the person? Do professional ethics and values drive our decision making about intervention? Would other professional values and ethical considerations be wrong for the person? (Value-free axiology versus value-laden axiology)

Social work, health, substance misuse, mental health, occupational therapy, housing and various other professions that may be involved in supporting someone who self-neglects each have their own professional values and ethics, which differ from one another, and each individual will add their own interpretation to these values and ethics based on their own experiences. These differing perspectives can to some degree be described within social theory, exploring the nature of social science and society. These social paradigms can be viewed in terms of four broad paradigms (Burrell and Morgan 2014). Figure P.1 is adapted from Burrel and Morgan's chart of social paradigms to attempt to identify why there may be conflicting perspectives, passionate debate and emotive responses from practitioners when trying to support someone who self-neglects.

Believe in the sociology of radical change. Feel that change can be brought about through creating conflict – often to change entrenched ideas.

Raisers of conscious-ness

Radical humanists
(Raisers of consciousness)

Radical structuralists
(The revolutionaries)

The revolutionaries

Person-centred – the person is central to their own issues and is self-determining

A capacitated person constructs their own view of reality and can take action themselves

Diversity of life and life choice is valued

May be a 'lifestyle choice' or one caused by barriers, oppression, trauma, abuse or discrimination

The person is able to take action where they see fit

The person is capable of transformation

Critical analysis of dominating factors, barriers to personal development and achieving goals

Psychoanalysis helps to explore historical abuse, neglect, trauma bereavement, attachment

Behaviourist approaches reinforce positive behaviours

Self-actualisation can be achieved

Society must change in order that it can support the person self-neglecting

The systems must be effectively developed to support the individual

The person is affected by outside factors such as barriers to accessing services at the right time

Financial restraint on services affects the outcome for the individual

Time and resource allocation should support the individual needs

Lack of political recognition in self-neglect results in less funding to support research, service development and awareness raising. This results in the structural and cultural challenge to prevent further discrimination of an already marginalised group of people

The person's definition of problems is the most important

The person self-neglecting should be supported to take control and regulate what occurs and when, at their own pace

The person creates their own boundar-ies, determining when to address their behaviours, consider and make change

Therapeutic approaches should be available to support the person in understanding what is affecting them, interpreting how and why they make choices and behave in the way that they do, in order that they can recognise the need for change

Understand the person's history and how they have developed coping strategies and methods of keeping themselves safe

Assumes that humans act in a rational manner and behaviour can be understood by hypothesis testing

Self-neglect is defined by underlying mental illness

Hoarding is a disorder

Behaviours are to be changed and meet societal norms

Behaviour requires adjustment; illness requires treatment

Self-neglecting behaviours impact on others and therefore require change – social stability and shared public values

A person exists to form a role or function within society. If they are unable to perform a specific and beneficial function they will not survive

Professionals influence the person and determine outcomes

The seekers

The interpretivists
(The seekers after meaning)

Functionalists
(The fixers)

The fixers

The sociology of regulation. See society as requiring control

Figure P.1: The sociological paradigms of self-neglect

INTRODUCTION
– AN OVERVIEW

'I look at every surface and see piles of paperwork; where would you start? I try to prioritise, what is the most important, what am I really passionate about, what poses the greatest risk. In the end, everything is important – that is why it is there.'

'I try to speak with people, get them to help out, offer their knowledge, but really they are too busy, have too many competing demands and my issues are not a priority for them.'

'It all takes time, you have to explore your own emotions and feelings, you have to decide why you chose this path in the first place, you have to explore and separate sentimentality from practicality. When you are feeling overburdened, isolated and alone, this can be very hard to achieve.'

'I feel lost. I seem to be going around in circles, so I cling to information, articles and things that might make a difference, and they make me feel safer. Something to rely on should things go wrong. I guess that it is just a kind of defence mechanism because there is so much to do.'

'They just tell me to clear the clutter and focus on the most important things, but what is important to me and what is important to another person are two different things.'

You could be forgiven for thinking that the quotes above are from people who hoard. However, these are the kind of quotes that I hear in training from practitioners on a daily basis, and they more frequently come up when they are faced with someone who hoards.

The practitioners are feeling very similar emotions to the people who hoard. Read the quotes again – whether it's you in your work, or the person hoarding that is saying these things, the issues are similar: conflicting views and perspectives, different ideas in terms of what is important, time and volume pressures, not allowing a focused perspective on the situation.

Practitioners have difficulty separating emotional feelings, caring feelings from responsibilities, and knowing how and when to intervene. The consequences of something going wrong create additional burden and it becomes easier to say that it is unachievable, particularly when there is little co-operation. Practitioners find themselves going round in circles with these cases and repeating the behaviours that did not work over and over again. They work so hard in such a frustrating situation and can waste a lot of time and energy working with people in this manner, as they will achieve very little without focused and intentional interventions. This book aims to clear the clutter in decision making around self-neglect and hoarding.

Consultation undertaken by the Law Commission in 2011 regarding adult social care identified a lack of understanding of self-neglect resulting in inconsistent approaches to support and care. In addressing risk assessment and management of people who self-neglect Gunston (2003) identifies the 'grey areas' for workers who have high tolerance levels, lack of clarity, lack of policies, procedures and legislation. The lack of clarity has been demonstrated in the different ways that local authorities have supported people who self-neglect, with some reporting self-neglect within safeguarding procedures and others under general social work practice. This has resulted in a lack of multi-agency response, which is essential when there are complex needs associated with self-neglect, such as health, social care, housing, fire risk, potential abuse, environmental health and social isolation. Practice in relation to self-neglect draws from a wide remit of legal frameworks, but with agencies working in isolation, knowledge and sharing of potential legislative frameworks often does not occur. Many dedicated and compassionate practitioners are left struggling with complex cases.

To explore social workers' tolerance of self-neglect we must consider the remit of social work. The diagnostic process of self-neglect is subjective and specifically centred around the issues of normality (Lauder 2001). Household normality is perceived as clean, ordered, tidy and generally healthy, and implicit within this is the presumption that similarity rather than diversity applies (Gerhardt 1989). Social workers aim to challenge social concepts of 'normality' in favour of diversity and may struggle to utilise more assertive methods of intervention and to involve other agencies when clear legislative guidance has not been available, providing thresholds for intervention.

Social workers are involved in the lives of some of the most socially oppressed people within society – people who have little access to community resources and are unable to provide their own care. Due to disability or illness, these are people who are perceived to have little choice over their circumstances – people with physical disabilities, learning disabilities and mental health problems. Often people with little access to resources and who are unable to care for themselves have little access to household cleaning services, or the ability to achieve this and therefore the social worker can become accustomed and tolerant to social isolation, poor hygiene and poor self-care. However, they can often break down these barriers to help a person make positive changes.

People who self-neglect often do not accept the social consensus about hygiene, to get well and seek medical health and some can see this as a lifestyle choice. Freidson (1970), in exploring the concept of illness, considered the difference between those who were responsible and those who were not responsible for their situation and determined that more privileges were afforded those who were not responsible for their illness/disability than those who made lifestyle choices. Where someone who self-neglects appears to be making an autonomous decision to live a certain way and does not appear to have obvious needs that can be addressed by providing services, this can pose a challenge. Being the author of their own events, the person who is self-neglecting is in control and therefore the need, relevance or direction of intervention can be unclear. Practitioners often refer to a 'lifestyle choice', but this book will challenge the assumption of lifestyle choices in relation to self-neglect.

Research into self-neglect has been sporadic and usually via either mental health services or older person's services, making statistical information within Britain difficult to collect. Definitions of self-neglect are inconsistent and responses defined in risk assessment equally inconsistent. There is little demonstration of the balance between the self-neglecting person's autonomous decision making and the safety needs of the individual.

In October 2013, a scoping study of workforce development for self-neglect was commissioned by Skills for Care (Braye, Orr and Preston-Shoot 2014) to review evidence from research literature, case studies and serious case reviews. This research reiterates the difficulties in addressing self-neglect, the inconsistent approaches, lack of definition and therefore little statistical information regarding prevalence of self-neglect. There are increasing numbers of serious case reviews/safeguarding adults reviews demonstrating failures in responses to people who self-neglect and require care and support.

To address the inconsistent approaches, the Care Act statutory guidance 2014 formally recognised self-neglect as a category of abuse and neglect. This enables local authorities to provide a safeguarding response to self-neglect including; the duty to share information for safeguarding purposes; the duty to make enquiries (S42) and the duty to provide advocacy, where a person does not have anyone else to advocate on their behalf. The change in eligibility criteria for social services and the focus on wellbeing create a clear basis for social work intervention with people who self-neglect.

Safeguarding duties apply to any adult who:

- has care and support needs (whether or not the local authority is meeting any of those needs)

- is experiencing, or at risk of abuse and neglect (including self-neglect)

- as a result of those care and support needs is unable to protect themselves from either the risk or the experience of abuse and neglect.

The duties apply equally, regardless of whether a person lacks mental capacity or not. This means that while the wishes and feelings of the individual are central to their care and support, agencies must share information with the local authority for initial enquiries to take place. Enquiries may take place even when the person has capacity and does not wish information to be shared, to ensure that abuse and neglect is not affecting other people, that a crime has not been committed, or that the person is making an autonomous decision and is not being coerced or harassed into that decision. Safeguarding duties have a legal effect in relation to many organisations and the local authority may request organisations to make further enquiries on their behalf. In 2016, the Care Act guidance update identified that not all cases of self-neglect needed to go to an S42 enquiry. This was to direct preventative work or care management responses towards other more appropriate forms of intervention.

The purpose of a safeguarding enquiry is initially for the local authority to clarify matters and then decide on a course of action to:

- prevent abuse and neglect from occurring

- reduce the risk of abuse and neglect

- safeguard in a way that promotes physical and mental wellbeing

- promote choice, autonomy and control of decision making

- consider the individual's wishes, expectations, values and outcomes

- consider the risks to others

- consider any potential crime

- consider any issues of public interest

- provide information, support and guidance to individuals and organisations

- ensure that people can recognise abuse and neglect and then raise a concern

- prevent abuse and neglect from re-occurring

- fill in the gaps in knowledge

- coordinate approaches

- ensure that preventative measures are in place

- coordinate multi-agency assessments and responses.

To achieve this, it is necessary to:

- ensure that everyone, both individuals and organisations, are clear about their roles and responsibilities

- create strong multi-agency partnerships that provide timely and effective prevention of and responses to abuse or neglect

- support the development of a positive learning environment across these partnerships and at all levels within them to help break down cultures that are risk averse and seek to scapegoat or blame practitioners

- enable access to mainstream community resources such as accessible leisure facilities, safe town centres and community groups that can reduce the social and physical isolation which in itself may increase the risk of abuse or neglect.

These safeguarding responsibilities apply to people who self-neglect and whose health and wellbeing are at risk as a result of self-neglecting. People who self-neglect may not engage with professionals, or may not be aware of the level or extent of their self-neglect. For social workers, this provides a significant challenge in developing relationships that empower the individual, and safety plans that are based on what makes a person feel safe and well cared for and respects autonomous decision making.

Self-neglect manifests in different ways. It may be that a person:

- is unwell and cannot physically meet their own care needs

- is mentally unwell and cannot meet their own care needs

- has a disorder that means that they do not or cannot meet their own care needs

- has suffered trauma or loss, resulting in the person neglecting themselves

- does not recognise the level of self-neglect.

Self-neglect can occur as a result of dementia, brain damage, depression and psychotic disorders. It may be as a result of substance use or abuse, or misuse of prescribed medications. In the past, extreme self-neglect has been referred to as Diogenes syndrome, which includes the hoarding of goods and domestic squalor that impacts on a person's wellbeing. According to the 2013 version of the *Diagnostic and Statistical Manual of Mental Disorders* (DSM-5) (American Psychiatric Association 2013), hoarding disorder is described as a pattern of compulsive behaviour, involving accumulating numerous possessions that are not really needed. This identifies those who severely self-neglect, or those who hoard, as in need of care and support and therefore meeting criteria for safeguarding adults.

Symptoms of hoarding disorder can include:

- emotional attachment and distress over parting with possessions, regardless of monetary value or worth, usefulness or need

- allowing possessions to interfere with daily life, relationships, friends, family and social interaction.

Often these attachments can begin with trauma and loss, parental attachment and control issues and information processing deficits. Often people who hoard suffer from anxiety (Jantz 2014).

With the self-neglecting person, it is important to explore their history and listen to the way that they talk about their life, difficulties and strategies for self-protection. By doing this, we can begin to assess why the person self-neglects and offer support in replacing attachment to objects with interaction and relationships with people and the community.

I demonstrate this through a case study of John, who was raised in a house where his parents hoarded large quantities of goods. John often talked about not being able to have friends round to play, being bullied for having recycled clothing, not having access to a good diet and therefore eating large quantities of free school meals and having limited access to friendship, family care and support. John felt neglected, isolated and alone and so he spent many a childhood hour wandering around his garden, clearing spaces to grow seeds and plants. John collected gardening books, compost bins, plant cuttings, waste food for composting, egg shells and a huge hoard of garden-related paraphernalia. Following the death of his parents John inherited the house with his gardening goods and his parents' hoarded goods. John didn't want to throw away his parents' belongings as they were his memories of them. He could not throw away his own books and gardening equipment, because that was his identity, although he no longer had any space to do gardening in due to the amount of goods that were stored in the garden.

A local gardener took an interest in John as he tried to clear a small space for plants. John's knowledge astounded the gardener, who grew to value his advice. The gardener asked John round for tea and John gladly accepted. During his next visit the gardener asked John to come and talk to his local allotment association, who also valued his knowledge and advice. The allotment association regularly popped by to seek John's wisdom and advice. The gardener supported John to gain two days' work at the local garden centre. Coming home John felt sad that he could not use his own garden and enjoy his own plants. Little by little the allotment association brought plants for

John and supported him in clearing his garden. Gaining his trust, they eventually helped him to organise areas of his home so that he could read his beloved books and access the useful resources required for gardening. John became more attached to his own gardening-related goals, valued by his community, and the purpose he sought in life was fulfilled.

When people self-neglect and feel distressed, they may seek comfort in obtaining and keeping possessions; when faced with isolation they may seek proximity to things that they are attached to, and when faced with chaos, they may seek predictability, and might not wish to change that which is familiar. Early relationships can have quite an effect on how a person perceives the world and why someone may not recognise that they are self-neglecting and may even be finding comfort and safety in the situation. There are many tools for the assessment of attachment, but the adult attachment interview is the most relevant for working with adults (Main *et al.* 2008; George *et al.* 1985, 1996; Steele and Steele 2009a, b). See Baim's *Guide to Using attachment Theory to Work with Adults* (2015).

When considering people who hoard and self-neglect, it is important to explore the characteristics and beliefs the person has regarding the objects, their emotional responses and how this relates to attachment to the objects and the excessive collection of them. Table I.1 offers some examples to consider.

One of the reasons why people who self-neglect may not be supported as effectively as they could be, may be down to a lack of confidence by professionals in using appropriate legal frameworks such as the Mental Capacity Act 2005 and the Human Rights Act 1998 (Gunston 2003; Lauder, Anderson and Barclay 2005). In its post-legislative scrutiny of the Mental Capacity Act 2005, the government select committee identifies that, 'Implementation has not met expectations. The Act has suffered from a lack of awareness and a lack of understanding. For many who are expected to comply with the Act it appears to be an optional add-on, far from being central to their working lives' (House of Lords 2014). Social workers and other professionals have also been concerned about sharing information without the explicit agreement of the person self-neglecting. This has resulted in a lack of action and response in situations that not only pose significant danger to the person but also, potentially, to others.

Table I.1: Examples and beliefs of people who hoard and self-neglect

Characteristics and beliefs that affect decisions	
Characteristics – difficulties with:	**Beliefs about:**
• Self-perception and self-identity • Self-determination • Attention • Memory • Impulse control • Decision making • Processing information • Categorising things • Working out chronologies • Childhood/family experiences • Socialisation • Phobias • Trauma • Loss and grief • Mental health • Mental capacity • Health and wellbeing	• Helplessness • Worthiness • Perfectionism • Waste and the environmental value of reusing objects • Personal power and control • Sentimental value of objects • Perceived beauty in objects • Perceived feelings of safety – being surrounded by things providing a barricade to external influences • Objects creating an opportunity to make something useful, or a connection to someone • It being hurtful to discard something • Emotional attachment to objects that offers some perceived reciprocity • Discarding of objects results in feelings of guilt, loss or remorse • The objects providing meaning to life • The objects being part of a cause or a passion that defines identity
Perceived benefits of hoarding	
• Pleasure obtaining goods • Pride in collection • A sense of purpose • A sense of belonging • A sense of security	• A sense of familiarity • Attachment to things • Feeling safe among the objects • Sentiments are evoked • Pride in not being wasteful
Emotional responses	
• Pleasure • Shame • Guilt • Loss • Emptiness inside • Sadness	• Grief • Embarrassment • Depression • Anxiety • Other coping mechanisms such as drugs/alcohol

Results of hoarding	
• Acquiring more things to stimulate positive emotions • Difficulty discarding objects • Isolation • Depression • Anxiety • Poor hygiene • Fire risk • Loss of social contact • Loss of family and friends • Breakdown of relationships • Rats, vermin, flies and other health risks	• Lack of work, education or leisure pursuits • Poor self-worth • Increase in phobias • Increased sensitivity to other people's responses • Little access to community resources • Denial of impact • Denial of care and support • Rejection of services • Poor mental health care • Poor health care

These legal frameworks are key to working with someone who self-neglects. The Mental Capacity Act 2005 provides a statutory framework for people who lack capacity to make decisions for themselves. The Act has five statutory principles and these are the values that underpin the legal requirements of the Act:

1. A person must be assumed to have capacity unless it is established that they lack capacity.

2. A person is not to be treated as unable to make a decision unless all practical steps have been taken without success.

3. A person is not to be treated as unable to make a decision merely because he or she makes an unwise decision.

4. An act done or decision made, under this Act for or on behalf of a person who lacks capacity must be done, or made in his or her best interests.

5. Before the act is done, or the decision is made, regard must be had to whether the purpose for which it is needed can be as effectively achieved in a way that is less restrictive of the person's rights and freedom of action.

When a person's self-neglect poses a risk to their health and safety, intervention will be required. With the exception of statutory requirements identified within the Care Act 2014, such as risk to others, criminal activity, domestic abuse resulting in the person being coerced, intimidated or controlled, and mental ill health requiring a

Mental Health Act assessment, any intervention or action proposed must be with the adult's consent. In extreme cases of self-neglect, the very nature of the environment *should* lead professionals to question whether the adult has capacity to consent to the proposed action or intervention and trigger a capacity assessment. This is confirmed by the Mental Capacity Act Code of Practice, which states that one of the reasons why people may question a person's capacity to make a specific decision is 'the person's behaviour or circumstances cause doubt as to whether they have capacity to make a decision' (Mental Capacity Act Code of Practice 2014, p.52). Arguably, extreme self-neglect or hoarding behaviour meets this criterion and an assessment should take place. Consideration must be given where there is dialogue or situations that suggest a doubt regarding a person's capacity to make decision with regard to their place of residence, treatment or care provision.

Any capacity assessment carried out in relation to self-neglect must be time specific, and relate to a specific intervention or action. The professional responsible for undertaking the capacity assessment will be the person who is proposing the specific intervention or action (wherever possible), and is referred to as the 'decision maker'.

The decision maker may need to seek support from other professionals in the multi-disciplinary team, and they are responsible for making the final decision about a person's capacity. The decision maker will be the person who understands the intervention required and therefore can recognise whether the individual who is self-neglecting understands what this means to them, the pros and cons of the intervention, or of non-intervention.

If a person lacks capacity to consent to an action or intervention, then the decision maker must demonstrate that they have supported the person to understand the decision to be made and that any decision made is in the person's best interests. This may often require a multi-agency meeting and in very complex cases a referral to the Court of Protection. The Care Act 2014 states that information sharing should be consistent with the principles set out in the Caldicott Review published 2013, *Information to share or not to share: the information governance review*, and that:

- information will only be shared on a 'need to know' basis when it is in the interests of the adult

- confidentiality must not be confused with secrecy

- informed consent should be obtained but, if this is not possible and other adults are at risk of abuse or neglect, or the person may be coerced or harassed, or a crime may have been committed or a safeguarding concern identified, it may be necessary to override the requirement

- it is inappropriate for agencies to give assurances of absolute confidentiality in cases where there are concerns about abuse, particularly in those situations when other adults may be at risk

- where an adult has refused to consent to information being disclosed for these purposes, then practitioners must consider whether there is an overriding public interest that would justify information sharing and wherever possible the Caldicott Guardian should be involved

- decisions about who needs to know and what needs to be known should be taken on an individual basis, within agency policies and the constraints of the legal framework

- principles of confidentiality designed to safeguard and promote the interests of an adult should not be confused with those designed to protect the management interests of an organisation.

The decisions about what information is shared and with whom will be taken on a case by-case basis. Whether information is shared with or without the consent of the adult at risk, the information should be:

- necessary for the purpose for which it is being shared

- shared only with those who have a need for it

- accurate and up to date

- shared in a timely fashion

- shared accurately

- recorded demonstrating why a course of action was chosen: I did this because… I ruled this out because… I chose this because…

- shared securely.

(National Data Guardian 2013)

Chapter 1

WHAT IS SELF-NEGLECT AND HOARDING?

Defining self-neglect and hoarding

The statutory guidance to the Care Act (2014) identifies self-neglect as a safeguarding responsibility, covering a wide range of behaviours. It is neglecting to care for one's personal hygiene, health or surroundings, and also includes behaviour such as hoarding.

There are no prescribed characteristics of a person who self-neglects and no 'evidence-based' risk factors identified within the UK. There is no screening tool for practitioners, therefore all tools and models are currently developed and utilised from practice and experience, including those identified within this book. The Care Act 2014 definition of self-neglect is limited in its scope and definition. The National Adult Protective Services Association (NAPSA) combined definitions of self-neglect from 28 States of America and defined self-neglect as:

> The result of an adult's inability, due to physical and/or mental impairments or diminished capacity, to perform essential self-care tasks including: providing essential food, clothing, shelter and medical care; obtaining goods and services necessary to maintain physical health, mental health, emotional wellbeing and general safety; and/ or managing financial affairs. (Bozinovski 2000, p.38)

People who self-neglect can go without food, water, adequate clothing, warmth or appropriate housing, access to the toilet or bathing facilities and required medication or treatment. Problems may (but not always) include poor personal hygiene, not paying bills and neglecting the safety of the individual or others. Gibbons, Lauder and Ludwick (2006) identify that self-neglect includes decisions made by capacitated people, as well as those who lack capacity to make decisions with regard to self-care.

The impact of self-neglect can be significant, not just for the individual but also for the family and wider community. Public health issues such as toxic substances, rats, flies or vermin, exposed wiring, mould, structural decay of the property and an increased fire risk can pose a risk to others. Children or other adults living or visiting the property may be at risk, as well as those living nearby.

Social isolation presents a significant risk to the individual because it is difficult for humans to exist without personal contact. The additional medical and environmental risks mean that self-neglect can lead to the death of a person if appropriate support is not offered or accepted (Dong, Simon and Evans 2012; Dyer, Pickens and Burnett 2007).

In assessing whether someone may be self-neglecting there is an element of judgement, which is particularly noticeable at the lower end of the self-neglect scale. Many practitioners have anecdotally described to me these differences when exploring self-neglect within training events. A social worker (mental health), nurse and paramedic were all exploring their concepts of self-neglect. The paramedic described a smelly and dirty house, the nurse described someone who was capacitated and not accepting medical treatment and the social worker described self-neglect as the person's physical and mental wellbeing affected due to inability or refusal to accept support and she described quite extreme elements of self-neglect, such as excessive hoarding, deteriorating physical wellbeing, often exacerbated by substance misuse. Self-neglect may be a social construct (Lauder 2001; Lauder, Anderson and Barclay 2002; Orem 1991) influenced by social, cultural and professional values and that self-neglect is not an objective phenomenon. Bozinovski (2000, p.52) concurs with this belief and states, 'Self neglect is not an objective, measurable entity or process', going on to describe self-neglect as being a social construct, with the labelling of self-neglect defining this social construct as a problem.

In the absence of operational definitions some researchers have tried to establish common concepts of self-neglect across practitioners. This concept mapping was utilised by Iris, Ridings and Conrad (2010) and addressed the need for a validated psychometrically reliable assessment. While this study focused on older people who self-neglect, these clusters may be useful in assessing all those who self-neglect. Their review produced 73 individual indicators which they clustered into seven conceptual areas:

1. Physical living conditions

2. Mental health

3. Financial issues

4. Personal living conditions

5. Physical health

6. Social network

7. Personal endangerment.

This concept of self-neglect moved from the psychosocial models described by Bozinovski (2000) to a wider concept, influenced by the individual's physical, cognitive, functional, social and financial status. Iris *et al.* (2010) considered risk levels within each cluster. Many studies have considered variables and factors within self-neglect and have been largely unsuccessful in determining specific reasons for self-neglect. I shall utilise six of the seven concept areas identified by Iris *et al.* (2010) to describe some of these potential variables (personal living conditions have been incorporated into the other concepts):

Economic resources available
Social resources available

Mental health

Poor mental health
Depression
Autistic spectrum disorders
Impaired cognitive functioning
Alcohol/substance misuse
Anxiety and stress disorders
Traumatic histories and life-changing events
Frontal lobe dysfunction
Impulse control disorders
Psychosocial history
Attachment issues
High perceived self-efficacy

Financial issues

Financial exploitation
Targeted financial abuse
Inability to manage finances
Debt
Economic resources available
Social resources available

Physical health

Poor physical health
Impaired physical functioning
Economic resources available to enable good health
Nutrition and vitamin deficiency

Social network

Diminished social networks
Isolation
Work
Leisure
Contact with the family
Contact with the community
Acceptance of help

Personal endangerment

All variables mentioned above.

There are many more variables that could contribute to someone self-neglecting and many of these variables coincide with each other or overlap and therefore, 'there is no typical case of self-neglect' (Bozinovski 2010). The complexity of working with someone self-neglecting comes from the barriers presented by the person, access to services, conflicting perspectives and judgements and no definitive assessment process. These barriers are affected by our judgements, values and professional attitudes towards self-neglect.

One of the greatest barriers presented to practitioners is the person themselves, not accepting help and support in increasingly difficult or dangerous circumstances. Looking at the variable reasons for self-neglect, the reasons for not accepting help may be equally variable: a person who is self-neglecting after suffering abuse or neglect may not wish to disclose their abuse or subject themselves to describing the issues and how they affect them. A person suffering from loss and bereavement may not wish to disclose the strength of their emotions and the sensitive issues around relationships. It can be very difficult for people who require care and support to accept that there is a need for intervention, that they are no longer in control of an aspect of their ability to look after themselves.

Having life is about creating opportunities, developing personal identity, feeling safe and secure, and having the ability to be autonomous and independent. These skills are developed over a lifetime, beginning in childhood and are an elemental aspect of human function around creating happiness, security and a sense of belonging. When these skills deteriorate, or are not functioning to support people in their concept of a good life, people can hold on to a need to remain independent. A person self-neglecting may not want to admit to themselves that they are no longer able to provide for themselves and try to maintain independence at the cost of their physical and emotional wellbeing. Many people who have major and multiple impairments or disabilities continue to feel that their self-interest is best protected if they control self-care decisions and activities. This therefore can affect the willingness of the person to accept assistance (Rathbone-McCuan and Fabian 1992). Perhaps the lack of time afforded to develop a rapport with the individual before any action is taken can present a barrier in itself.

Dyer *et al.* (2007) identified that elder self-neglect is one of the most common types of abuse reported in American adult protective services, finding it three times more common than physical abuse. Accurate statistics are difficult to gather from the UK as there is no singular forum for collecting this data. It is easy to recognise why self-neglect is such a huge area and is further complicated by elements of hoarding and the risks associated with hoarding behaviours.

Hoarding disorder

The *Diagnostic and Statistical Manual of Mental Disorders* (DSM-5) (American Psychiatric Association 2013) identifies hoarding as a distinct disorder. The first DSM was published in 1952 and has been regularly revised since. It is an American publication used to varying degrees by professionals around the world. Psychiatrists, psychologists, policy makers, pharmaceutical companies and insurance companies all use the DSM and make reference to it.

The DSM-4 listed hoarding as a subtype of obsessive compulsive disorder (OCD) and referred to it as 'compulsive hoarding'. Studies have shown that about one third of people diagnosed with OCD have a hoarding disorder; however, in studies involving people who hoard, just under a quarter of them report to have OCD symptoms (Frost and Steketee 2011). OCD symptoms feature intrusive thoughts which provoke compulsive actions to alleviate the distress, discomfort and anxiety created by the intrusive thoughts and the person does not experience any positive emotions throughout this process. Many people who hoard report that they feel calm, safe and happy in acquiring objects, sometimes referring to this as being in 'their zone'. The positive experiences can often turn to bad experiences of anxiety, guilt and shame when faced with the daily difficulties of managing their acquisitions. The positive feelings experienced by people who hoard differentiate them significantly from those who have OCD. Frost and Steketee (2011) also found that genetic linkage studies show that hoarding and OCD have a different pattern of heritability and that brain scans on people who hoard show a different pattern of cerebral activation. They concluded that people who hoard show more severe family and social disability, less insight into their problems and, mixed with the pain and pleasure of hoarding, this distinguishes hoarding disorder from all other anxiety and mood disorders. Growing evidence identified that hoarding was a disorder in its own right (Mataix-Cols et al. 2010) and led to its inclusion as a separate disorder in the DSM-5 (APA 2013).

The DSM-5 identifies hoarding disorder as a psychiatric condition that produces symptoms such as the compulsive urge to acquire unusually large amounts of possessions and the inability to voluntarily get rid of the possessions collected. Characteristics may include:

- difficulty discarding things

- a need to save items and the thought of getting rid of them is distressing or causes anxiety

- the creation of crowded and cluttered areas, making it difficult to use the space for its intended purpose

- clutter causing significant distress and problems with isolation, social functioning and safety of the person/others

- hoarding not due to other medical conditions that can be addressed such as physical disability, other mental disorders, or brain injury.

Frost *et al.* (2009) investigated excessive acquisition (part of a broader spectrum of disorders) in a large cohort of self-identified participants with clinically significant hoarding. They identified that 80 per cent of the participants met the criteria, with 95 per cent of their family members noting that the people concerned had traits of excessive acquisition. Frost, Steketee and Tolin (2011) explored this a little further and found that in a study of 217 people diagnosed with hoarding disorder, 80 per cent met the criteria for acquisition-related impulse control disorder. Frost *et al.* (2009) identified that impulse control disorders (ICDs) were characterised by the inability to resist an urge or impulse, even though the behaviour may be dangerous or harmful and identified that 'compulsive buying', a major component of hoarding disorder, is considered to be an ICD. A further study revealed that people who have serious gambling problems (also an ICD) reported problems with clutter, excessive buying and difficulty discarding things. This led to the conclusion that in addition to a lack of impulse control the psychology of opportunity was also important.

Is it collecting or is it hoarding?

Collecting things is a part of everyday life for many people, and children in particular have a propensity to create collections (Baker and Gentry 1996). Pertusa, Frost and Mataix-Cols (2010) identify a continuum of collecting from normal/adaptive to excessive/pathological and Subkowski (2006) identifies characteristics for collecting of tangible objects as:

- the search for, selection and storage of objects
- the collection being systematic and limited to a defined area
- additional interests in the background of things collected
- having a passion for, or dedicated interest in the collection
- a fairly long-term behaviour.

Comparing this in contrast to people who hoard, Nordsletten and Mataix-Cols (2012) identify a number of significant differences:

- People who hoard avoid discarding, while people who collect discard by trading to improve the collection.

- In people who hoard the difficulty with discarding objects is long term, while a collector's ability to discard fluctuates.

- People who hoard have unstructured and excessive acquisition across a number of categories, while people who collect are more discerning, have a theme and a structure and limit their acquisitions.

- People who hoard have a high sense of responsibility towards the objects and can be very sentimental about the objects, while people who collect have less responsibility and sentimentality towards their collection.

- A hoard is large in size and a collection is physically smaller in size.

- A person who hoards does not display their goods and the items are chaotically distributed, resulting in shame and humiliation, while there is organised display and pleasure and pride shown by the collector.

- A person who hoards demonstrates high emotional distress, high social, occupational and relational impairment, while the opposite is true of a collector.

- A person who hoards has few shared interests with others about the objects that they keep, while a collector has common interests with a group who also collect.

Attachment to objects

Many people who hoard items identify themselves as collectors and may not see themselves as having a problem with hoarding. The objects may be seen as a collection because the person has developed attachments to the items. Many of us have attachments to things and see objects as an extension of ourselves. This often begins in early childhood where relationships can be formed with a special object such as a particular blanket or toy. These attachments can be intense and consuming.

At the age of six a fire broke out in my family home, caused by a blockage in the chimney. We came home to find many items unsalvageable. I remember the day because it was very unusual for me to leave without a particular soft toy, a stuffed rabbit. I cried all day and wanted to go back home. When I got home my rabbit had burned feet, hands and ears. I sat with my rabbit in the middle of the garden and could not move. I felt devastated. I would not go anywhere or do anything without my rabbit. I guess that there were many practical things that my parents had to do and they could not address these things with an uncooperative child. My gran was called, not to help with the house fire, not to help with accommodation, but to bring along an emergency sewing kit and put the rabbit back together. My parents recognised the significance and importance of the rabbit being mended. I am sure that this story is not unusual and many parents would be able to identify that special object without which their child would not leave the house.

Psychology recognises the importance of these objects in our childhood development and they are termed as 'transitional objects' because they teach a growing child about gaining independence from parents. Many teenagers see possessions as a reflection of who they are and become preoccupied with getting the most up-to-date mobile phone, trainers, clothing or bags that reflect their personality and status (Jarrett 2013).

These emotions continue into adulthood. Objects can provide a feeling of security, familiarity and safety when feeling anxious. Emergency vehicles often have blankets, soft toys and objects that can provide this sense of comfort following a trauma or accident. Think of some items that you have within your home that have no significant value to another person – maybe a soft toy, your grandmother's button box, a particular photograph, your child's first shoe, or a picture that your child has drawn. You keep these objects because they invoke feelings, memories and personal connections and perhaps a sense of identity, grounding you in your history.

Some people who hoard may like to have objects around them and rather than their attachment to objects being the key issue it may be that they are afraid of an empty, or clear space. One person that I met identified that she had been sexually abused as a teenager and her family had chastised her for allowing the person into her house and not putting objects between her and her assailant. As she grew up she felt safer if she did not answer the door and had objects around her.

Sorting and organising

People who hoard often describe these attachments to the objects that they collect and struggle to separate objects for practical use, objects of aesthetic beauty, objects of sentimental value and a fear of waste and this is exacerbated by the allure of acquiring objects, the opportunities presented and the comfort and safety provided by objects. Detachment from these objects of safety can result in increased anxiety. Can you imagine if I were to say to you select three of those treasured possessions, the ones without monetary value and I want you to keep one, throw one away and recycle one. Which would you choose? How would you sort the objects? Would you be ascribing more value to one rather than another and what does this mean about the relationship you have with the person that created or gifted the object, or features in the object? This would create anxiety, a feeling that part of you and your history might be lost and a sense that people are not recognising the importance that these things have for you and therefore they do not know you. Many people who hoard describe such feelings about all the objects they collect (Frost and Steketee 2011).

Frost and Steketee (2011) have explored the extraordinary ability of some people who hoard to see every object as rich in detail, which creates a much more expansive world of limitless potential, limitless information, limitless utility and limitless waste. They identify why this can make sorting and organising a particularly difficult task. To offer an example of such difficulties I am going to describe a conversation that I had with my son, who would have a propensity towards hoarding if left to his own devices. My son has a diagnosis of autism and attention deficit hyperactivity disorder (ADHD, an impulse disorder) and deficits in motor control and perception (DAMP). He is 19 years old and studies graphic design.

As things begin to accumulate we sit together to sort one area of objects at a time and this is a shortened version of the discussion:

Me: Where would you like to begin?

Son: The shelves, top shelf first.

Me: Bring the things down to sort.

Son: Where do we begin?

Me: Let's just pick up an object at a time and see what you want to do with it. What about this magazine, what did you keep that for?

Son: (Looking through the magazine.) I like the way that the front cover is designed. The art is particularly good.

Me: OK then, shall we just keep the front cover in a file?

Son: No, I like the typography in this advert and I like the article written on pixilation in imagery. (He explains the article in detail to me.) I like the font used here, but I can use that picture there as a bad example of colour use.

Me: So you want to keep that magazine then. Let's move on to the next object. (It is one old trainer that he has outgrown many years ago.) Can we throw that out then?

Son: Ah, I remember those trainers, they were my favorite pair. Can you remember, Mum, how my brother and I used to make dens in the woods? I used to wear those trainers then and they even have some mud still on to remind me of the woods. (He tells me about the dens that he used to make and who was there and what they did.)

Me: How would it feel to get rid of this trainer?

Son: I might forget about the fun my brother and I had in the woods. No let's keep it.

Me: How about we put it in the loft and see if you can still remember the time with your brother when you are not looking at it?

Son: OK, we can try that, but I want to be able to get it at any time.

Me: What about this video?

Son: (He recalls most elements of the video and can tell me word for word many aspects of it.) You see, Mum, that was an important part of my childhood. That video made me who I am today. My friend and I used to watch it repeatedly and even you could say some of the words from the video after a while…

Me: We do not have a video recorder any more, can we get rid of it?

Son: No, it is too important to throw away.

Me: What about sending it to a charity shop, if they will take it?

Son: OK but only if they take it. If not, I want it back.

We have sorted three objects, kept one, stored one and potentially got rid of one and we have been sitting on the floor for two hours. By this time, I can no longer keep his attention, he is tired and wants to sort another day. This happens over a period of two weeks on a daily basis and usually we manage to sort the shelves into some order that he is happy with. We start again every couple of months to ensure that it doesn't accumulate. It is hugely frustrating if you are in a hurry, want something sorted quickly, or have limited patience. However, entering his world is fascinating, insightful, creative and quite extraordinary when I have the time, patience and ability to sit and listen.

Frost and Steketee (2011) identified similar responses in their case studies during research into people who hoard.

Links with other diagnoses

There may be links between attention deficit hyperactivity disorder and hoarding disorder (Hartl *et al.* 2005; Sheppard *et al.* 2010; Hacker *et al.* 2012). The inattentive and impulsive behaviours displayed by those who have ADHD are reflective of those described by Frost and Steketee (2011).

There may also be a link with people who have autism spectrum disorders and hoarding; however, much of the research again has centred around OCD and hoarding (Baron-Cohen 1989; Pertusa, Frost and Mataix-Cols 2010).

Links have also been created between post-traumatic stress disorder and hoarding, although many of the studies have involved patients who have also been diagnosed with OCD (Landau *et al.* 2011).

When to consider a referral for diagnosis

In assessing and working with a person who hoards we may need to consider whether a referral for diagnosis is required. Following the DMS-5 diagnostic criteria a structured interview process was developed

(Nordsletten and Mataix-Cols 2012). The principles of diagnosis were further explored using scaling as a method of assessment in assisting the person who hoards to self-reflect. (Steketee and Frost 2014)

To ascertain whether someone has a hoarding disorder we may need to consider their *ability to discard things and the impact this has on them emotionally*. This might include their ability to throw things away, give things away, sell things or recycle things. It is useful to know how a person feels about getting rid of things and the level of distress that this causes them. This would help determine whether there may be further psychological assessments required or whether the clutter has another attributable reason. It may be useful to use a scaling system of 0–10 to establish the level of distress a person feels when discarding or being asked to discard objects: 0 = little or no distress, 10 = severe distress and anxiety.

In considering *the impact of the clutter on the person*, how does the person feel obtaining the items (the positive aspects)? How would they feel if asked to stop acquiring the objects (again, you can use scaling to determine how they feel about this)? How does the person feel about the clutter, how do they feel about others seeing the clutter and how does this affect them on a daily basis? Please refer to the clutter rating scale and ask the person to identify the image that most reflects the relevant rooms of the house, or complete this yourself if the person is not able to. Some people may not have insight into the level of distress caused by the clutter, or the removal of objects. This may have to be sensitively tested in a hypothetical situation.

It's important to establish *when hoarding behaviours began*. If the hoarding has been problematic for a relatively short period of time, is there a reason why the person has so much clutter? Consider things such as a recent house move, inheritance, or other circumstances which might explain the clutter.

What kinds of things do they hoard and what do they find most difficult to discard? There are usually themes and patterns to the person's collecting that are not instantly recognisable. It is helpful to explore this in some detail with the person to establish their themes, such as animal hoarding, newspapers and books, food and food products, bric-a-brac, humorous items. It is useful to look at the differences between hoarding behaviours and collecting behaviours to determine this.

Does the person intentionally save the items? Does the person intentionally and actively seek to collect items, or do they passively allow the items to accumulate? This helps in determining whether the person has a hoarding disorder.

Can rooms be used for their intended purpose? It is useful to decide how well each of the main living spaces can be accessed and utilised. It may be helpful to ask the person how they feel about each room of the house, including hallways, garages and loft areas. You might find it helpful to use a rating scale of 0–10, with 0 being 'I can easily use and access all the facilities in this room' and 10 being 'I cannot access this room and safely use the facilities'. Has anyone recently helped the person to remove any items and if so what, how and what volume? This helps to judge whether the situation would usually be worse.

Does the person have difficulty sorting objects, or identifying appropriate places for objects? How would the person feel about organising a small area? Are they able to identify a specific purpose for the object or are there multiple reasons for keeping it?

Is the person's ability to function socially and occupationally affected? Some people who hoard can interact well with others outside the home environment and their friends and colleagues may be unaware of the difficulties they face at home. Family member perspectives can be useful. It is also very useful to determine the roles that family members play, i.e. do they live with the person, do they regard themselves as a carer for the person?

Is the hoarding associated with an inability to complete the tasks, such as a learning disability, physical disability, autism spectrum disorder or other psychiatric problem? If a person is hoarding because they cannot physically achieve the task, or because their mental health condition prevents them from achieving the task and they have little or no emotional connection to the items and therefore could discard the items without distress, a referral to the local authority will be required. This could be a safeguarding referral that would most likely result in a social work assessment to determine how these needs can be met.

The reasons for a person hoarding are as multifaceted as the reasons for all aspects of self-neglect. It is important to understand a person's history and their narrative of how their life has developed.

Chapter 2

HOW SELF-NEGLECT AFFECTS PEOPLE'S LIVES

Fire

Hoarding increases the risk of fire because hoarded items become fuel for a fire and have a greater opportunity to ignite. There is potential that the fire could burn hotter than usual house fires and there is difficulty in targeting the water to stop the fire. Applying water could also make any hoarded goods unstable and could provide additional weight that could overload structures causing ceilings and floors to collapse. If gas or electricity in the property is not functioning effectively and alternatives are used for cooking, this could post significant hazards around collected goods. Blocked exits and difficulty manoeuvring around the property could mean that access for fire fighters is difficult and dangerous. Escape routes for the person living within the property can also be difficult. Fires in properties where people hoard are far more likely to rapidly become out of control, causing a risk to anyone within the property, fire fighters and neighbours. It can be difficult to locate someone when a fire occurs in a property where there are hoarded goods and there are many trip hazards.

The fire service can provide a valuable source of advice and support. In relation to minimising harm the fire service recommend:

- installing smoke alarms and testing them

- ensuring that smoke alarms are clear from clutter so that they can detect smoke

- unblocking exits as a priority

- enabling easier access through the property

- checking that utilities are all connected appropriately

- prioritising the removal of goods around any cooking areas or heaters

- discouraging the use of open flames within the property

- discouraging the use of extension cables and overloaded sockets.

Leicestershire Fire and Rescue Service identifies that between 2 and 5 per cent of properties in the UK are classified as properties where hoarding is problematic and account for 25–30 per cent of fire fatalities. If you are worried about fire risks please get in touch with your local fire service. They can offer advice to the person, and services that could lessen the risk. The fire service should be part of any multi-agency response.

Ann Bradshaw hoarded goods at her property in Newton Aycliffe, County Durham, in 2012. A fire broke out at the property and Mrs Bradshaw's 37-year-old son was saved but unfortunately fire fighters were unable to get to Mrs Bradshaw in time to save her life. An inquiry was conducted and changes to services made as a result of Mrs Bradshaw's death. The Durham and Darlington Fire and Rescue Service identified how quickly a fire can spread in a property where hoarding is an issue. An initiative begun where local housing providers identify potential fire risks and the fire service maintain contact and give advice to residents. The fire service also keeps a log of high-risk properties.

The extent of the potential fire risk to others must be assessed as part of the inquiry process. People are entitled to make autonomous decisions and realise their own life plan without interference, so long as the safety and rights of others are not affected.

Falls

Self-neglect, substance misuse, increased clutter, poor physical health, frailty, disorientation and dyspraxia can all increase the risk of falls. Falls can be particularly dangerous when a person is socially isolated and the clutter levels mean that access into the property and around the property is particularly difficult.

An adult serious case review in 2014 undertaken by Cornwall and the Isles of Scilly regarding Mr L, highlights the risk of fires, risk of falls and the risk from the collapse of hoarded goods. The executive summary identified an 81-year-old man who lived in accommodation that was deemed unsafe by fire services due to excessive and prolific hoarding of items/rubbish. Fire, police and ambulance services were alerted by neighbours, concerned that Mr L had fallen and was trapped in his home by the amounts of items hoarded. Three fire crews, totalling 16 fire fighters attended to free Mr L and the ambulance service conveyed him to hospital for treatment. Despite concerns and specific detail about living conditions, Mr L was discharged home without follow-up care. Seven months later Mr L was found dead in his property after neighbours again raised concerns. It was thought that Mr L had fallen backwards and his belongings had caved in around him. The only part of his body visible was his face.

It is important that the potential risk of falls is assessed alongside other risks in houses of people who hoard. A number of serious case reviews/safeguarding adult reviews have highlighted limited consideration of the impact of hoarding on the person's physical or mental wellbeing and the potential risks within the property at the point of hospital discharge. Environmental visits may be required by an occupational therapist to consider the person's ability to manage their home environment following discharge from hospital.

Housing

A housing provider must be confident that anyone signing a tenancy agreement has the capacity to understand the requirements and conditions of the tenancy, recognise what they can and cannot do and the consequences of not complying with the agreement. If a person does not understand the tenancy agreement in the first place, then it is unlikely that they will or can comply with it and therefore it may be difficult to take action against a person who is non-compliant. In many cases of self-neglect, it is difficult to determine whether the person neglecting themselves and their home environment understood the conditions of the tenancy agreement at the time of signing it.

The Mental Capacity Act 2005 applies where a housing provider is unsure about whether the person does or does not understand and a capacity assessment should be conducted. The housing officer is often best placed to conduct this capacity assessment regarding the tenancy agreement because they understand the requirements of the tenancy and therefore are best placed to determine whether the person themselves can understand the agreement. The housing provider would also be best placed to try all possible methods of enabling the person to understand the requirements.

The Court of Protection (2012) offered guidance regarding capacity and consent in relation to signing a tenancy agreement:

> If a person lacks the mental capacity to make his or her own informed decision about whether or not to accept a tenancy offer, then an appropriate person can make the decision through the best interest process outlined in the Mental Capacity Act 2005.
>
> Alternatively, if there is a registered enduring or lasting power of attorney in place; or a deputy for property and affairs has already been appointed, then the attorney or deputy would usually make that decision.
>
> Although the Mental Capacity Act 2005 enables the making of certain decisions without the need to obtain any formal authority to act, it does not extend to signing legal documents, such as tenancy agreements. Someone can only sign a tenancy agreement on the person's behalf if they are:
>
> - an attorney under a registered lasting power of attorney (LPA) or enduring power of attorney (EPA)
>
> - a deputy appointed by the Court of Protection
>
> - someone else authorised to sign by the Court of Protection.
>
> In some circumstances, landlords may be willing to accept unsigned tenancies.

This means that the housing provider will have to determine whether it is in the best interests of the person to have the tenancy and whether they are happy to record a best interest decision rather than have a signed tenancy agreement. It is important that people with mental ill health and disabilities are not discriminated against as a result of this process. In circumstances whether there is dispute or a lack of clarity about whether the housing offered would be in the person's best interests, then an application can be made to the court for decision-making purposes.

If a person is believed to be capacitated at the point of signing the tenancy agreement, but there is reason to believe that they have subsequently lost capacity to make decisions relating to the upkeep of the property, then a review of the agreement should take place and the above rules followed if the person is assessed as lacking capacity to recognise or understand the terms and conditions of their tenancy agreement.

Housing providers recognising that someone is not maintaining a tenancy agreement – for example the house is falling into a state of disrepair, there are issues with hoarding or other risks – should consider sharing this information with appropriate authorities such as the local authority and fire service.

If housing providers recognise early indicators of self-neglect this helps to create enough time to develop rapport with a person self-neglecting. The person can be supported and agencies can put in place preventative strategies, assess the person's capacity to make all relevant decisions, access care and support to maintain their mental and physical wellbeing and prevent more drastic and intrusive forms of intervention further down the line. Consider the level of self-neglect and whether a safeguarding referral is required (see eligibility criteria for safeguarding adults, Chapter 4).

Hoarding and neglect of the home environment can lead to fire risk, structural damage, rats, flies, vermin and potentially toxic substances within the property. Housing providers must consider the person's capacity to consent to any repairs carried out. If the person is assessed as lacking capacity to consent then concerns must be shared in a multi-agency safeguarding forum. The balance of best interest decisions (including least restrictive options) and the impact that any imposed intervention may have on the person must be weighed appropriately and proportionately with the risk to others. This decision may require the gathering of information from a number of sources. Whether a person is capacitated or not in making these decisions, a safeguarding referral to the local authority should be considered (follow local authority safeguarding procedures).

Physical and mental health

The first case of self-neglect that I experienced was an elderly lady (Mrs X) who had psychosis. I was a student social worker in my final year and it was my first independent statutory home visit. I knocked on her door and no one answered. I walked around the back of the property and knocked on the back door, still no answer. The garden was littered and unkempt and something blocked any view through the windows. The lady lived alone and records identified that she rarely ventured out as her mobility had deteriorated. GP records showed that she had chronic and painful arthritis, but rarely engaged to seek treatment or medication. I knocked on the neighbours' doors and they told me that they had not seen or heard her in a while. I eventually called the police.

When we entered the property, there were bags about three-foot-high on the floor and flies lifted from them with every footstep. Old newspapers were laid on top to create a pathway through the house. Many of the bags were filled with used incontinence pads. Mrs X must have ran out of pads at some point as faeces and urine was found in a number of receptacles around the property. The window, walls and sockets were lined with tin foil. Records showed that Mrs X believed that aliens were trying to get to her and that they would not be able to find her if she blocked all outlets with tin foil.

The kitchen was inaccessible, and rotting food sat on top of boxes and plastic containers. The room as filled with mould. The bedroom was also inaccessible.

Following the trail of old newspapers into the living room I could see an old armchair on top of all the newspapers and bags. In the armchair sat Mrs X with her feet in a bucket of water. Mrs X had been dead for quite some time. She had become so physically unwell that she was no longer able to navigate her way across the living room, no longer able to get food or water and so mentally unwell that she had been too afraid to leave the house. The combination of lack of physical and mental wellbeing had not been considered. In the doorway were piled numerous letters, many stamped with the hospital or health logos, but Mrs X had not opened any of them, as she couldn't make it to the door. Mental health records had focused on her mental health issues and while they referenced her physical wellbeing, they did not make any plans in relation to this.

Mental and physical wellbeing must not be seen as distinct separate entities and often poor physical health and isolation can impact on a person's mental wellbeing, or a person mental wellbeing makes it difficult for them to access treatment for physical conditions.

The interface between mental health and substance misuse can often be difficult to navigate. A person's mental wellbeing cannot be assessed while they are heavily intoxicated and a person cannot be made to change behaviours relating to alcohol or drugs. They must be encouraged and motivated to engage in the process.

Services need to support each other, rather than working in silos. This can be achieved in cases of self-neglect via well-coordinated, multi-disciplinary safeguarding strategies and the support of senior managers in breaking down access barriers to services when risks are increasing. Pathways between services should be clear in policies and procedures.

Families and carers

Caring for one or more people can pose significant constrictions on a person's ability to care for themselves. Braye *et al.* (2014) explored policy and practice in self-neglect and interviewed a range of people to understand how local authorities and partner agencies work with people who self-neglect. One respondent referred to a survey of carers, carried out every two years, which asked whether they experienced difficulties in looking after themselves. In the last survey, 56 carers (18.5 per cent) had indicated that they felt they were neglecting themselves. Many respondents in this survey recognised the difficulties in identifying a consistent definition of self-neglect and for carers, this can cover a wide range of issues such as overuse of alcohol to manage difficulties, or little time to see to their own physical and mental wellbeing.

As a preventative measure, all carers' assessments should seek further information about a carer's wellbeing and ability to provide for their own mental and physical wellbeing. Where self-neglect is apparent, a whole family approach to assessment may be required to assess the interface between meeting the needs of the cared for, as well as the carers. This should also include the carer's ability to provide or continue to provide care and, where appropriate, should include capacity assessments. In the case of Adult A in South Tyneside in 2015, the son took a lead role in advocating for his mother; however, no assessment of his ability to provide care took place. The son did not live locally to his mother. In the case of Mrs Q and Mrs W, in South Tyneside in 2010, family members were relied on to ensure that the women's basic needs were met. There was no assessment of the families' ability to provide this role. This appears to be a common theme in serious case reviews/safeguarding adults reviews (see Chapter 3).

Sometimes more than one person in a household is self-neglecting and a whole-family approach is required. Sometimes one person is self-neglecting and the other is neglectful. Where carers have responsibilities to meet particular needs, these identified needs, along with the carer's responsibilities to meet the need, should be recorded on any care and support plan. This clearly establishes the caring duties and responsibilities. We should be informing the carer that if anything changes they should get in touch with the local authority or health care professional managing the care. The duty to provide care in relation to meeting a need will have to be clearly explained to the person with caring responsibilities. Wilful neglect of anyone lacking capacity to make a decision about their own care provision may be seen as a safeguarding issue, or even a crime. Capacity assessments are required to determine whether a case is self-neglect (capacitated person) or neglect (a non-capacitated person with carers). Where there is suspicion of the latter, all possible support should have been offered to the carer to ensure that they are able to manage care provision and recognise the potential consequences of not seeking appropriate support at the right time.

Where family members are obstructive, reside in the same house but do not identify as carers, or are hostile towards service intervention, serious case reviews/safeguarding adults reviews have identified potential prosecution of carers. The death of Adult D in Newcastle upon Tyne in 2014 identified this in relation to the son's repeated attempts to prevent access to his father for the purpose of care and support.

Chapter 3

THEMES FROM ADULT SERIOUS CASE REVIEWS OR SAFEGUARDING ADULT REVIEWS

The purpose of a safeguarding adults review is described within the Care Act statutory guidance (2017) as to 'promote effective learning and improvement action to prevent future deaths or serious harm occurring again'. The Social Care Institute for Excellence (2015) identifies the need to agree an incident causation model that contextualises individual practitioner decision making, actions and inactions. Its report warns against 'hindsight bias' and recognises that knowledge of the tragic outcome could affect how decisions and actions are judged. The report also asks safeguarding adults boards to gain an understanding of what happened in a case and why, considering what causes failure to protect adults effectively, in order that safeguarding actions can be informed by these experiences.

To gain an understanding of common themes in cases of self-neglect, a framework for thematic review was developed considering 30 safeguarding adults reviews, domestic homicide reviews and safeguarding adults reviews (executive summaries) since 2010 that relate to self-neglect and wider literature identified within the bibliography of this book. Themes were correlated into particular clusters from the identified findings and lessons to be learned:

1. Identifying self-neglect

2. Care Act compliant enquiries (S42)

3. Risk to others

4. Risk assessment

5. Carers' assessment

6. Mental health and substance misuse

7. Capacity and consent

8. Advocacy and representation

9. Multi-agency response

10. Comprehensive and holistic assessment

11. Person's compliance and insight

12. Imposed sanctions, compliance or penalties

13. Information sharing

14. Personalised safeguarding

15. Management support and response

16. Defensible decision making.

The reviews were considered in relation to an ethical balance of:

1. beneficence (the doing of good; active kindness; caring)

2. non-maleficence (doing no harm; not inflicting harm on others)

3. justice (being fair, moral and equitable)

4. autonomy (freedom from external control and influence; independence).

Ethical decision-making considerations
Beneficence (the doing of good; active kindness; caring)

Practitioners often cite their 'duty of care' and their need to intervene when someone is making choices that affect their health, happiness or fulfillment in life, resulting in harm, illness, suffering or neglect. Under Article 2 of the Human Rights Act 1998 we have a duty to protect life. If someone believes that the intervention is life saving then they can intervene with the consent of the person, or in the best interests of an incapacitated person. A valid advanced decision can prevent intervention, even in lifesaving situations where the refusal of the specific treatment is identified. If someone holds a lasting power of attorney for the person's health and wellbeing and the person is incapacitated then the lasting power of attorney will be the decision maker. Any conflicts within these processes may require a court decision.

The Mental Capacity Act 2005 identifies that capacitated people are entitled to make unwise decisions. People have the right to autonomy and a private life. Our duty of care should not be confused with overly intrusive interventions into a person's private life, including autonomous decision making.

In making any best interest decision for an incapacitated person, we must weigh the benefits and the risks of any proposed action with their wishes, values, identity and expectations, and ensure that the person is not subject to a life of misery as a result of our actions. Paternalistic responses must be avoided, interventions must be proportionate to the risk presented and the practitioner must identify the least intrusive or restrictive intervention for the situation, creating all possible opportunity to maintain a life course chosen by the person.

This can be difficult to achieve, as we must first ensure that we have assessed the person and their wishes effectively enough to differentiate between their identity, wishes, values and expectations and their defence mechanisms after suffering loss, trauma, bereavement or being a victim of crime. We must also consider whether the person's mental health is stable enough to make these decisions, or whether a Mental Health Act assessment is required. We may also need to consider fluctuating capacity and the impact that this has on decision making, for example when someone misuses substances. These enquiries will take time and will need the cooperation of a number of agencies.

The benefits of the intervention are weighed against the risks and costs. For example, large-scale clear-ups in a property where someone is hoarding are not beneficial to the person concerned. A person who is attached to their objects, using their objects as a form of comfort, security or as a coping mechanism, is not going to stop collecting objects unless the underlying reasons are addressed. Often people collect goods as a way of maintaining some control and if we remove these things without exploring with the person other methods of gaining power and control in their lives, then the loss of the goods will only exacerbate any loss already experienced. The collecting will become worse, the trust will be lost and it is likely that the self-neglect will worsen. In monetary terms, the cost of clearing the goods may be substantial, with very little reward. The risk to others must be considered in proportion to the situation and the least intrusive intervention proportionate to the risks must be considered.

Non-maleficence (doing no harm; not inflicting harm on others)

A person self-neglecting cannot choose to place others at risk. The safeguarding process must establish the risk to other people at the property, or visiting the property. This may include children, other vulnerable adults or the interplay between caring responsibilities within the place of residence. A person self-neglecting cannot pose a fire risk to others or a public health risk to others. Our responses to these risks must be proportionate and consider the least restrictive and intrusive intervention.

Justice (being fair, moral and equitable)

There are three basic elements to justice:

- Fair distribution of resources

- Respect for people's rights to be free from oppression and discrimination

- Respect for the law.

People who self-neglect are often labelled as problematic, eccentric, obstructive, difficult and challenging and rarely are the qualities or strengths of a person identified. The barriers in working with the person can be seen as 'too difficult' and they are passed from service to service without justifiable reason and with no key lead person to coordinate the care provision across the services. Cases are regularly closed when risks are escalating. The intensive work required to engage someone who is refusing services is not readily available within the current economic climate. Resources are often redeployed to those more accepting of help.

The allocation of resources must be balanced alongside the risks. If you were a doctor and you had ten patients who required a variety of minor operations totalling 15 hours' work, or one person who was going to die if you did not intervene, despite it being time consuming, there would be no question about allocating resources to lifesaving interventions. There have been safeguarding adults reviews where the escalation of self-neglect would certainly lead to death without intervention, but resources were redistributed to others who had less immediate need for intervention.

Any assessment process when safeguarding a person must consider the cultural and religious background of the person and whether this impacts on their decision making. Historical or current abuse or neglect must be explored with the person to determine whether the impact of the abuse or neglect has resulted in them neglecting themselves. Caring responsibilities and the ability of the person to afford time to care for themselves should be explored. These are all issues where power, control and the understanding of diverse responses to things such as medicine, acceptance of care and support must be understood to assist us in understanding the person and breaking down barriers of oppression and discrimination.

It may be that a person is self-neglecting as a result of trauma or abuse. There may be domestic abuse, anti-social behaviour directed towards the person, or historical abuse. Circumstances may mean that the person is too intimidated or distressed to report a crime. A safeguarding referral may still be required to rule out capacity issues, consent, coercion and a potential risk to others. A person cannot choose to break the law and once we identify a potential crime this information should be shared with the police, or other appropriate bodies, unless the sharing of information would increase the risks to the person or others. The police will make enquiries and determine whether it is in the public interest to prosecute.

Autonomy (freedom from external control and influence; independence)

Autonomy falls under Article 8 of the Human Rights Act 1998 – the right to a private life. The obligation is to refrain from interference and this encompasses the importance of personal dignity. Autonomy is rooted in the deontological traditions established by Immanuel Kant, which emphasise respect for an individual and their ability to establish and realise a life plan without interference, so long as the rights of others are not denied (Rathbone-McCuan and Fabian 1992).

Autonomy also means that a person is entitled to make a decision free from outside influences, coercion, intimidation or interference. This means that if individuals are capable of making decisions, can understand the consequences of those decisions and are able to communicate this to us, and the welfare of others is not affected, then they are entitled to make those decisions and we must respect any autonomous decision made. We do not have the right to interfere with their self-determined course of action, otherwise we may be violating their right to a private life.

The legislation that predominates decision making in relation to capacity and consent is the Mental Capacity Act (2005). We must assume that someone has capacity unless there are circumstances that lead us to question this. We must then assess the capacity of that individual for that particular decision at that particular time. This means applying the two-part capacity assessment – the diagnostic and functional tests under the Mental Capacity Act 2005.

Article 8 of the Human Rights Act (1998) identifies that:

Everyone has the right to respect for his private and family life, his home and his correspondence. There shall be no interference by a public authority with the exercise of this right except such as is in accordance with the law and is necessary in a democratic society in the interests of national security, public safety or the economic well-being of the country, for the prevention of disorder or crime, for the protection of health or morals, or for the protection of the rights and freedoms of others.

The Care Act (2017) guidance identifies that information may be shared on a need-to-know basis where the person lacks capacity to make that decision and it is deemed to be in their best interests to share relevant information with relevant people. The guidance stresses that confidentiality must not be confused with secrecy and states:

Informed consent should be obtained but, if this is not possible and other adults are at risk of abuse or neglect, it may be necessary to override the requirement; and it is inappropriate for agencies to give assurances of absolute confidentiality in cases where there are concerns about abuse, particularly in those situations when other vulnerable people may be at risk.

Abuse, crime, capacity and risk to others all need to be explored via a safeguarding enquiry. This may take a little time to develop a rapport, identify risks and coordinate and conduct the relevant capacity assessments. It is also important to understand the underlying reasons for self-neglect and identify any possible associated crime such as anti-social behaviour, domestic abuse, historical abuse, hate/mate crime or other forms of abuse that may have led to self-neglect. If domestic abuse is suspected then the potential coercion of the person in relation to their decision making needs to be considered and ruled out. These actions will require the sharing of relevant information with relevant people in a coordinated safeguarding enquiry, with a key identified lead. A decision is not autonomous if the person has been coerced or intimidated into making that decision.

Frank lived on a large council estate and following the death of his mother he remained a tenant in the property. Frank struggled to come to terms with the death of his mother and talked about a life full of loss. Excessive alcohol consumption left Frank with memory and coordination problems. Local youths befriended Frank and used his house for drinking and partying. Frank was afraid of the youths and was intimidated into paying for alcohol. The youths threatened Frank saying that bad things would happen to him if he told anyone about their activities. Frank told services that he did not want their help. He was desperate to get help and rid his life of the torment caused by the youths, but it took many years of abuse before he was served with eviction and finally confided in the housing worker.

Jenny lived with her husband who was controlling and abusive, regularly deriding her abilities. Jenny stopped looking after herself and the house, giving greater rise to aggressive and controlling behaviours. Jenny was told how to wash a dish, how to clean an item, but the cleanliness of each item was to be achieved to such a meticulous standard that she never managed to achieve very much and the house remained cluttered and difficult to manage. Jenny's husband refused any help or support offered. Jenny became ill, depressed and anxious and feared people asking after her, as this often resulted in further insults about her own ability to cope. Eventually a referral was made to the local authority by concerned neighbours, the telephone call was to Jenny to see if she would consent to an assessment. Jenny wanted care and support but was too afraid to allow anyone into her life as she feared the repercussions and she declined the assessment.

A person cannot choose to inflict harm on others and therefore the enquiry must rule this out. All decisions where a person is assessed as lacking capacity, best interest decisions will need to be made. Those decisions where the person has capacity and no one else is at risk then practitioners should provide information, advice and guidance, record what the person said that confirmed the capacitated and autonomous decision and provide the person with information about contacting services.

Safeguarding adults reviews often identify the reluctance of people to make referrals to the local authority without the consent of a capacitated person. The purpose of the enquiry is to determine whether the person has capacity, to rule out risk to others, or potential crime and consider any risks to the public. It is good practice to discuss the referral with the person; however, even if they do not consent you may still need to make a referral for safeguarding purposes. You will need to pass on any concerns with the local authority and inform the person that someone will be in touch, ensuring that you have safe contact details. We have a duty to protect the public (others) and report when there is reasonable suspicion of a crime. Safeguarding is about ensuring the safety not just of the victim but also anyone else who may be affected by the situation. Once the referral is received we may not have the cooperation of a person, but this does not necessarily prevent further assessment and enquiries to determine the risks. If the person is assessed as capacitated to make all their own decisions then we have no right to intervene in their autonomous decision making relating to decisions about their own care and support needs, but may still require a multi-agency meeting to rule out all possible interventions and risks to others.

A balance of beneficence, non-maleficence, justice and autonomy must be applied to ensure least restrictive, least intrusive and proportionate responses. These ethical debates may require further discussion in a multi-agency meeting. Applying these ethical principles to practice in thematically reviewing the cluster groups provides a basis for analysis of key themes in self-neglect, but can also be useful for self-assessment purposes in safeguarding, or as a reflection tool for supervision.

Identifying self-neglect

Has self-neglect been appropriately identified and a safeguarding referral made to the local authority?

Guidance

Practitioners need to recognise the definition of self-neglect. Self-neglect covers a wide range of behaviours:

- Neglecting to care for personal hygiene.

- Neglecting to care for health.

- Neglecting to care for surroundings.

- Behaviours such as hoarding.

No additional thresholds should be applied to safeguarding referrals. The response will be different depending on the extent of self-neglect. Some people may only require advice and guidance, some may require social work or nursing support and some people will require a full safeguarding enquiry. The responses are assessed in relation to an identified process, but this should not prevent a safeguarding referral. A safeguarding referral should be made in cases of self-neglect where the three-part test is met:

- The person has needs for care and support.

- The person is experiencing or at risk of abuse or neglect (including self-neglect).

- As a result of those care and support needs, the person is unable to protect themselves from either risk or the experience of abuse and neglect.

It is good to be open and transparent with the person concerned and enable them to understand why a referral may be necessary; however, you do not need consent to make a safeguarding referral:

- Checking out the person's consent is part of local authority S42 duties, therefore a referral can be made without consent.

- Enquiries can be made about the issues affecting the person/ others, including whether the person consents or not.

- If they do not consent, this simply means that the local authority does not have their cooperation, but this does not prevent agencies from taking any steps that they can.

- Any potential risks in making your decision need to be considered.

The purpose of the enquiry is to establish a person's capacity to make certain decisions, determine the level of risk to the person and others, to coordinate personalised responses to abuse and neglect and to explore potential crime.

Barriers can include:

- Not recognising or identifying the issue as self-neglect or neglect.

- Not recognising appropriate threshold criteria for safeguarding, or applying additional thresholds.

- Where a person's self-neglect is impacting on their emotional or physical wellbeing, then it is no longer questionable whether they have needs for care and support – they meet the three-part test.

- You do not need consent to make a safeguarding referral to the local authority. Lack of consent for safeguarding purposes should not be a barrier.

Remedies to consider:

- A Care Act-based definition of self-neglect across all procedures.

- All safeguarding training includes the identification of self-neglect and how agencies might recognise self-neglect.

It is important that any subsequent safeguarding responses consider the ethical balance of beneficence, non-maleficence, justice and autonomy and that the principles of safeguarding are applied throughout practice.

Empowerment

- People are supported and encouraged to make their own decisions.

- The person is asked what their expectations are and what outcomes they would like.

- The person is asked the miracle question, 'If you were to wake up tomorrow and you and your home are as you want them to be what would that look like, feel like and be like?' Ask the person to describe this in some detail – this establishes personal goals and helps the person to move away from an identity as a self-neglecter/hoarder.

Prevention

- It is better to take action before harm occurs.

- The person receives clear and simple information about what abuse and neglect are, how to recognise the signs and how to get help.

Proportionality

- The least intrusive response appropriate to the risk presented.

- Proportionate response.

- The person is involved to the extent that they require.

- Best interest decisions are not made for capacitated people.

- Where a person lacks capacity a best interest decision does not necessarily mean removing all risk, but it is balancing the identity, wishes, values and opinions of the person proportionate to the risks presented.

Protection

- Support, advocacy and representation for those in greatest need (those who would have substantial difficulty being involved in the process without advocacy or representation).

- A voice in the process.

- Equal access to justice, including criminal justice.

Partnership

- Local solutions through services working with their communities.

- Communities have a part to play in preventing, detecting and reporting neglect and abuse.

- 'Circles of support' – the person is supported by family, friends, neighbours or community members in addition to any professionals and this is identified on the care and support plan.

- Coordinated multi-agency response as required.

Accountability

- Accountability and transparency in safeguarding practice.

- The person understands the roles of everyone involved.

- Professionals are accountable for their actions (responsibility for capacity assessments is acknowledged in addition to other actions).

Care Act compliant enquiries (S42)

Have Care Act (2014) enquiries been implemented appropriately?

Guidance

The purpose of an enquiry is to:

- get a picture of the abuse/neglect/self-neglect

- make sure that the person is safe (consider Mental Capacity Act and personalised response)

- consider capacity assessments required and by whom

- rule out additional or historical abuse and neglect,

- explore potential crime

- identify any coercive or controlling behaviours

- explore any mental health and substance misuse concerns

- consider risks to others

- determine the care and support needs of the individual

- consider advocacy and methods of communication

- determine whether a multi-agency response is required.

The local authority must have oversight of safeguarding procedures, but can request another agency to make enquiries on its behalf (as long as there is not a vested interest or a conflict of interest), or chair multi-agency meetings for safeguarding purposes. Information and outcomes must be shared with the local authority.

The benefit of invoking safeguarding procedures is that safeguarding duties and responsibilities apply. These are duties to:

- share information for enquiry purposes

- cooperate with the local authority and for the the local authority to cooperate with other agencies for safeguarding purposes

- assess where there is an identified need

- determine consent

- provide appropriate advocacy

- assess carers' needs.

This requires all agencies to share relevant information with relevant people for the purposes of safeguarding the person.

Barriers can include:

- Lack of understanding about what a S42 enquiry is.

- Reluctance to coordinate a multi-agency response to prevent further neglect or self-neglect.

- A lack of confidence in coordinating, delegating and utilising all partnership agencies to make enquiries and respond to abuse or neglect.

- Local authority wanting to maintain control of safeguarding responses, rather than a multi-agency response, or being overwhelmed with safeguarding referrals and referring back to single agency to deal with case without multi-agency support or coordination.

- No clear safeguarding procedures on self-neglect – including when to manage self-neglect as a single agency and when to make a safeguarding referral.

- No specific training in self-neglect.

- No clear risk-assessment tools.

- No clear models of intervention.

Remedies to consider:

- Clear procedures for safeguarding in cases of self-neglect.

- A Care Act-based definition of self-neglect across all procedures.

- A specified model for intervention.

- Tools to assess the level of risk.

- Specific multi-agency training.

- Practice that works on the strengths of the individual and solutions rather than defensive practice.

- Clear training on when consent is not required for safeguarding purposes.

- Multi-agency training in chairing safeguarding meetings in cases of self-neglect.

- Single point of contact/access trained and qualified to effectively triage safeguarding cases, including cases of self-neglect.

Risk to others

Has the risk to others been considered?

Guidance

Risks to others may include but are not exclusive to:

- fire risk

- rats, vermin, flies

- faecal matter, vomit or other bodily fluids
- toxic substances
- open wires, unsafe gas, structural issues
- oxygen tanks where someone smokes, or other medical equipment
- drugs paraphernalia (uses needles, spoons, knives)
- weapons
- people using the property who may target other vulnerable people
- anti-social behaviour
- animals at the property
- others to whom there is a risk including people who may have needs for care and support also residing at the property and/or children residing or spending time at the property.

Barriers can include:

- A strong focus on individual rights and needs without consideration of the needs and rights of others to be safe.
- Not reporting, or poor response to potentially criminal activity.
- Other forms of abuse are explored without consideration of self-neglect.
- Local authorities wait until self-neglect escalates to a severe situation before intervening – often this is too late.

Remedies to consider:

- Earlier multi-agency response.
- Coordinated responses with a key identified agency.
- Early rapport development with individual and family and carers.
- Address issues impacting on others via relevant legal frameworks.
- Safeguarding enquiries explore risks to others.

Risk assessment

Has the appropriate risk assessment been completed?

Guidance

Risk assessments should include:

- Historical abuse and past knowledge of the person.

- Previous safeguarding referrals.

- Cumulative risk.

- The vulnerability of the person (capacity, mental ill health, physical disability, learning disability, autism spectrum disorder, age and frailty of the person, social isolation and support the person has, acceptance of care and support, insight the person has into their problems and difficulties).

- Type and seriousness of self-neglect/hoarding.

- Level of self-neglect/hoarding (clutter rating scale).

- Background to self-neglect/hoarding (does the person have a disability or mental health problems that prevents self-care and has this been a long-standing problem – when did it begin and was there a trigger? Does the person engage with services and was there a time when this was different, is social isolation a concern?).

- Impact on others.

- Reasonable suspicion of abuse (could self-neglect be an indicator of abuse/neglect, is the person targeted for abuse/anti-social behaviour/mate crime, is the person neglected by someone responsible for their care?).

- Legal frameworks (is the person at risk of eviction, are there pressing environmental concerns or public health concerns, debt issues that may lead to prosecution, other criminal convictions, child protection proceedings?).

- Is there anyone obstructing or preventing work with the person (family members, other people at the property)?

Barriers can include:

- Services identifying risk but not identifying the risk-management plan.

- Services recognising level of risk but not implementing defensible decision making, for example evidence of capacity assessments and outcomes, use of Human Rights Act, recognition of someone being deprived of their liberty in the community.

- Lack of escalation process and, in particular, support where strategic barriers are presented such as access to services.

- Cases being closed with escalating risks identified.

- The person being moved from service to service without a safeguarding oversight and coordination of services.

- Lack of consideration of the person's Mental Health Act status, for example S117 aftercare services.

- Discharge from hospital back to unsafe premises and insanitary conditions not considered (unsafe discharge).

Remedies to consider:

- Clear safeguarding risk-assessment training.

- Recognition of the 'duty to assess' where there is reasonable suspicion of abuse or neglect, irrespective of whether the person engages or not.

- A clear process for identifying people subject to Mental Health Act provisions.

- Clear procedures for case closure – requirements and considerations.

- Clear guidance on safe hospital discharge.

- Clear escalation processes for cases that are increasing in risk and intervention is not addressing concerns.

- Executive strategy meetings or executive risk-assessment meetings should cover multiple abuse or serious risk of harm to an individual with an overarching strategic response that supports individual operational responses.

- Training in models of assessment – assessment needs to explore potential mental disorder, trauma and trauma response, historical issues impacting on the person, social networks, physical health and nutritional requirements, personal philosophies and the identity of the person beyond what is observed and utilise cognitive and solution-focused assessment alongside risk-management approaches.

Carers' assessment

Have carers' needs been considered and a carers' assessment completed? Have carers been identified on care and support plans where they are meeting an identified need of the person for whom they care? Are carers aware of their duties and responsibilities and the potential consequences?

Guidance

Carers' assessments to consider:

- Carers' needs in continuing to support the person.

- Capacity issues relating to the carer and their ability to provide care.

- People residing at the property who may not consider themselves carers, but may still have a duty of care.

- Obstructive or aggressive carers and family members.

Note: If there is an identified carer, then this may be a case of neglect rather than self-neglect. Wilful neglect is a potential crime.

Barriers can include:

- Carers not identifying as carers.

- Carers not being identified on the care and support plan as meeting a need.

- Not recognising carers who self-neglect – eligible for safeguarding.

Remedies to consider:

- The whole-family approach to assessment.

- Training including assessing carers' needs and working with obstructive or complex carers.

- Safeguarding training including the need to assess carers' needs and make safeguarding referrals where the eligibility criteria is met.

Mental health and substance misuse

Have referrals for mental health and substance misuse services been considered and recorded? Have all legal duties under the Mental Health Act been considered (for example, S117 aftercare, community treatment orders, guardianships)?

Guidance

In assessing mental health and substance misuse consider:

- Does the person require mental health assessment?

- Has a referral been made?

- Are there barriers to assessment?

- Does the person misuse substances?

- Would they engage with substance misuse services?

- The impact of substance misuse on physical and mental wellbeing and daily functioning and the increased risks.

- Assessment, including that of executive functions of the brain.

When someone self-neglects there may be a range of psychological issues impacting on them, for example attachment issues, issues of neglect in childhood, executive function difficulties, trauma and loss issues, agoraphobia. Mental health services should consider access to psychology support even if there is not a defined medical treatment route. Access should be defined as accessible to the person, for example someone with agoraphobia is not going to make it to a clinic appointment and someone self-neglecting is unlikely to respond to appointment letters.

Psychiatry and psychology intervention is very important when working with someone who has a hoarding disorder. Barriers can include:

- Sending appointment letters to someone who is not engaging (not an appropriate form of communication).

- Maintaining that someone needs to attend a clinic appointment when this is clearly not accessible to the person, for example a person who has agoraphobia.

- Unclear pathways between services.

- Case closure – no risk or capacity assessments.

- No clear pathways when there are multiple low-level disabilities, mental health problems, substance misuse, or when the person was a previously looked-after child, homeless, or there are other factors present that increase vulnerability.

- Lack of engagement and accountability of services in the safeguarding process.

- Lack of identification and consideration of domestic abuse within the assessment process.

Remedies to consider:

- Pathways between services clear and available to all practitioners.

- Multiple disabilities and risks are assessed holistically and an agency made accountable for the assessment.

- Training to address the need to consider domestic abuse as part of safeguarding procedures where eligibility criteria for safeguarding is met and support is offered to access those services.

Capacity and consent

Are all relevant capacity assessments up to date and recorded within one support plan for monitoring?

Guidance

List capacity assessments required, for example:

- Tenancy agreement

- Tenancy support

- Tenancy review

- Medication offered

- Treatment offered

- Safeguarding referral

- Assessment and support planning

- Services offered (identified individually, including each individual care and support service)

- Finance

- Aids and adaptations.

Are proportionate and least restrictive interventions being considered?

Where a person lacks capacity to make a decision are we balancing their rights, wishes and expectations with the actual level of risk, or are we being too risk averse? You assume capacity unless there is reason to believe otherwise.

The Mental Capacity Act Code of Practice states that one of the reasons why people may question a person's capacity to make a specific decision is that 'the person's behaviour or circumstances cause doubt as to whether they have capacity to make a decision' (Mental Capacity Act Code of Practice, p.52). Arguably, extreme self-neglect or hoarding behaviour meets this criterion and assessments should take place.

In determining who assesses capacity, or who is accountable for assessing capacity there are some issues you should consider:

- If you are the person who requires consent, agreement, understanding or a signature from the person self-neglecting for a proposed treatment, care provision, course of action or tenancy agreement/compliance, then you need to assess whether the person is capable of consenting by undertaking a capacity assessment.

- Any capacity assessment carried out in relation to self-neglect must be time-specific and relate to a specific intervention or action. The professional responsible for undertaking the capacity assessment will be the person who is proposing the specific intervention or action (wherever possible), and is referred to as the 'decision maker'.

- The decision maker may need to seek support from other professionals in the multi-disciplinary team, and is responsible for making the final decision about a person's capacity.

- When the person is assessed as lacking capacity the decision maker is responsible for the best interest decisions.

- If the person is deemed to have capacity, this should be clearly recorded along with the things that the person did and said that made the decision maker think that the person had capacity, and the information and advice given.

- If the person self-neglecting is refusing to engage with certain professionals, anyone who has access and has developed a rapport with the person self-neglecting should be supported by the actual decision maker to carry out the capacity assessment and best interest decisions.

- Safeguarding principles should be considered in relation to any decision or intervention.

List all the aspects of care, treatment, service provision or intervention that require the person's consent, agreement, understanding or signature. Identify the person/agency that requires consent as the decision maker. Safeguarding plans should detail the capacity assessments required and the person/agency responsible, with timescales for completion and follow-up monitoring. Once the capacity assessments are complete then agencies are looking to see whether there may be a change in the person's ability to consent. If there are a number of agencies involved that do not have access to assess the person, they may need to support whoever does have access, to conduct the capacity assessment to the best of their ability on their behalf.

Barriers can include:

- Capacity assessments being too generic, not issue-specific enough and not undertaken by the appropriate agency.

- The person/agency requiring consent to provide an aspect of care, a treatment or a service has not taken responsibility for that capacity assessment.

- Lack of understanding where a person has capacity and is making an unwise decision (they entitled to do this).

- Confusion about what 'duty of care' means. A duty of care does not mean that we prevent risk and protect the person no matter what. It means respecting the wishes, expectations, values and outcomes of a capacitated individual, including their right to make what others might consider unwise decisions. If the person has capacity to make a particular decision and this is not criminal or posing a risk to others, they are not being coerced or intimidated into making this decision and they are not detainable under the Mental Health Act, then we have no right to intervene in that decision, but can offer support advice, guidance, therapy to enable the person to understand more and perhaps reconsider their decision.

- Lack of defensible recording when a person has capacity and their decision could have a significant impact on wellbeing.

- Lack of coordination of capacity assessments in the safeguarding process.

- Lack of access to the person – for recording what is known and sharing knowledge across agencies.

- Mini-mental state tests and diagnostic tests being used instead of a capacity assessment.

- Lack of awareness across agencies about when a case may need presenting at court.

Remedies to consider:

- The safeguarding adults board to audit multi-agency capacity assessment standards.

- Multi-agency training in who does capacity assessments, when they are required, how to record capacity assessments and the consequences of not doing a capacity assessment. (Consider, for example, a hospital ward where nurses and doctors are refusing to undertake capacity assessments. This potentially becomes a safeguarding matter that requires further enquiries relating to organisational abuse. If staff never conduct capacity assessments, how would they ensure that they had valid consent when a patient appears confused? How would they know who the decision maker is? How could an autonomous, unwise decision be differentiated from a decision made by someone potentially lacking capacity to make that decision? This may be a violation of a person's human rights or an act or negligence if staff are not supported to recognise when to do capacity assessments and how to do them.)

- Enquiries consider social isolation, appropriate advocacy and a coordination of capacity assessments at an earlier stage of intervention.

- The inherent jurisdiction of the court should be identified in policies and procedures as a consideration.

Advocacy and representation

Does the person have suitable representation and support?

Guidance

The local authority has a duty to arrange for an independent advocate to be available to represent and support the person self-neglecting in order to facilitate their involvement in the process. This duty applies when the person has substantial difficulty in being involved in any part of the safeguarding process. Substantial difficulty is defined as the person having difficulty in:

- understanding the relevant information

- retaining that information

- using or weighing up that information

- communicating their views, wishes and feelings.

This duty does not apply if the local authority is satisfied that there is someone who would be appropriate to represent and support the person to facilitate their involvement (a friend or family member who is not part of any safeguarding procedures and does not have a vested interest in any potential outcomes). This individual must not be engaged in providing care or treatment for the person in a professional capacity.

The duty also does not apply where the person has capacity and is competent enough to consent to a course of action.

Barriers can include:

- Lack of knowledge in relation to the duty to find support or advocacy under the Care Act 2014.

- Automatically deferring to family as appropriate advocates.

- Lack of advocacy resources.

Remedies to consider:

- All training to include the need to have appropriate representation of the person's wishes, values, expectations and outcomes.

- All training to consider relevant and up-to-date case law.

Multi-agency response

Has a multi-agency response been coordinated early enough to prevent the deterioration of physical and mental wellbeing? Has a key person been identified to liaise with the person self-neglecting?

Guidance

Multi-agency response to:

- consider capacity issues in relation to a range of matters affecting the person and who should/can do them

- rule out additional or historical abuse or neglect

- explore potential crime

- identify any coercive or controlling behaviours affecting the person

- examine the person's mental health and how this may be affecting them

- explore any risks to others

- determine support needs of the individual, including appropriate advocacy.

Earlier intervention assists in developing a rapport, access to community, circles of support around the person, and solution-focused, strengths-based processes. Multi-agency meetings should consider a number of issues:

- Police-led enquiries coordinated alongside any required assessment processes.

- In criminal cases – the preservation of evidence.

- Referrals to necessary services.

- Involvement of services not already involved, such as domestic abuse, substance misuse, mental health services, fire service, anti-social behaviour services, multi-agency public protection arrangements (MAPPA), multi-agency risk-assessment conferences (MARAC), sexual assault referral centres (SARC), public health.

- Coordination of assessment methodology.

- Therapeutic assessment and intervention processes.

Barriers can include:

- The person being passed between agencies without oversight or coordination.

- Where there are issues of severe neglect short-term intervention services are not appropriate, for example the case being held solely with the GP, a single point of access or duty team.

- Lack of consistency – developing a rapport with the person is of prime importance. An agency, or if possible an individual, should be identified as the key agency to undertake the long-term work.

- Barriers in sharing information, coordinating approaches, access to appropriate support, and the duty to cooperate with the local authority and the local authority to cooperate with other agencies not being carried out. When meeting a number of barriers from a particular organisation, concerns should be escalated. Board members should be supportive and offer advice and guidance to ensure that safeguarding duties are being met within their organisation.

Remedies to consider:

- Safeguarding adults board ensuring accountability for allocated actions within safeguarding procedures.

- Accountability across agencies for capacity assessments and agencies being actively held accountable when they refuse to undertake appropriate capacity assessments, or support others to do so.

- Training in chairing safeguarding meetings and multi-agency responses offered to managers within all relevant agencies.

- Examples of good multi-agency working shared and positive lessons learned from the experience.

Comprehensive and holistic assessment

Has a comprehensive and holistic assessment of need been conducted with or without the consent of the individual where self-neglect is impacting on physical and mental wellbeing? Is there a duty to assess? Have non-commissioned services, other agencies, carers, friends and other parties meeting an identified need for the individual all been recorded as meeting that need on the care and support plan?

Have culture, values and religious beliefs been explored with the person?

Guidance

Where a person self-neglecting refuses an assessment, S11 of the Care Act identifies that the local authority has a duty to carry out the assessment if:

- the person lacks capacity to refuse that assessment and carrying out the assessment is in the person's best interests (this must be recorded)

- the person is experiencing or is at risk of abuse or neglect.

When assessing someone who self-neglects, do not assume that this is a lifestyle choice. Ask the 'miracle question': 'If you were to wake up tomorrow and your house was miraculously changed into the type of house you would like to be living in, what would it look like, what would you see, what would you be doing and what would be different?' or 'If you were to wake up tomorrow morning and you did not feel so low in mood, what would you be doing, what would things look like, what would be different?'

Has the assessment covered enough detail to understand the reasons for self-neglect, when self-neglect began, for example any triggers, loss bereavement, abuse? What are the goals of the person and are there any barriers to these?

Barriers can include:

- Overly simplistic assessment that does not consider why a person is self-neglecting, how the self-neglect began and what the person gains from the self-neglect.

- Some individuals believe in alternative medicines and therapies, rejecting western medicine. Where a person has capacity to make decisions about medical intervention and treatment and has differing cultural beliefs from traditional western medical perspectives, this needs to be explored thoroughly and support plans established in a culturally sensitive manner.

- Family members, friends and non-commissioned services meeting the needs of the individual are not identified on the care and support plan – ensure that if a person or organisation agrees to meet a need they understand the accountability for meeting that need.

Remedies to consider:

- Safeguarding training that includes the duty to assess if there is reason to suspect that the person may lack capacity to consent to assessment.

- Training that includes the duty to assess where there is reasonable suspicion of abuse or neglect, irrespective of whether the person engages.

- Policies and procedures that reflect the above duties and maintain contact with someone who self-neglects.

- Training in models of assessment – assessment needs to explore potential mental disorder, trauma and trauma response, historical issues impacting on the person, social networks, physical health and nutritional requirements, personal philosophies and the identity of the person beyond what is observed. Cognitive and solution-focused assessment should be used alongside risk-management approaches.

Compliance and insight

Does the person have insight into their behaviour? Is the person accepting of care, support and services? Is there a plan to maintain engagement and contact? Has potential loss, trauma and grief been considered in the widest context and how can the person be supported through this?

Guidance

When someone is not accepting of services, explore the reasons why. What prevents the person from accepting support? Consider the following issues:

- Harm minimisation – what can be achieved and how much will this lessen the risks?

- Has there been a negative experience of services?

- How can negative experiences be changed: be prompt, remain engaged, be on time, communicate in ways that the person can respond to, do not send letters if this is inappropriate to the needs of the person, do not impose actions if at all possible, work with the person and their timescales, do not instigate a clear-up before other issues have been explored, and undertake any clearing at the pace of the person (dependent on risks to others).

- Is there someone who has a relationship with the person and are they willing and able to support services in providing care and support?

- Can a rapport be developed with someone?

Barriers can include:

- Recognition of loss and grief – this is not merely about bereavement and can include, for example, loss of childhood through neglect, loss of mobility or ability, loss of independence in older people, loss of confidence as a result of abuse.

- Not recognising the process of change – if you are suggesting change then a person may experience a range of emotions and anxieties about leaving something that they feel safe with behind. Do not suggest taking something away from the person without exploring what they gain from it and how they feel this emotion can be replaced.

Remedies to consider:

- Training in motivational interviewing techniques to help a person begin contemplating their current situation and the incongruence with the desired outcomes.

- Support to assist the person in engaging in their local community resources – Care Act responses should be identified in training.

- Circles of support identified around the person – and procedures for this.

- Key person identified to engage with the person self-neglecting.

- Earlier intervention via a coordinated approach.

- Be wary of labelling people as anti-social, criminal or a nuisance without exploring the reasons behind these behaviours. Safeguarding training should address this.

Imposed sanctions, imposed compliance or penalties

Are there any legal considerations or imposed compliance considerations and have these been clearly recorded?

Guidance

A person is unlikely to change when power and control are removed from them. In some cases, sanctions must be imposed and the effects of these must be considered by professionals intervening. Consider:

- Eviction notices
- Child protection proceedings
- Imposed housing sanctions
- Criminal proceedings
- Debt and debt recovery
- Other.

Barriers can include:

- Lack of capacity assessments – sanctions cannot be imposed on someone who did not understand the requirements in the first place, unless there is a risk to others or there are criminal proceedings.

Remedies to consider:

- Clear and justifiable recording of the legal frameworks used, why they were used, what was ruled out and why.

Information sharing

Is information being shared across all agencies to prevent deterioration in physical and mental wellbeing and to safeguard the person?

Guidance

Relevant information can be shared with relevant agencies without consent when there is reasonable suspicion of:

- risk to others
- crime
- public interest issues

- coercive and controlling behaviours/domestic abuse

- the need for an assessment under the Mental Health Act.

Confidentiality must not be confused with secrecy. It is inappropriate for agencies to give assurances of absolute confidentiality in cases where there are concerns about abuse, particularly those situations where vulnerable people may be at risk. Any response to information shared must consider the ethics of that response; for example, any response should not place the person or others in increased danger.

The Data Protection Act is not a barrier – it supports this form of information sharing.

Remedies to consider:

- Follow Caldicott guidance and look out for new updates relating to information sharing responsibilities.

Personalised safeguarding

After risks to others, potential crime, public interest issues, coercive and controlling behaviours have been ruled out, is there evidence of person-centred care and support planning? Have the wishes, views and values of the person and their expectations and desired outcomes been identified and recorded?

Has the reason why a person is refusing treatment, care and support been explored? Have cultural, ethnic, religious and personal perspectives in relation to care, services or treatment been explored? Have capacity assessments been conducted in relation to each treatment decision? Have the person's relationship, cultures and values been assessed alongside family and community cultures and values?

Guidance

When a person has capacity to make a decision and they are entitled to make an unwise decision, consider:

- the reasoning behind this decision

- whether this is impacting adversely on anyone else

- whether information and advice has been offered in a format that the person understands (and has been recorded).

We should explore the reasons why a person is refusing care, support or treatment. This needs to include possible correlation with past caring responsibilities and let-downs, cultural issues, and the previous interface with professionals. We should not make assumptions based on our own culture and values; for example, a person may have strong beliefs about non-traditional forms of medicine that impacts on their acceptance of traditional western medicine.

Barriers can include:

- Lack of understanding of the Mental Capacity Act.

- Anxiety about unwise decisions.

- A feeling that we are in trouble if we do not protect people when they are making capacitated, unwise decisions. Although we are not the decision maker and they are responsible for their decisions and the consequences, we must demonstrate why we think that this is a capacitated decision (what information and advice was offered and the person's reasoning).

Remedies to consider:

- Safeguarding training identifing how the safeguarding principles are applied in practice.

Management support and response

Are escalating risks taken seriously and addressed at the appropriate level of management and intervention? Is there clarity regarding when to escalate concerns and to whom?

Guidance

It is helpful to have a strategic layer of safeguarding sitting between safeguarding multi-agency response and safeguarding adult reviews. This may be called an executive strategy, executive safeguarding or overarching strategy. This may be chaired by a senior manager within the local authority who can look at the strategic elements of the safeguarding process to support the removal of any barriers, feed the outcomes and actions down to operational staff and up to the safeguarding adults board for action. Individual safeguarding meetings will still be held looking at the needs of the individual or people involved and feeding information back to the senior manager.

Barriers can include:

- No clear escalation process in safeguarding where a person is continuing to deteriorate as a result of self-neglect.

Remedies to consider:

- Supervision identifing cases of self-neglect, where the supervisor has a clear framework of reflection and assessment within which to explore the cases.

- Caseload pressure and distribution of work considered within supervision.

- Managers attending self-neglect training – to provide more consistent responses.

- Services identified to support work with people who self-neglect.

Defensible decision making

Is recording defensible (or justifiable) rather than defensive (offering reasons for failure)?

Guidance

Defensible or justifiable decision making follows the word 'because':

- I chose this course of action because…

- I ruled this out because…

And following 'because' should be recorded the legislation used to make the decision. In the absence of legislation use policy, model, method, theory or research that informed the decision. This should be balanced with what the person did or said that made you think this was or was not an appropriate course of action, alongside attempts to enable the person to understand consequences, pros, cons, risks, alternative options and information and advice given.

Intervention should be justified in recording logs:

- Who is intervening?

- What is the purpose of the intervention?

- What actions were taken?

- What were the outcomes of the action?

If a professional is struggling to identify outcomes from intervention they need to raise this during supervision and consider:

- Why am I going around in circles with this case?

- What might possible solutions be?

- Who do I need to help me with these solutions?

- Is the mental and physical wellbeing of this person significantly deteriorating and does this case need escalating?

A summary of work, progress, barriers and how those barriers have been addressed can support defensible decision making. Issues to consider include:

- Referrals made

- Appointments offered

- Information and advice given

- Capacity assessments

- Access to advocacy

- The person's wishes, choices, expectations and outcomes

- Support given to help the person recognise and understand the situation

- Duty to assess and how this has been achieved

- What was considered, what was ruled out and why

- Legal frameworks used

- Models, methods, theory and research used in practice

- 'I' statements of the person (what the person said) or indicative responses (what the person did).

Barriers can include:

- Professionals stating 'I did this in my head' – a major barrier to defensible decision making. It is important to see the justification for actions taken – what was considered and why it was appropriate, what was ruled out and why.

- Lack of knowledge of legal frameworks available.

- Lack of discussion at safeguarding meetings about potential legal remedies.

Remedies to consider:

- Policies and procedures to reflect the legal frameworks available in cases of self-neglect.

- Multi-agency meetings and responses developed to extract information from all professionals about legislation available.

- Legal literacy training that presents the information in a way that enables the practitioner to understand how to put learning into practice.

Other

Are we trying to impose large-scale clear-ups, and sanctions that are neither cost effective, nor support the person?

Guidance

Practitioners to consider the barriers and explore in supervision the possible solutions to barriers. Ensure that intervention is not overly intrusive and involves the person as much as possible. Consider the emotional impact of any decision and whether this may have a negative or positive impact.

If a person has an emotional attachment to their actions or hoarded items then removing the items will only serve to increase the sense of loss and powerlessness. It will exacerbate the problem, not remove it. The wellbeing of others must be factored in but if we can achieve this working with the person, rather than against them, it will more likely be sustainable. The cost of clear-ups to the local authority is substantial and the problem will only begin again elsewhere and with less positive intervention.

Barriers can include:

- Services imposing control with no recognised benefits.

Remedies to consider:

- Training to address ethical decision making.

Chapter 4

SAFEGUARDING THOSE WHO SELF-NEGLECT UNDER THE CARE ACT 2014

The safeguarding referral

People may experience a sense of what self-neglect is like during a traumatic event or major loss. Consider for example a time where you have split up from your partner, lost your job, or experienced a bereavement. You may not feel like eating, you may drink too much alcohol, you may not bathe or care for your personal hygiene as you usually would. The dishes may pile up and you may not feel like meeting up with family or friends. Well-meaning comments can seem irritating, or not quite right, and a sense of disconnect occurs. Imagine this continuing until your physical and mental health suffers. At what point along this process would you define yourself as having needs for care and support and at what time would others define you as requiring care and support?

The Care Act 2014 identifies self-neglect as a safeguarding responsibility covering a wide range of behaviours, such as neglecting to care for one's personal hygiene, health or surroundings and including behaviour such as hoarding. The Care Act 2014 also states that we should delay or prevent the need for services by offering advice, information and guidance and signposting someone to appropriate services. A person having a short-term period of self-neglect may require 'safeguarding' through the support of family and friends who encourage them to re-engage with activities and guide them back towards happiness, fulfilment, contentment and achievement. A person who is losing weight and becoming depressed and disengaging may require advice about counselling and support services, medication or short-term therapeutic intervention to safeguard them. A person whose physical and mental wellbeing is affected, is no longer paying bills, not eating a healthy diet, or whose drinking is affecting their ability to function may require a number of services to support them. Someone whose self-neglect has become entrenched and whose mental and physical wellbeing is affected to the extent that they are not able to address daily functions, keep themselves or others safe or maintain their home for its intended purpose may require well-coordinated and sensitive support.

Safeguarding is everyone's business, whether you are a neighbour, family member, friend or professional. We try to provide support in a way that enables the person to live a happier and healthier life. Safeguarding a person is not making a referral to the local authority and expecting a meeting to wave a magic wand and make everything better. It is about the need to consider the complexity of the person within the complexity of the situation and help them to find a pathway to their own defined outcomes, as far as it is practicably possible to do so. To safeguard someone who is self-neglecting we need to understand their journey up to the point at which we met them.

Eligibility criteria for safeguarding adults

The eligibility criteria for safeguarding identify that safeguarding duties apply to an adult who:

- has needs for care and support (whether or not the local authority is meeting any of those needs)

- is experiencing or is at risk of abuse or neglect

- as a result of those care and support needs is unable to protect themselves from either the risk or experience of abuse or neglect.

This is often referred to as the 'three-part test'.

This definition of eligibility for safeguarding is significantly different to the government's previous *No Secrets* guidance (2000) which sought to protect vulnerable people from abuse or neglect. Vulnerability was mainly interpreted by local authorities as those who required community care, or those eligible for social work support. The Care Act 2014 definition is distinctly different, as the word 'safeguarding' is defined as an action that anyone can be involved in, rather than a task undertaken by the police and local authority, with the support of other agencies to protect the individual. All elements of all work to maintain health and wellbeing, justice and equality and protect autonomy are (when working with someone who has care and support needs) an act to safeguard the person from illness, isolation, injustice, degrading treatment and mental ill health. All agencies in health, social care and the police therefore safeguard people on a daily basis when there would be a risk of neglect or abuse if they did not intervene to provide care and support. A safeguarding referral is made to the local authority when the agencies' efforts to prevent abuse or neglect appear to be failing or faulty and external support may be required. It could also be when someone previously unknown to services appears to be struggling to prevent abuse or neglect, or to protect themselves. This is defined as the point where there is reasonable suspicion of abuse or neglect. A disclosure, observation or indicators of abuse or neglect would raise concern that elicits further exploration of the situation until there is sufficient concern to involve other agencies.

Enquiries (S42)

Once a referral has been made to the local authority it is required to identify the gaps in its knowledge and create enquiries to fill those gaps. This could be anything from a telephone conversation to a police investigation. The local authority must then determine a course of action appropriate and proportionate to the needs, wishes and expectations of the person and the risks involved in the situation. The responses to the enquiry findings may be varied. For example, a person who has a physical disability and is self-neglecting as a result of not physically being able to manage may require an assessment of need, and a social worker may be allocated.

Following the referral to the local authority, there may be no further need for enquiries for this person, as the assessment and support planning process would meet their outstanding needs to enable physical and mental wellbeing.

A person suffering short-term distress may need signposting towards the appropriate service. Someone with increasing risk and complex needs may cause the local authority to make further enquiries.

The local authority may identify an appropriate service to conduct those enquiries on their behalf and coordinate multi-agency services under safeguarding procedures. In cases where agencies have failed to prevent abuse or neglect from occurring and there is a significant impact on the mental and physical wellbeing of the person, local authorities may seek a specialist safeguarding team, or a specialist worker to lead the process and chair any multi-agency meetings.

Police enquiries will take precedence, although the care and support needs of the individual must be addressed throughout any enquiry. Enquiries conducted for safeguarding purposes fall under Section 42 of the Care Act and can often be called Section 42 enquiries. The safeguarding duties have a legal effect in relation to organisations other than the local authority, for example the NHS and the police. Agencies have a duty to share information with the local authority for safeguarding purposes, and the local authority has a duty to make enquiries or cause enquiries to occur.

While it is good practice to be open and honest with the person about any sharing of information, we do not necessarily need consent to share information with the local authority. Checking out a person's consent is part of Section 42 duties, therefore a referral can be made without consent. The referral must be considered if the three-part test is met. Once the referral has been received, enquiries can be made into capacity, consent, crime, abuse and neglect. If the person does not consent to the safeguarding referral this simply means that the local authority does not have their co-operation, but this does not prevent agencies from taking any steps that they lawfully can. The duty to make enquiries (or cause them to be made) does not depend on the request or consent of the adult concerned. This duty cannot be overruled by a third party's refusal to allow access to the person concerned.

The Care Act guidance identifies that the local authority has a duty to assess the needs of the individual where an adult may lack mental capacity to make the decision and that carrying out the assessment would be in their best interests. The local authority also has a duty to assess whether the person is experiencing or is at risk of abuse and neglect, even if they have capacity and are refusing the assessment. Local authorities are required to remain in contact with the person, assess as far as is possible and document this. This could require a multi-agency meeting to consider who has the best rapport with the person concerned and who may be able to achieve the assessment, including relevant capacity assessments, and to determine the support provided from other agencies to achieve this.

Knowledge of reporting duties and assessment duties under the Care Act are particularly important in cases of self-neglect and hoarding, where there can be difficulty in establishing communication and the person refuses assessment. When a person is feeling lonely, down, possibly humiliated by the house and contents, may have suffered trauma and abuse, they may not always answer the telephone or open the post because they do not want people to have a derogatory opinion of them and potentially they may feel out of control and powerless. To have someone knock on the door and say that they are there as a result of a safeguarding referral may just be overwhelming and frightening. The initial contact must be sensitively communicated and the feelings and responses of the individual considered. It is highly unlikely that Section 42 enquiries will have all the required answers without establishing the best person to speak with the person hoarding, the best time to call, the development of a rapport with the person and the beginning of an assessment. This process will take time, requires compassion for the needs of the person concerned and must comply with the principles of safeguarding (see the section on building a rapport in Chapter 5).

Every agency must be accountable for their role in engaging with the person, and if they are not able to undertake relevant capacity assessments, because the person is refusing them access, then they should support the person who has access to the individual to undertake the relevant capacity assessments. Details must be given to the person who is self-neglecting about what information is being shared, with whom and why. The person who is hoarding/self-neglecting has a right to understand the role of everyone involved. Working in partnership with the local community and local services to support the person concerned enables the person to re-engage with people and reflect on their own circumstances.

Principles of safeguarding

In all aspects of our work to safeguard someone self-neglecting we must ensure that the safeguarding principles are considered. Safeguarding principles of empowerment, prevention, proportionality, protection, partnership and accountability apply to each and every action and intervention. The key considerations related to these issues are detailed here.

Empowerment

- There should be equitable access to services, including the criminal justice service.

- There is recognition of potential domestic abuse, hate/mate crime and anti-social behaviour.

- Oppression and discrimination are prevented.

- Strength-focused intervention seeks to place the person as the expert in their own wellbeing.

- The person is well informed about any safeguarding process and the roles of those involved in support.

- There is an assumption that the person has capacity to consent to interventions. Where there is reason to believe that an individual may not have capacity to consent, this will be assessed by the person requiring consent (or relevant person). Any capacity assessment will be recorded and any decision made will be proportionate and least restrictive, ensuring that the person has a safer, but also happier, life with their own best interests central to decision making.

- The expectations, wishes, values and outcomes expressed by the person are central to any action or intervention.

- The Human Rights of any individual are maintained.

- Information is shared in line with Caldicott principles and any local information-sharing agreement. We cannot assure absolute confidentiality, and where there is reasonable suspicion of a crime, a potential risk to others or matters of public interest, information may have to be shared. If a person has potentially been coerced or intimidated into making a decision then information may need to be shared. Where a person's mental ill health may require assessment under the Mental Health

Act, relevant information may need to be shared with relevant people. The duty of candour means that we should be open with people about when and how information will be shared.

Prevention

- People are supported to recognise and report abuse and neglect in a manner that they can understand.

- People are informed of their rights to be free from abuse and neglect and supported to exercise these rights, including access to advocacy.

- The experience of care and support is positive and equitable. Packages of care do not distinguish between those perceived as deserving or undeserving, obstructive or receptive.

- Dignity, compassion and respect in care and support is evidenced.

- Least restrictive interventions are evident. Practice and recording reflects the practitioners' attempts to reduce restrictions.

- The practitioner can recognise the difference between a restriction, a restraint and a deprivation of a person's liberty and respond to the person's needs and rights, irrespective of environment.

- There is a recognition of culture, religion and personal values in assessment and planning.

- There is understanding of the Mental Capacity Act and its principles in practice.

- The links between commissioning and provider services and the need for consistent and coordinated care planning and review are evident.

- Holistic assessment, care and support planning is coordinated and specific to the needs of the individual, family and in the context of the community in which the person lives.

- There is a whole-family approach to care and support. Carers' assessments that identify and address carers' needs, comprehension, communication skills, memory, risk factors and ability to meet the identified needs of the person for whom they are caring.

- Risk-assessment processes that are not risk averse are evident.

- There is recognition of abuse and neglect, including self-neglect at an early stage, and steps are taken to engage with the person and provide advice, guidance and appropriate community links.

- There is a recognition of the need for strong leadership and management in supporting practitioners when working with someone who self-neglects. Early identification of interventions that may not be working for the person concerned and support to consider alternative interventions utilising multi-agency skills, knowledge and abilities are vital.

- Methods to prevent or delay the needs for services by utilising community resources and circles of support around the person are evidenced as far as is possible and lawful.

Proportionality

- The least intrusive and restrictive response relevant to the risk presented is actioned as appropriate and recorded.

- The ethical considerations are discussed and evidenced in practice, considering a balance of *beneficence* (the doing of good; active kindness; caring), *non-maleficence* (doing no harm; not inflicting harm on others), *justice* (being fair, moral and equitable) and *autonomy* (freedom from external control and influence; independence).

- Understanding of capacity and consent across all decision making is evidenced.

- Application of the principles of the Mental Capacity Act in practice is evidenced in relation to the person concerned.

- There is evidence of the support offered to help the person understand the decisions to be made, in order that they can make an informed decision.

- Best interest decisions are only made in relation to those decisions where the person is assessed and recorded as lacking capacity and there is evidence of balanced best interest decisions that are not risk averse.

- There is evidence that practitioners have considered those decisions that may be seen as unwise decisions made by a capacitated person. If there is concern about potential capacity, a mental capacity assessment is conducted. The assessment is recorded alongside the advice, support and information given and access appointments with relevant services. The expressed or indicated outcome chosen by the capacitated person is recorded in their own words.

- Practitioners recognise and report when they have 'reasonable suspicion' of abuse, neglect or crime and responses proportionate to the potential risk.

- There is evidence that practitioners have considered the human rights of the person concerned.

Protection

- The person is protected from abuse and neglect via safeguarding procedures. Any care provided is considered in relation to potential neglect rather than self-neglect.

- Eligibility criteria are evidenced against the three-part test.

- Other forms of abuse are considered and identified.

- Circumstances that increase risk are identified and proportionate plans put in place.

- Capacity and consent are integral to protection planning.

- Safeguarding is everyone's business – roles and responsibilities are clarified and coordinated with a key lead person identified.

- Agencies recognise when to share information and what information to share.

- The enquiry process considers the risks, the capacity and consent issues and a wide breadth of potential legislation covering crime, housing, environmental health, care, support, health and wellbeing.

- Risk assessments are undertaken and risk-management plans are put in place.

- Therapeutic and other support is considered where someone has suffered abuse, neglect, loss or bereavement.

- A whole-family approach is considered.

- Criminal investigations and working to support equitable access to justice enable potential victims to be supported in line with the victims' charter and victims' codes of practice.

- The credibility of evidence and credibility of the witness is not determined by a diagnostic judgement. The principles of the Mental Capacity Act apply in supporting the person to understand and in supporting the police to determine credibility.

- Defensible decision making is evident based on legislation, models, methods, theories or research and aligned with what the person did or said that made the practitioner think that this was the appropriate course of action. Recording evidences decision making.

- There is evidence that lessons from serious case reviews, safeguarding adult reviews, domestic homicide reviews and other serious injury or death-related reviews have been learned and any public bodies have acted in accordance with those previous lessons learned.

- The person has access to advocacy where appropriate.

Partnership

- Partnership includes community services and involvement of those services.

- Local solutions are found within the person's chosen community, where possible, to support them in maintaining contact with community resources and facilities.

- Consideration is given to the person's past occupational interests, recreation or leisure interests and they are supported to re-engage with past occupational, study and leisure pursuits to reduce social isolation and regain purpose.

- There is evidence of all partner organisations taking responsibility for decision making and that they recognise accountability for actions or inaction.

- There is evidence that partners have supported each other in breaking down barriers in access to services that could prevent or delay the need for more intrusive or restrictive intervention in the future.

- Safeguarding policies and procedures are recognised and enacted across the partnership.

- All parties are clear about who has oversight and guidance and who will take the lead within any enquiries.

- The person is aware of all agencies involved and recognises the roles and responsibilities of those agencies.

Accountability

- There is informed, transparent practice and decision making across all aspects of care, support and intervention.

- Effective partnership governance in safeguarding is evidenced.

- Partnership accountability for recognising and determining capacity and consent in safeguarding practice is recognised and actioned in safeguarding plans.

- Accountability for sharing of information to prevent or protect a person from abuse or neglect is recognised and actioned in safeguarding plans.

- Accountability in recognising the human rights of an individual and preventing oppression and discrimination is recognised and actioned in safeguarding plans.

- There is support and guidance regarding when to escalate concerns to appropriate strategic or decision-making forums.

- The role of the Court of Protection is recognised and utilised appropriately.

- Wider partnerships such as multi-agency public protection arrangements, multi-agency conferences, sexual abuse referral centres, hate and mate crime initiatives, counter terrorism reporting and the interface between these services are considered, as appropriate.

- Reporting accountability, such as Deprivation of Liberty Safeguards, Care Quality Commission, Disclosure and Barring Service, Trading Standards, is recognised and responded to.

- Clear and transparent care and support planning in one holistic plan is evident.

- All agencies are accountable for lack of early intervention to prevent the deterioration of mental or physical wellbeing.

Information recording and sharing

Information should:

- be drawn up in partnership with the person whose record it is whenever possible

- record the views of the person whose record it is, including whether they have given permission to share information

- include views and a summary of assessment of professionals involved, such as occupationa therapist, nurse, housing officer

- be an accurate up-to-date record of work, which is regularly reviewed and summarised

- include a record of decisions taken and the reasons for these decisions, what has been ruled out and why, why you have chosen the course of action taken. This could be based on legal frameworks, policy frameworks, methods and theories or multi-agency discussions

- include a chronology of significant events

- be evidence based and ethical

- be separate fact from opinion

- incorporate assessment, including all capacity and risk assessments

- include an up-to-date support/care/action plan

- record race/ethnicity, gender, religion, language, disability.

In cases of safeguarding and self-neglect each agency is responsible for its own record keeping, assessment processes and risk-management recording. You may be asked for a report and you will need to ensure that you:

- plan carefully before starting to write. An outline should ensure that all assessment areas are covered

- organise reports into sections, including a chronology of events

- use every day standard English, avoiding technical or legal jargon

- record those consulted to inform the assessment

- explain any technical terms used

- take care to use accurate grammar, spelling and punctuation. Do not rely on spell checkers, as they can 'let through' words that may be correctly spelt but used in the wrong context, such as 'there' and 'their'

- always check that the report is accurate, clear, concise and readable

- write in the first person and use the 'I' statements or words that the person said, and what you determined as a result of their statement. In the absence of statements from the person, record what was observed

- keep the sentence length down to an average of 15–20 words. Stick to one main idea in a sentence

- use active verbs as much as possible

- are concise and avoid needless repetition

- think of the reader. Write sincerely, personally and in a tone that is suitable

- always date and sign written communication

- include identifying details of the writer – name, address, telephone number and email address so that the reader can contact them

- incorporate an appropriate title for the report and include the date

- are aware of the legislation: Data Protection Act 1998, Human Rights Act 1998, Care Act 2014, and the implications for practice.

How the local authority responds

Once a safeguarding referral has been made to the local authority, the response will be determined by the level of self-neglect, the nature of risks involved and the level of care and support needs (see assessment/ risk-assessment process, Chapter 6). In some cases, an assessment for care and support will be required. If initial enquiries determine low-level self-neglect, low-level risk and low-level care and support needs then it is likely that the person will need support to re-engage with family, friends and community. Community support services may be offered advice and guidance from the local authority. The actions requested and the outcomes met will be fed back to the local authority. If these actions fail to prevent deterioration of health and wellbeing, then a new referral to safeguard the person will be required.

Figure 4.1: Levels of self-neglect, risk and care and support needs

Where there are moderate levels of self-neglect, moderate risks and moderate care and support needs it is likely that a multi-agency response will be required to coordinate outcomes and expectations of the person, involvement of the person and feedback to them, capacity assessments, risk assessments and legislative frameworks applicable to the situation. The local authority must determine the best placed agency or person to coordinate these enquiries. Where there are major health concerns, it may require a nurse, doctor or GP to make enquiries and conduct multi-agency meetings to safeguard the person. Where the key issues relate to the home environment, then a housing officer may be best placed to make enquiries and coordinate the response, using support, advice and guidance from the local authority. If these interventions have failed to prevent further self-neglect, or to protect the person from harm, and self-neglect has become severe, the risks and care and support needs have increased, impacting on the person's mental and physical wellbeing, it is likely that the local authority will coordinate safeguarding responses in a multi-agency forum.

A safeguarding referral is made regarding the person who has suffered abuse or neglect, although the safeguarding process considers all those involved, including family, friends and others affected and any potential perpetrators of abuse or neglect. The local authority and health service will need to determine whether the person self-neglecting has capacity to make decisions regarding their own care and support needs and whether they reside with someone or someone is providing care and support for them. If someone is providing care and support to the person, a capacity assessment may also need to be carried out to determine whether they have capacity to understand the care and support needs of the person and how to meet those needs. The outcomes of these assessments will determine whether enquiries are made into neglect or self-neglect.

It is every agency's responsibility to safeguard and, particularly when working with people who self-neglect, access, rapport and knowledge regarding the person will determine the best-placed agency to manage enquiries and coordinate responses. Too often a referral is made to the local authority and agencies determine that this is the end of their safeguarding responsibility. If the person, or their situation is better supported by the expertise of a particular profession, then they may be best placed to convene multi-agency meetings and lead enquiries and to involve the person and support them in a manner that they wish to be supported.

Defensible decision making

What is defensible decision making?

A defensible decision follows the word 'because'. It is a way of justifying an action.

I chose this course of action because...
I ruled this out because...

Following the 'because' word will be what the person did or said that made you consider this course of action or rule something out – the law, policy, models, methods or theory that informed the course of action and what the course of action was proportionate to the situation.

An example of this may be: I chose this course of action because Mrs Johnson said that she did not want to be referred to substance misuse services. Mrs Johnson said that she was not ready to make a change in her drinking at the moment, because after speaking with the fire service recently, she was concentrating on giving up smoking due to the identified fire risks. Mrs Johnson has agreed to see the smoking cessation nurse. Mrs Johnson recognises that she falls when intoxicated and with goods piled high (clutter rating scale 9) the risks are significant; however, she sees the fire risks as a priority. She has agreed to wear a call pendant to press for help until she is ready to consider addressing her drinking problems. Using the Mental Capacity Act 2005 it was determined that Mrs Johnson had capacity to make this decision about a referral to substance misuse services and has made it clear that she understood the risks. The fire service has the property recorded as a high fire risk property. Mrs Johnson declined further assistive technology and a telephone call service to check her safety, but has agreed to call in to see her neighbour every day to ensure that she is safe.

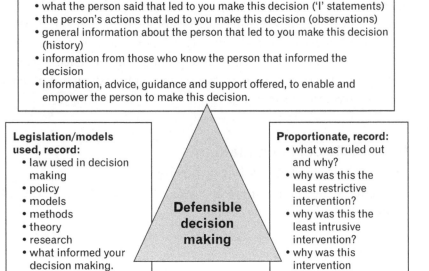

Figure 4.2: The triangle of defensible recording

If using a risk assessment, identify against each section of the risk assessment what the person did or said, what others said and why the response was proportionate. This model can be used to ensure that any legislation, policies, procedures and tools used are justified.

Information sharing and defensible decision making
Risk to others, reasonable suspicion of a crime and public interest
The philosopher Kant described humans as having the unique capacity to make reasoned and rational choices and decisions. As a result of humans being regarded as rational thinkers, Kant identifies that humans should not only consider meeting their own needs and happiness through their actions and choice, but also have moral regard for others'. Autonomy is described by Kant as a significant and important right. When people have the capacity to make decisions that

realise their own vision of how they should live their life they should be entitled to do this without interference. Kant emphasised that in planning your own life events, you should not adversely affect the rights of others. These values are based within deontological ethics and it is largely these moral principles that we instruct our children in today. As our children grow up we enable them to make more and more autonomous decisions. We also tell them that in making these decisions they should not create a risk for others, should not make people overly worried or concerned, should not be party to or commit a crime and they should be caring and supportive of others.

A person who self-neglects can choose to live life in a way that they see fit (as long as they are capable of making these decisions) and they should be entitled to do this without interference, as long as it does not adversely affect the rights of others. A person self-neglecting has a moral obligation not to impose toxic substances on someone, and an obligation not to create a fire risk, or a public health risk due to rats, flies vermin or bodily fluids. There is a legal obligation not to place anyone else in danger, or to commit a crime, and a right not to have a crime committed against them.

This fine balance of needs, rights and responsibilities can be described by making an analogy with a three-legged stool. In choosing our life pathway we are like a three-legged stool. If we do not equally balance our needs, our rights and our responsibilities then the stool will fall over unsupported. For example, the person self-neglecting may have:

- a need to have their belongings around them

- a right to have access to suitable housing

- a responsibility to prevent risk to others by maintaining compliance with the tenancy agreement and maintaining that house.

Many caring practitioners are happy to discuss the needs and rights of individuals and worry about the sensitive aspects of discussing responsibilities, but by not discussing these necessary topics early we are playing a role in the person's deterioration. If we can support a person to recognise their responsibilities before self-neglect escalates and provide very early preventative safeguarding measures exploring the consequences of meeting or not meeting these responsibilities, this may prevent hoarding and self-neglect from escalating. These principles can be seen in relation to all aspects affecting a person's self-care. To offer another example let us take a look at needs, rights and responsibilities in relation to social isolation, where a person may have:

- a need to live their life without worrying about people's responses

- a right to have access to family and friends

- a responsibility to provide parental support, or to not cause other family members excessive worry or concern.

If we can support a person to maintain family contact before this breaks down and provide carers' support, this will meet the person's needs and rights to have access to family. If we encourage a person to engage in community activities it will support the development or maintainance friendships and if we identify responsibilities at an early stage and support the person to make choices that do not adversely affect others, then we may be able to prevent self-neglect from escalating.

Where the responsibilities of the person to maintain the law and keep others safe break down, public sector workers have a duty to consider the level and extent of this risk and act to prevent harm from occurring. Article 2 of the Human Rights Act identifies the right to life and the positive obligation placed on authorities to take preventative operational measures to protect an individual whose life may be at risk from the criminal acts of another individual. Public bodies violate their obligations to prevent and suppress offences against the person when they know or ought to have known that there was at that time a risk to the life of an identified individual or individuals from criminal acts of a third party and that they failed to take measures within the scope of their powers which reasonably might be expected to avoid that risk (Osman and another v Ferguson and another CA 1993).

Legislation pertaining to police, environmental health, child protection and safeguarding adults reinforces the need to share information where there is reasonable suspicion of a crime.

We can therefore share relevant information with the police and local authority where further enquiries are required to consider risk to others, potential crime, and public interest issues. If the person does not consent to the referral then this means that services may not have their cooperation and they are free to make autonomous decisions that do not adversely affect others. Actions taken by public sector services must ensure that there are benefits to those concerned and that actions do not increase risk.

Domestic abuse and severe mental ill health

A person cannot be seen as consenting if they are being coerced or controlled into making a decision. Consent requires an autonomous decision to be made by the person. Domestic abuse and coercive and controlling behaviours that may have led to the victim self-neglecting may be a line of enquiry, made in a sensitive manner that diminishes rather than increases risk. It is likely that this enquiry will be police-led. If there is suspicion that coercive and controlling behaviour is affecting decision making, the police will make enquiries regarding S76 of the Serious Crime Act 2015. If domestic abuse cannot be ruled out this will form part of the initial enquiry process.

If a person's mental health requires assessment under the Mental Health Act 1983, amended 2007, consent is not required for detention purposes. Family and advocates would be sought.

The Caldicott principles apply to all information sharing:

- Justify the purpose.

- Do not use personal information unless it is absolutely necessary.

- Use the minimum amount of personal information necessary.

- Access to personal information should be on a need-to-know basis.

- Everyone should be aware of their responsibilities with regard to personal information.

- Actions should be taken to ensure that those handling personal information are aware of their responsibilities and obligations to respect and individuals' confidentiality.

- Understand and comply with the law.

The Care Act and information sharing

S14.43 of the Care Act's Care and Support Statutory Guidance identifies:

> Early sharing of information is the key to providing an effective response where there are emerging concerns. To ensure effective safeguarding arrangements:
>
> 1. All organisations must have arrangements in place which set out clearly the processes and the principles for sharing information between each other, with other professionals and the SAB; this could be via an Information Sharing Agreement to formalise the arrangements.
>
> 2. No professional should assume that someone else will pass on information which they think may be critical to the safety and wellbeing of the adult. If a professional has concerns about the adult's welfare and believes they are suffering or likely to suffer abuse or neglect, then they should share the information with the local authority and, or, the police if they believe or suspect that a crime has been committed.

S14.95 identifies:

> Whether or not the adult has capacity to give consent, action may need to be taken if others are, or will be put at risk if nothing is done, or where it is in the public interest to take action because a criminal offence has occurred. It is the responsibility of all staff and members of the public to act on any suspicion or evidence of abuse or neglect and to pass on their concerns to a responsible person or agency.

The British Medical Association's adult safeguarding toolkit reinforces this:

> ...where a competent adult explicitly refuses any supporting intervention, this should normally be respected. Exceptions to this may be where a criminal offence may have taken place or where there may be a significant risk of harm to a third party. If, for example, there may be an abusive adult in a position of authority in relation to other vulnerable adults, it may be appropriate to breach confidentiality and disclose information to an appropriate authority. Where a criminal offence is suspected it may also be necessary to

take legal advice. Ongoing support should also be offered. Because an adult initially refuses the offer of assistance he or she should not therefore be lost to or abandoned by relevant services. The situation should be monitored and the individual informed that she or he can take up the offer of assistance at any time (p.28).

S14.187 of the Care and Support Statutory Guidance identifies:

Agencies should draw up a common agreement relating to confidentiality and setting out the principles governing the sharing of information, based on the welfare of the adult or of other potentially affected adults. Any agreement should be consistent with the principles set out in the *Caldicott Review published 2013* ensuring that:

- information will only be shared on a 'need to know' basis when it is in the interests of the adult

- confidentiality must not be confused with secrecy

- informed consent should be obtained but, if this is not possible and other adults are at risk of abuse or neglect, it may be necessary to override the requirement

- it is inappropriate for agencies to give assurances of absolute confidentiality in cases where there are concerns about abuse, particularly in those situations when other adults may be at risk.

S14.188 identifies:

Where an adult has refused to consent to information being disclosed for these purposes, then practitioners must consider whether there is an overriding public interest that would justify information sharing (for example, because there is a risk that others are at risk of serious harm) and wherever possible, the appropriate Caldicott Guardian should be involved. Confidentiality: NHS Code of Practice sets out guidance on public interest disclosure.

S14.189 states: 'Decisions about who needs to know and what needs to be known should be taken on a case-by-case basis, within agency policies and the constraints of the legal framework.'

The Crime and Disorder Act 1998

S115 of the Crime and Disorder Act allows information to be shared for the purpose of community safety between a number of relevant authorities:

- Police forces
- Police authorities
- Local authorities
- Probation boards and trusts
- Fire and rescue authorities
- Health authorities
- Registered social landlords
- Transport for London.

Under S17 of the Crime and Disorder Act, relevant authorities have a duty to share relevant information with relevant people to reduce or prevent crime and disorder, including anti-social behaviour (England and Wales).

Relevant information can be shared with relevant people where there is reasonable suspicion of abuse (reasonable suspicion of a crime).

Information may need to be shared for enquiry purposes, to determine whether abuse or neglect is occurring, whether the person is self-neglecting due to historic abuse or neglect, current or historic domestic abuse, whether they are being targeted for hate/mate crime, whether there is anti-social behaviour and to rule out other potential crime.

Case law judgments

There have been a number of cases that have highlighted the need to share information without the consent of the individual. This includes when:

- it needs to be shared by law
- it is needed to prevent, detect and prosecute serious crime
- there is a public interest

- there is risk of death or serious harm

- there is a public health interest

- it is in the interests of the person's health

- it is in the interests of the person concerned.

There still needs to be careful consideration to ensure that the disclosure is justified on the basis of an overriding interest.

Ten steps to information sharing

A safeguarding referral can be made without the consent of the person. Enquiries would be to consider the following aspects:

1. Is there a risk to others (children, other vulnerable people, neighbours)?

2. Is there reasonable suspicion of a crime (domestic abuse, historical abuse, hate/mate crime, exploitation, financial, etc.)?

3. Are there public interest issues to consider?

4. Could there be a domestic abuse situation involving coercive and controlling behaviours?

5. Could the person require a Mental Health Act assessment?

6. Does the person have capacity to make each relevant decision and has the appropriate agency assessed capacity to consent or decline the proposed course of action?

7. Has the person been provided with the appropriate advocacy and support to make relevant decisions?

8. What are the person's wishes, expectations and desired outcomes?

9. Do agencies need to get together to discuss risks, legislation and capacity assessment coordination and accountability?

10. Have all agencies recorded in a defensible manner how, where and why information has been shared? If information has been refused that is necessary to safeguard a person, has the legislation and duty to share information for safeguarding

purposes been considered and ruled out? How has this been justified?

Some local authorities have confused the need to share information for safeguarding purposes with the autonomous decision-making processes that do not affect others. A person is entitled to make decisions about themselves and their care provision, treatment or services when they have the capacity to make autonomous decisions. In cases of self-neglect it is rare that on first being approached a person will disclose potential crime, abuse, historical abuse or neglect, risks that their hoard poses to the public, the extent of their mental ill health or the impact of domestic abuse. It is very important that the information is shared with the local authority and police where required so that enquiries can be made during the process of getting to know the person.

To give an example of how the ten-step approach relates to the decision-making process I shall give two scenarios.

In the first scenario, a young man who has autism is groomed for suicide bombing. You go out to meet with the man who tells you that he has capacity to make his own decisions. He tells you that he understands that he will die and that he will kill others. Do you state that he has capacity and does not consent to the referral?

No. You make the referral because the enquiry needs to:

- determine the risk to others

- consider potential crime

- explore whether it is in the public interest to monitor and observe him more closely

- determine whether he has been coerced or intimidated into making this decision

- assess his mental wellbeing.

In addition, further capacity assessments may be required, a multi-agency meeting will need to be convened and appropriate representation may be required.

In the second scenario, an elderly lady living on the tenth floor of a black of flats, smokes 50 self-rolled cigarettes per day. The house is filled with newspapers and magazines. Piles of papers between four feet and ceiling height create gangways between the armchair and the cooker. None of the rooms can be accessed and so the lady sleeps in the armchair. The lady has breathing difficulties and has a large oxygen tank in front of her. She stubs her cigarettes out on the arms of the chair. The lady describes the risks and clearly understands that she could cause a major explosion or fire hazard, but refuses any referrals to services.

Do you state that the woman has capacity to make this decision and walk away?

No, because your enquiry will have to rule out each of the ten steps before coming to that conclusion. Safeguarding considers all affected by the situation.

Figure 4.3: The ten-step approach

Chapter 5

THERAPEUTIC INTERVENTIONS

A comprehensive assessment can include therapeutic interventions, or the focus may be specifically therapeutic. In any event, the professional will have to determine the factors impacting on the person, when and why the self-neglecting behaviours began and the person's own narrative regarding these events. This will assist in identifying the forms of therapeutic work required to support the person concerned. In most cases of severe self-neglect, it is highly beneficial to have psychological intervention. Where this is not possible the occupational therapist, health worker or social worker may be able to receive psychology supervision to support their interventions with the person. I have worked with victims of severe trauma, while working within mental health and substance misuse social work and found that regular psychology supervision supported my work with those individuals and also enhanced my toolbox of skills and interventions. While I am not psychologically trained, I was able to undertake some work that provided long-term support.

Some local authorities have specialist workers who engage with people self-neglecting; however, this is not available to everyone. It may be that the social worker will have to become more creative in care and support planning, identifying funding and supporting the person to advertise for the right individual to assist them, or enlisting the assistance of someone close who is capable of establishing a good working relationship. There may be complex underlying factors that have resulted in self-neglect that require more intense support, or there may be simple factors that require the person to re-engage with others. The assessment process will have to determine the level and extent of trauma or loss that the person has experienced, and meet that need as appropriate.

During my work, I often hear people comment that this type of long-term work is unrealistic and unsustainable, that inevitably if the person does not engage with services then the case will be closed. So far, we have considered the reasons why a person may not be engaging and why we need to explore this in more detail through section 42 enquiries. In my view the full extent of the Care Act 2014 and implications for change have not yet fully infiltrated all aspects of health and social care. Creative use of family, friends and community resources is not always an alternative to traditionally commissioned services and, as a result, social care professionals remain involved in the provision of services where there are low-level needs better addressed by enabling the person to remain in touch with their local community and services. Conversely, high-risk cases that are complex and require multi-agency approaches are closed due to increasing pressures and the demands placed on staff.

In training, I ask the social care professionals and their managers and senior managers to consider an analogy with health care responses to cases. If a person has influenza or a moderate ailment, they are offered treatment, medical support and directed towards resources that will prevent deterioration of health. This may amount to a few hours of health care support. If a person has a brain tumour or a life-threatening illness, many hours of health care are offered to medically assess the person, test what the cause is, determine where the tumour began and the dangers posed by the tumour. There will be a coordinated response across a variety of health care services leading up to the potential operation itself. The operation will last a considerable amount of time involving a variety of professionals, directed by the lead consultant and then there is rehabilitation, follow-up support, potentially therapeutic support and eventually community health interventions. The time that is afforded a person who is potentially going to die is vast. This relates back to Article 2 of the Human Rights Act, the right to life and the need for public sector services to prevent death. It is also a balance of ethics, including beneficence, non-maleficence, justice and autonomy.

A person self-neglecting is on a pathway of deteriorating mental and physical wellbeing and, in some cases, it may be evident that the possibility of death is not far away. I have made it clear within this book that early intervention is of paramount importance; however, where this has not successfully occurred to prevent deterioration, we have an obligation to consider the human rights of the person and to demonstrate that we have done everything that the power of all agencies involved can lawfully think of to support the person concerned and prevent death. In such circumstances, it is inevitable that these cases will be resource-intensive and this must be acknowledged when coordinating responses. To build an initial rapport with the person will take time before any real intervention work is even considered.

Building a rapport

Many people who hoard and self-neglect feel embarrassed and ashamed about their circumstances. Can you imagine a time when you have felt low in mood, your self-esteem is low and you have felt that you cannot face the world? I call this 'duvet time', perhaps when you have split up with a partner, lost your job, fallen out with someone close to you, or someone close to you has died. Think about how you felt, how you acted and who you saw during this time. Often we shut the door, take to our bed and build a nest of things around us and will not even speak to our best friends. The house may become untidy, dishes go unwashed, we do not bathe as regularly as usual and we hang on to things that have sentimental value, value in distracting us from our feelings, value in easing the pain somehow. What happens when someone knocks on the door? During my duvet times I have not wanted to open the door to anyone, and I certainly would not want someone coming into my house, particularly a stranger.

Imagine these feelings exacerbated and developing as a pattern of behaviour over years and years. For some people who hoard and self-neglect they have never left this stage of self-preservation. You want to develop a rapport with a person in difficult circumstances and so you need to be very sensitive to the feelings of the person concerned.

When people feel anxious or ashamed they appreciate a friendly, non-intrusive, non-judgemental introduction with someone who is patient, attentive and understanding (Silverman 1969; Barker 2009).

When initially meeting someone, *do*:

- talk about things that the person enjoys and is interested in

- use the person's given name early in conversation

- choose non-threatening and safe topics

- reflect the person's language and do not use language that may be perceived as derogatory in relation to the home, or personal appearance, such as clutter, hoard

- be an active listener and reflect back some of the key points to check your understanding

- be conscious of your body language and other non-verbal signals – consider how you are going to manage any smells, seating arrangements and infestations prior to attending and arrange a suitable place for both parties to comfortably engage with each other

- create eye contact and use non-verbal open communication methods

- ensure that you are speaking on the same level and not where one person is standing or sitting higher than the other. Try to sit at a 45-degree angle rather than 180-degree angle to the person. Sitting opposite can feel a little like an interview

- avoid talking too much about yourself and your concerns

- avoid asking direct questions

- use encouraging language and highlight strengths

- be aware of methods of communication used by the person – do they use a mobile phone, the internet, read their letters

- if it feels comfortable, begin using the miracle question: 'If you were to wake up tomorrow and a miracle had occurred, what would things be like for you? What would you hear, feel, see, eat, be doing?'

Do not:

- discuss the hoarding or self-neglect

- make suggestions about their possessions

- try to persuade or argue with the person

- touch the person's belongings without prior permission. People often have strong feelings about their possessions and can find it upsetting when someone touches them

- launch into assessment questions on the first visit. Work on establishing the person's likes, interests and strengths

- be unreliable – this may appear to the person as a lack of respect and may also reflect other poor experiences

- send appointment letters, if the person does not open their mail. Thank the person for meeting with you, tell them what you have enjoyed about your discussion and ask if you can call again. Establish a form of letting the person know that you would like to see them and make an appointment.

Trauma, abuse, neglect, loss and bereavement

People who self-neglect often do so as a result of trauma, abuse, early neglect, domestic abuse or bereavement. It is therefore useful to consider the level and extent of the trauma suffered, if the person can recall a specific time or event. Traumatic memories are often stored in a person's brain without them being able to directly recall the event. This is because traumatic memories are devoid of context or chronology. The part of the brain that helps us to respond to trauma stimulates the senses to keep us alive, so the person can often recall sights, sounds, smells, tastes or sensations, but not detail about what happened, or when it happened. Herman (1997) describes memories as, 'lacking verbal narrative and context, rather they are encoded in the form of vivid sensations and images' (p.38). It is worth considering that a seemingly insignificant experience that invalidates a large part of a person's values, identity or view of the world in which they live may cause major trauma.

Traumatic events can cause a person to question human relationships. The psychological processes that enable a person to develop human attachments and link the individual to their community are affected. Trauma also affects how safe a person feels and can damage self-esteem and concepts of order and meaning. A sense of safety is developed through early relationships with parents, or caregivers. If there is a lack of care in childhood, childhood neglect, or parents who hoarded and didn't provide a safe environment, it may be difficult for the person to imagine a caring world, and identify what they would want in their own world. This is because if a person is feeling traumatised and cries for help, they would usually call for the person they are closest to.

When abuse or neglect occur this cry often goes unheard, leaving the person feeling, lost, alone or abandoned. This sense of being different and disconnected can have a significant impact on later relationships. In some cases of childhood neglect, the child struggles to recognise self-care, order and maintenance of themselves and their home, as they get older. Usual sorting and caring processes are not offered to the child and the adult grows up without experience or resources to draw on often leaving them feeling different, misunderstood, frustrated and sometimes angry. Attachment may move from people to objects, a favourite toy, blanket or object.

In my work with people who have suffered domestic abuse and people who had been raped, I often came across people who stopped taking care of their own health and environment. There were different explanations, but the essentially similar component was a lack of self-esteem and in some cases a lack of self-awareness. A lack of care and respect can lead us to reflect on our own sense of self, with negatives constantly affirmed by the abuser. The person focuses on these negatives and can even seek them out, further confirming their negative suspicions of themselves.

Often people who suffer trauma feel guilt. A rape victim may question what they could have done differently, what they should have done, the choices and decisions that they made. Following a bereavement, grieving families identify feeling guilty because they had not been able to see the person at the time of their death, or about medical attention that they fear could have been sought sooner. These feelings of guilt may be initially more palatable than powerlessness and helplessness to people who have experienced rape or suffered loss. There was little they could have done to change the situation; however, the impact of guilt and shame can be significant in affecting self-worth.

Post-traumatic stress is well recognised as a result of war, sexual violence and childhood physical abuse, but can also be triggered by assault, being threatened, an accident or the death of a loved one. The person may relive the memory repeatedly, traumatic memories can be triggered by any form of sensory stimulus, and so the person may withdraw, socially isolating themselves. They may fear talking about the traumatic event in case this increases anxiety, sleeplessness and emotional distress. Some people who have suffered a trauma turn to drugs or alcohol to manage their distress, others may self-harm in a variety of different ways. The person could become detached from family, friends, lose interest in activities, find it difficult to experience positive emotions, be easily startled, appear angry or irritated, and in general disengage from society.

The first step is to help the person regain a sense of safety and security. It is important that assurances of safety form part of the initial discussion, but more importantly, you should not make assurances that you cannot keep. Maintain appointment times, do not cancel or change appointments at the last minute. This may exacerbate the negative feelings associated with the trauma. The person may need assurances that they are not going to be abandoned or left to cope with traumatic emotions alone. Be clear about your appointment times and the amount of intervention offered, what will happen next and how support will be provided. The next step is to support the person to regain a sense of control over what has happened and be able to bear the feelings associated with the trauma. To achieve this, you will need to develop trust and support re-engagement with the wider community. This will assist in the person developing a sense of power and control, connectedness and autonomy. It may also help them reflect on their current heath or living conditions and contemplate change.

We have already explored the concept of trauma as an incident that stimulates the person's sensory interpretation and understanding of the event. The association between the sensory interpretation and how the person interprets that meaning and their emotional responses is called the metadata. The exploration of metadata can assist the person in placing data in a chronology and recognising that the traumatic event is in the past by analysing the information via cognitive behavioural therapy (CBT).

In addition to trauma therapy, other therapeutic interventions may be considered and are explored in more detail within this book. Utilising psychotherapy, the person may come to understand the narratives they have about themselves from childhood and potentially how self-neglect developed. Neuro-linguistic programming may also help them to transform the narrative of traumatic incidents and change their negative narrative about themselves. In addition, motivational interviewing can assist the person in exploring their own identity as being separate from the collection of clutter and help them in establishing purpose in their own lives.

The sensory stimulus of trauma can produce intense responses that are difficult for the person to interpret and address. Supporting the person to identify the trigger for these responses that starts the sequence of events can be effective in supporting the person to prevent the rapid and frightening trauma response. This can be very scary for the person as they may feel that by talking about the event they lose control and fall into the post-traumatic emotions, feelings, anxiety and stress. The experience of the trauma triggered by a stimulus is more intense than the original experience and can persist for decades. People have their own pace for processing trauma, and it is important to recognise the dangers in pushing people to address issues too soon, or in introducing a number of traumatic incidents in one session. This can be particularly difficult for practitioners trying to assess the needs of an individual who is self-neglecting. The competing time demands of human resources, the deterioration of the person's mental and physical wellbeing and the desire to solve the perceived problems compete with the slow pace of a person's ability to consider trauma and change. It may not be possible for the person to consider all elements of the assessment within the traditional health and social care assessment timeframes. This could cause further trauma symptoms and become counterproductive for the person concerned.

Symptoms of trauma can include overwhelming anxiety, panic attacks and the ability to separate the person from their bodily experiences (disassociation). These symptoms are triggered by a stimulus, which may be a sensory stimulus, photograph, word or television programme. It may be someone who reminds the individual of the perpetrator of a traumatic event. The person may or may not know what the stimulus is, or there may be a number of stimuli. This can be a sudden, unwelcome and unexpected intrusion and may be a 'flashback'. Professionals often expect flashbacks to be a memory of the traumatic event, but because the event is stored without context, the person experiences the emotions intensely, as if the event is happening at the time of the flashback, but it may not come in traditional memory format. It may be a flicker book of sounds, words, images, without faces or meaning. A person may be able to tell you what it feels like when they start to have a flashback; often people describe a sensation in their upper arms or thighs, or sensations experienced at the time of the traumatic event. Some people may not be able to recognise the beginning of a flashback and may have little memory of what occurred following the event. In some more extreme instances, people can experience voices telling them to do things such as harm themselves or others.

If a person is experiencing flashbacks it is always advisable to have some psychological support for them wherever possible. When working with anyone who has experienced loss, bereavement or trauma, it is useful to learn how to disengage them from the negative experiences before leaving them; this is called 'anchoring'. Anchoring techniques may be used prior to assessment or therapeutic intervention to try and prevent flashbacks or to bring a person back from a flashback more quickly and should be used prior to leaving a person. During an assessment or therapeutic intervention try to get the person to sit on a seat with their feet flat on the ground and arms rested on the arms of the chair. Encourage the person to know that their feet are firmly on the ground and to feel the material of the chair arm. Ask the person to tell you what they can hear within the room or what tells them that they are present within the room. It may be helpful to ask the person to name things of a certain theme in the room such as five round objects that you can see. A helpful question may be to ask the person to tell you something that they know is real now and that helps them to recognise that the traumatic event is in the past.

Find out from the person the things that they enjoy as an independent adult, things that have always been associated with positive and happy memories, but nothing that led to or was associated with a trauma. It may be helpful for the person to gather a box of objects that they can talk about that invoke happy memories. Each session a new object can be taken from the box and described.

Ask the person to place their hand just above their belly button and breathe so that their hand is pushed up and down, to try and breathe from their diaphragm. This can assist in preventing a panic attack. Knowing that you can help the person to prevent the negative and frightening impact of trauma responses will help them to feel able to discuss events with you. Talking about traumatic events can be exhausting for a person, because of the emotional effort and the associated muscle tension and stiffness. Remind them of how well they are doing, how these feelings and emotions are their way of getting through a very difficult experience and that they should try to relax afterwards and treat themselves with something that will make them feel calm. It is important that the method of relaxation is not associated with the hoarding or self-neglect behaviours and should not involve drugs or alcohol if possible.

Trauma may cause a person to fluctuate between passive and aggressive emotions, appearing to engage and then disengage. This may be part of the process of change, with the person beginning to test out how they feel, thinking and responding differently to people and environments. Positive reinforcement and a focus on a person's strengths can be very helpful. People need to be supported to mourn the loss of a relative or the loss caused by a traumatic event. Recognition of the struggles, difficulties and resources used by the person to get through trauma can help. A person may have needed to shut themselves down a little, become attached to something, not people, and recognise beauty elsewhere in order to keep themselves feeling safe; however, these coping mechanisms can become counterproductive and even destructive the longer they are utilised. To consider change on this scale, you need to develop a good working relationship with them.

Systemic approaches

People cannot be seen in isolation; they are part of their family group, friendships, community and formal networks around work and leisure pursuits. These are all dynamic aspects of a person's support network and places for support and comfort, particularly when contemplating change. The interdependency of the people within each network ensures support and reassurance. Maintaining social systems requires input and energy, and these systems eventually break down if there is not sufficient support from others. Social systems can create energy for survival through synergy, meaning that the sum of the group support is greater than each of its member's individual input. A social system that lacked synergy is in trouble unless it draws energy from others – in other words it is difficult for one person to support their emotional and physical wellbeing in isolation, or when support systems lack impetus or energy to provide support.

Exploring the systemic relationships of someone who self-neglects can provide information about how those relationships broke down, the impact on the person and the development of social isolation. In working with someone self-neglecting the dynamics of family life, past friendships, access to community resources, past and present work relationships can be drawn on. Look for what changed, why a relationship broke down, what the present barriers are. Once the systemic relationships have been assessed, a key factor in supporting a person to make change must be to help them identify and plan for future networks that are not dependent on professional input. Re-engaging with people and having successful, meaningful personal relationships is one of the most important things to support the person to achieve.

The cycle of change

People seek to make choices that protect them from feeling vulnerable and will adapt their behaviours to changing circumstances. Change may be caused by grief or loss, adapting to life following abuse or coping in abusive situations. Elderly people may have to make changes due to deteriorating physical and mental wellbeing. All people wish to maintain control of their own lives, but the impact of becoming more frail and elderly, managing after abuse, coping with a disability or following a loss may make traditional coping mechanisms difficult.

Grief, loss, bereavement, diagnosis, abuse and neglect or major change in a person's life all impact on their ability to respond in ways that maintain their identity, contact with others, proactive involvement and achievement within a work or community life and physical and mental wellbeing. No one likes to be dependent and no one likes to admit the extent of their dependency, and the more a person's identity and self-esteem are based on their independence, the less likely they are to accept help. The person's perceptions of the relationship between independence and support can be explored by asking them to consider the key questions related to the areas shown in Figure 5.1 and encourage them to talk about their responses.

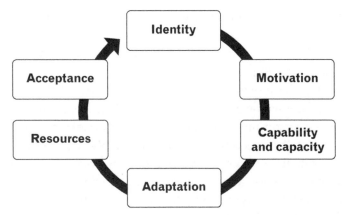

Figure 5.1: Key areas for assessing the relationship between independence and support

Identity

Ask the person the answer these questions about themselves:

- Who am I?

- What would I consider as my identity?

- What do I need?

- What are my goals?

- What are my expectations?

- What are my aims?

- If I could change my life, what would it look like?

Motivation

- What is my motivation to care for myself?

- What is my motivation to be independent?

- What would I like to achieve?

- What motivates me in other aspects of my life?

- How do I maximise my independence?

Capability and capacity

- Can I manage all the decisions that I need to make?

- Do I get overwhelmed and confused by some decisions?

- Do I recognise the risks involved in the choices that I make?

- Can I identify the risks and benefits of the choices that I make?

- Can I identify the consequences or potential consequences of my choices?

- Can I recognise why others may worry about me?

- Can I perform the tasks to keep me well?

- Can I get a good night's sleep?

- Can I eat a varied and balanced diet?

- Can I get medical attention when I am unwell?

- Can I manage to maintain my home?

- Can I maintain personal hygiene?

- Can I recognise choices that may be a danger or cause a risk to others?

Adaptation

- Can I learn a new skill?

- Can I adapt my existing skills?

- Can I get the support required to adapt to any health changes (physical and psychological)?

- Can I make new friends?

- Can I access community resources?

- Can I make use of my existing skills?

- Can I take action and respond to new situations?

Resources

- Can I get in touch with family members?

- Can I accept support from family members?

- Can I get in touch with friends?

- Can I accept support from friends?

- Can I offer my skills to the community where I live?

- Can I be involved in community activities?

- Can I identify how I feel about engaging with family, friends and services within the community?

Acceptance

- Can I accept support?

- Can I identify any benefits of gaining the support that I need?

- Do I feel that I am able to maintain control when accepting support?

- Can I identify things that might make me feel safe in accepting support?

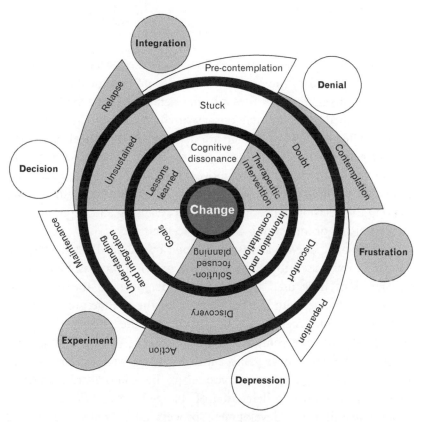

Figure 5.2: The wheel of change

Prochaska and DiClemente (1983) used a transtheoretical model of behaviour to demonstrate the process of change. The model describes how people can modify their behaviours that are seen as problematic, in order to create positive behaviour, or change. The decision-making processes of the person are central to the model and the activities that people use to move through the process of change. There are five stages identified in the cycle of change, with the potential for a sixth stage of relapse:

- Pre-contemplation

- Contemplation

- Preparation

- Action

- Maintenance

- Relapse.

What this transtheoretical model does not describe very well is the emotions invoked by the process of change and how practitioners can support someone to work through these emotions. Elizabeth Kübler-Ross described the emotional journey of change in her Change Curve Model. The emotions of change are depicted in the wheel of change by circles spinning off from the wheel itself. Starting with denial, emotions change as the person moves through the process becoming angry and frustrated, depressed and then experimenting with change, making the decision to change and either relapsing and beginning the process again, or integrating change into their life.

The change curve was first developed by Kübler-Ross during the 1960s and was used to demonstrate the grieving process. Since then, organisations have used this model to demonstrate the emotional process of change, with the last element of the change process being integration with acceptance, hope for the future and trust (Kübler-Ross 1998). Anyone going through a process of grief or change will recognise that sometimes you seem to be doing well and then out of the blue something hits you and you relapse back into distress, anger or denial. The emotional rollercoaster of change is never a linear process, more a learning and development process until finally the change is accepted. I have therefore added the emotional responses to the change wheel connected to the actions towards change identified by Prochaska and DiClemente (1983). The emotional response to change is important to understand alongside the decision-making processes, because we cannot address the actions required without considering the reactions invoked.

In social care situations where the practitioner is attempting to motivate change, consideration must be given to the dynamics of power and control, with the end goal being that the person regains power and control within their life. Sherry Arnstein, writing in 1969, developed a ladder of citizen participation to identify where the power lies during a time of change, a time when important decisions must be made. Arnstein (1969) identified that the initial stages of attempting to initiate change with a person involve a process of manipulation and therapeutic intervention. In the change wheel, the emotion experience is denial, as the person is not yet ready to consider change. This pre-contemplation stage is where the practitioner and the person self-neglecting perceive the situation as stuck, nothing is changing and the person's physical and mental wellbeing continues to deteriorate. A stuck person would have changed the 'stuckness' and the debilitating aspect of their situation if they knew how to. On our wheel of change, the person will remain stuck without assertive intervention. During this stage, you may hear a person say things such as, 'As far as I am concerned this is just me, this is how I live, I don't have any problems that need changing.' Even when a person begins contemplating change they can feel stuck just considering the change process, pondering the difficulties of change.

To stop a person feeling stuck, an internal conflict must be created to instigate the desire to change and ensure that the need for change becomes greater than the effort to change. To move a person from pre-contemplation to the contemplation of change, the practitioner must create a dissonant discourse – communication that creates a conflict between the person's actions and their self-identity. Not many people would describe themselves as dirty, untidy, disorganised and chaotic as part of their identity and therefore understanding how a person describes their own identity is a starting point for cognitive dissonance. The difference between their identity and their behaviours creates a conflict that the person then wants to make congruent. This is the most intrusive element of change and should be carefully considered in relation to what the person wants to achieve. Asking the miracle question can assist in determining this and then we can be reassured that the means of achieving the objective of change are consistent with the desired outcomes identified by the person themselves. Raising consciousness and assisting the person to observe, interpret and reflect on the problems caused by self-neglecting is required. Prochaska and DiClemente (1983) describe raising consciousness as the first stage of promoting change.

I shall describe each therapeutic intervention in more detail later in this chapter; however, I shall explore the processes involved in supporting change here. During the pre-contemplation stage:

- if the person is in denial or stuck then you can confirm with them that you see they are not ready for change. This creates a little conflict within the person but also allows them to trust that you are listening and responding to them

- reinforce that you are going to work with them at their pace and that you will not impose change. You will have to be open and honest if there are legal reasons enforcing change

- encourage the person to reflect on and evaluate their behaviours (describe). The use of picture boards that demonstrate what a person wants to achieve can be powerful

- encourage self-exploration, without seeking change, to establish:
  - when self-neglecting behaviours began
  - when things were different
  - what changed
  - their personal narrative

- encourage the person to explore the risks posed by self-neglect and promote open communication about what the outcomes may be if change does not occur.

Once a person begins to consider change, they may begin to doubt whether change can happen, becoming frustrated by potential barriers. Helping the person to understand how things have become so problematic and why it all began, what they gain from these coping mechanisms and what they lose as a result enables a person to contextualise the need for change.

Considering the historical impact of loss and bereavement, trauma or neglect in addition to the potential forthcoming loss of current lifestyle is the beginning of the person preparing for change. This aspect of change can feel very uncomfortable and the person may at times feel depressed and overwhelmed. At any point in this process where you become concerned for the person you must consider making a referral for psychological intervention. Reinforce how the person has managed to cope and survive, despite the challenges that they have faced. It is possible that the person may fall back to denial or get stuck in contemplation again, but now you can remind them of the things that they have said that make life difficult for them and reflect on what has been learned so far.

Encourage the person to evaluate the pros and cons of behaviour change. Consider the person's strengths. Begin planning one small action, identified by the person. This is a good time to get a picture or mood board together that identifies what the change might look like. Support the person to identify how they will know that they have been successful with this task. Self-esteem may dip and so you will need to reinforce strengths, positives and small achievements and support the person to build a positive self-perception. Reinforce any described benefits of change.

Support the person to explore careers, hobbies, interests and educational aspirations that they have or have had. Support emotional resilience by helping the person to engage with others and reflect on the benefits of positive relationships with people. Family or advocacy support may be helpful if the person is willing to engage. Encourage talk about feelings and emotions and place emphasis on the solutions that the person has found to their difficulties and problems. Place as much emphasis on solutions to emotional difficulties as well as physical difficulties. Talk with the person about people they have cared about and listen to the empathetic discourse. Model the person's empathetic responses during appropriate times. Be reliable, open and honest. If you make a mistake or get something wrong, apologise. Show respect to the person and always treat the person with dignity and seek permission to touch any belongings.

When the person starts to take action and make changes they will need to explore their feelings and discover a little at a time. They will begin to experiment with how the change makes them feel. Focus on a positive narrative and encourage solution-focused discussion. Plan change a small step at a time and explore how the change makes the person feel. The anxiety about change is often greater than the reality of experiencing it, once the process begins. Focus on what the person is gaining by making the change and guard against promoting any loss that they may be feeling.

Maintaining motivation can be tiring, especially when faced with such complex emotional and physical dynamics. Reinforce all the benefits and develop the person's self-management skills. Revise targets and goals and encourage positive community and family relationships that have been reinvigorated, or that have developed. Continue to reinforce the benefits of change and support the person to develop emotional and physical resilience by continuing to support them to gain insight into themselves, how they cope and how empathetic they are towards others and themselves. Discourage negative internal narratives that destroy positive action. This will assist the person in integrating change and stabilising themselves, thus preventing relapse.

Solution-focused assessment

The miracle question can be used in many different ways, for example to discover how a person would like to live, what they aspire to be or do and what they woud like to achieve.

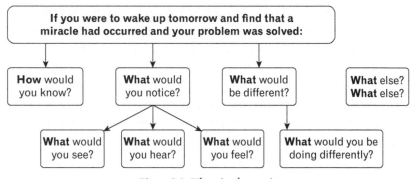

Figure 5.3: The miracle question

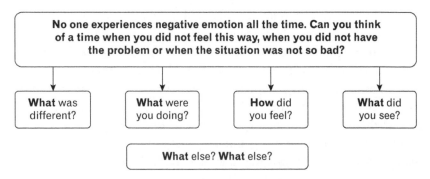

Figure 5.4: The exception question

This question may be phrased differently to establish when the person did not:

- have clutter – can you recall a time when you were able to stop collecting and when you could move around the house? What was different, what were you doing, how did you feel, what did you see?

- feel anxious – can you recall a time when you did not feel anxious and you felt safe and secure? What was different, what were you doing, how did you feel, what did you see?

Consider the exception question in any situation where it would be helpful to determine whether the person has managed things effectively in the past, even if it was only for a brief period of time. Exploring what was different then and how the person explains why the problem did not happen is insightful. It may also be helpful to ask how it was possible for the person to achieve that and how they did it. Scaling can be helpful to understand how important things are or how affected the person is by a situation. For example, on a scale of 0–10, how important is...to you? How anxious does that make you feel? How frightened are you? How lonely does that make you feel?

A seven-step model of solution-focused therapy was developed to consider the process of change (Visser 2013). It may be helpful when working with someone self-neglecting and hoarding who wants to change but is struggling. This should be completed only when the person feels ready and comfortable.

Clarify the desire for change

- Establish what has evoked that desire.

- Is this the presence of something positive or negative, for example a desire to reconnect with family or to prevent eviction?

- Acknowledge any difficulties or problems and how those problems came about to better understand the desire for change.

Define the desired state

- Help the person to describe this as vividly as possible and as positively as possible.

- It may be helpful to use story boards, for example ask the person to find pictures of how they would like their shelves to look. Create a mood board for how they would like their room to look.

- Identify how they would like things to be different and what the advantages would be for example 'If your shelves looked like this, what difference would that make? What could you do that you can't do now?'

Determine the platform

- The platform is the current state of play, the situation, the place in which change begins to move towards the desired state.

- Sometimes people like to take photographs when they are at the beginning of a change process. When they lose commitment or motivation to move forward the photographs are useful reflection tools to identify how much progress has been made. Remember that photographs should never be taken without the consent and involvement of the person and should remain the property of the person for this purpose.

Analyse past success

- Identifying when something has worked in the past helps to provide a confidence that it can be achieved again.

- Look for positive exceptions where the situation was not as bad or the time before the situation occurred.

- Ask the person to consider how that happened, what made it possible and what was different.

Take one small step forward

- Test the water without pressure. On the first few sessions looking at change do not ask the person to discard objects, just begin by sorting. While sorting, ask the person to place something that they choose in the bin. It doesn't have to stay there but begin to allow the person see how it feels to get rid of something. Explore the person's emotions and anxieties. You can remind them of Egor the devil (see Figure 6.8) on their shoulder, preventing progress, and ask the person to challenge Egor.

- Build a bridge between past successes and current/future success. Be experimental with responses.

Monitor progress

- What has worked?

- Do more of what works.

- Reinforce the achievements of progress and reflect back on the difference it makes to the person's life.

- Determine further desire for change.

Desire for further change

- Always go with what the person says.

- Concentrate on the person's ability to influence and change things (strength- and solution-focused), which will reduce anxiety and concern. Focusing on concerns will only decrease the person's influence and ability to change. We shall listen to the person and their Ida angel (see Figure 6.8) rather than the Egor devil who wishes to break down the person's power and control over the situation.

The beginning of assessment

Bream (2013) in the Vicious Shamrock Model describes a perpetual, vicious cycle of thoughts and responses with the hoarded goods at the centre and three key components: stuckness, acquiring and discarding. The model can be used as the beginning of an assessment, focusing on elements important to the person hoarding.

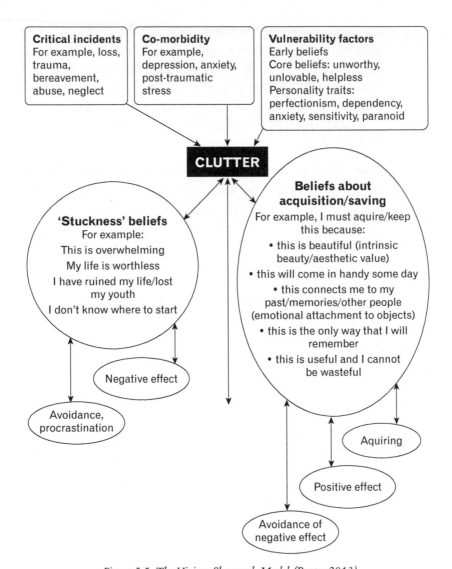

Figure 5.5: The Vicious Shamrock Model (Bream 2013)

Chapter 6

ASSESSMENT AND ENGAGEMENT

What is a good assessment?

A good assessment:

- is based within appropriate legal frameworks

- includes the views of the person and their carer(s)

- includes a carer's assessment where appropriate

- includes 'I' statements

- is outcome-focused and solution-focused from the person's perspective

- evidences capacity assessments throughout (identifies where a person has capacity to make decisions and where they lack capacity to make decisions/best interest decisions)

- refers to advocacy (family or commissioned)

- identifies the journey of support

- analyses assessment: defensible decision making stating what was considered, what was ruled out and why

- is evidence-based: legal frameworks, policy, models, methods and theories

- utilises multi-agency and collaborative working within one care plan

- has a range of people involved, including family, friends and neighbours, and they are identified with roles and responsibilities and contact details (circles of support)

- has transparency in relation to finance

- identifies eligibility criteria

- evidences responses to carers' needs as well as the needs of the individual

- demonstrates progress wherever possible

- identifies how needs are delayed and prevented

- recognises the values and wishes of the individual

- identifies prevention of and protection from abuse and neglect

- records concisely and proportionately

- is clear in how wellbeing is promoted.

Risk assessment

The risk-assessment tool and the self-neglect tool described here are to be used as a guide or checklist to determine the level of risk and response required.

In cases of self-neglect, other forms of potential abuse are often missed as the practitioner focuses on the most obvious issue of self-neglect. Some safeguarding adults reviews have missed opportunities to explore these other forms of abuse. For example, an elderly lady was self-neglecting, but was also neglecting her adult son who had autism. The serious case review (safeguarding adults review), focused on the key issue of self-neglect. The elderly lady was being financially exploited by a neighbour and when she died the neighhbour financially exploited and abused the son. This issue was missed within initial enquiries and within the serious case review.

A man was self-neglecting and there was anti-social behaviour with older youths using the property and drinking. The safeguarding adults review focused on the self-neglect and did not consider the potential financial abuse and mate crime.

A woman was severely self-neglecting and refusing services. The enquiry did not consider that the woman was self-neglecting as a result of domestic abuse and was refusing services as a result of her husband's coercive and controlling behaviour.

Other aspects of abuse and neglect must be therefore explored, including:

- Anti-social behaviour around the person and property.

- Financial abuse, often associated with but not exclusive to vulnerability or substance misuse.

- Domestic abuse leading to self-neglect.

- Sexual abuse leading to self-neglect.

- Historical abuse.

- Neglect or historical neglect – remember that if the person lacks capacity to make decisions regarding their own care and support needs and they have a person identified as their carer, that form of abuse to be considered would be neglect, rather than self-neglect.

- Other forms of abuse or neglect.

We must therefore consider the forms of abuse for safeguarding and the level of abuse:

- Physical.

- Neglect and acts of omission.

- Financial or material.

- Psychological.

- Organisational.

- Discriminatory, including hate or mate crime.

- Sexual, including sexual exploitation.

- Domestic abuse, including forced marriage, honour-based crime and female genital mutilation.

- Modern-day slavery and human trafficking.

- Grooming for terrorist activities.

Consider the following risk factors:

1. How vulnerable is the person?

   - Can the person protect themselves?

   - Can the person raise a concern themselves?

   - Does the person have capacity to make relevant decisions?

   - Is the person dependent on the perpetrator?

   - Is the person socially isolated?

2. Type and seriousness of abuse

   - What is the level and extent of the abuse?

3. The pattern of abuse

   - Is this a one-off isolated incident?

   - Is there a pattern of abuse?

4. Prevalence of abuse

   - Is this a recent incident in an ongoing relationship?

   - Is this repeated abuse that has gone on for a long time?

5. The impact of abuse on the victim

   - Has the person changed their behaviours as a result of abuse?

   - Are there indicators that the person is upset or distressed? Some seemingly minor incidents can have a significant effect when perpetrated by someone whom the person trusts or who is the only source of support.

   - What interventions are wanted by the person (be guided by their preferred outcomes and consider the potential for coercion)?

6. The impact of abuse on others

   - Are others affected by the abuse, for example children and other vulnerable people?

   - Is anyone else potentially involved?

- Is anyone witnessing the abuse and the impact on them?

- Is anyone upset or affected by the abuse?

- Are others intimidated and their environment affected?

7. The intent of the alleged perpetrator

- Was the abuse intentional or unintentional or ill informed?

- Was the abuse planned or deliberately malicious?

8. Illegality of actions

- Was this poor or bad practice? Was it illegal and could it be a potential offence? Seek advice if unsure of reasonable suspicion of a crime.

- Is there the possibility of neglect if there is a carer involved and the person lacks capacity (willful neglect is a crime)?

9. Risk of repeated abuse on the victim

- Is the abuse:

   – likely to happen again

   – less likely with significant changes

   – very likely, even if changes are made?

10. Risk of repeated abuse on others

- Are other adults or carers likely to be at risk of being abused?

- How likely is it that others could be abused?

- What changes could be made to prevent or limit this?

- What is the level of threat posed by the potential perpetrator?

In addition to assessing the risk relating to any potential abuse it is also helpful to assess the level of self-neglect and the risk surrounding the self-neglect. The following pages provide a basic tool.

The journey of support (following the self-neglect tool) is an overview of the key considerations throughout the journey supporting the individual.

1 The vulnerability of the person	Less vulnerable	More vulnerable	• Does the person have capacity to make decisions with regard to care provision/housing, etc? • Does the person have a diagnosed mental illness? • Does the person have support from family or friends? • Are family/friends obstructive to services? • Does the person accept care and treatment? • Does the person have insight into the problems they face?

2 Forms of self-neglect and hoarding	Low risk	Moderate risk	High/ critical risk	• Refer to the tables following. Types and seriousness of hoarding and self-neglect. Look at the relevant categories of hoarding and self-neglect and use your knowledge of the case and professional judgement to identify the seriousness of concern.
Self-neglect				
Hoarding – property				
Hoarding – household functions				
Hoarding – health and safety				
Hoarding – safeguarding				

• Incidents that might fall outside invoked adult protection procedures (low risk) could potentially be addressed via preventative measures such as engaging with the person, developing a rapport, supporting the person to address concerns, getting the person to engage with community activities and develop/ repair relationships, access to heal care and counselling (do not underestimate the value of community engagement.)

• If a social worker or nurse is involved in the care of the person, report concerns to them as part of the preventative measures in addition to the safeguarding referral.

This tool does not replace professional judgement and does not aim to set a rigid threshold for intervention. Note that professional decision making reflects the fact that the type and seriousness of hoarding and self-neglect may fall within the low-risk category, but other factors make the issue more serious.

3 Level of self-neglect/ hoarding (see clutter rating scale for hoarding)	Low risk	Moderate risk	High/ critical risk	Determine if the hoarding/self-neglect is: • a fire risk • impacting on the person's wellbeing • preventing access to emergency services • affecting the person's ability to cook and clean, and their general hygiene • creating limited access to the main areas of the house • creating an increased risk of falls for the person.
Self-neglect				
Hoarding – property				
Hoarding – household functions				
Hoarding – health and safety				
Hoarding – safeguarding				

4 Background to hoarding and self-neglect	Low impact		Seriously affected	• Does the person have a disability that means that they cannot care for themselves? • Does the person have mental health issues and to what extent? • Has this been a long-standing problem? • Does the person engage with services, support and guidance offered? • Are there social isolation issues? • When did self-neglect first begin? • What does the person want to happen?

5 Impact on others	No one else affected	Others indirectly affected	Others directly affected	Others may be affected by the self-neglect or hoarding. Determine if: • there are other vulnerable people (children or adults) within the house affected by the person's hoarding and self-neglect • the hoarding and self-neglect prevents the person from seeing family and friends • there are animals within the property that are not being appropriately cared for.

| 6 Reasonable suspicion of abuse | No suspicion | Indicators present | Reasonable suspicion | Determine if there is reason to suspect that:
• the hoarding self-neglect is an indicator that the person may be being abused
• the person may be targeted for abuse from local people
• a crime may be taking place
• the person is being neglected by someone else
• safeguarding is required for additional safeguarding reasons.
Follow your safeguarding policies and procedures. |

| 7. Legal frameworks | No current legal issues | Some minor legal issues not currently impacting | Serious legal issues | Try to determine if:
• the person is at risk of eviction, fines, non-payment issues
• there is an environmental risk that requires action – public health issues
• there are safeguarding and animal welfare issues
• there are fire risks that are a danger to others
• there are risks to others such as other adults or children. |

| Types of abuse and seriousness | These cases may be referred where the person has care and support needs and cannot protect themselves from abuse or neglect as a result of their care and support needs. | The examples below are likely to indicate the need for a referral for formal safeguarding procedures. If there is any immediate danger to an individual evident, call 999 straightaway for ambulance, fire or police intervention. Following your referral an enquiry will take place to explore whether there are any issues of historical or current abuse/neglect impacting on the person, to determine a person's capacity to make each decision, to rule out anyone else who may be affected by the circumstances and to identify whether there are any potential mental health issues that need addressing. The safeguarding team may do this or they may advise individuals of actions and feedback required, or they may ask the most appropriate agency to conduct a multi-agency meeting to achieve positive outcomes, have oversight of this and provide guidelines. |

Level of risk	Low risk	Moderate risk	High/critical risk
Self-neglect	Person is accepting support and services Health care is being addressed Person is not losing weight Person is accessing services to improve wellbeing There are no carer issues Person has access to social and community activities Person is able to contribute to daily living activites Personal hygiene is good	Access to support services is limited Health care and attendance at appointments is sporadic Person is of low weight Person's wellbeing is partially affected Person has limited social interaction Carers are not present or prevent intervention Person has limited access to social or community activities Person's ability to contribute towards daily living activites is affected Personal hygiene is becoming an issue	Person refuses to engage with necessary services Health care is poor and there is deterioration in health Weight is reducing Wellbeing is affected on a daily basis Person is isolated from family and friends Care is prevented or refused Person does not engage with social or community activities Person does not manage daily living activites Hygiene is poor and causing skin problems Aids and adaptations are refused or not accessed
Hoarding – property	All entrances, exits, stairways, roof spaces and windows are accessible Smoke alarms are fitted and functional or referrals are made to the fire services to visit and install them All services are functional and maintained in good working order Garden is accessible, tidy and maintained	Only the major exit is blocked Only one of the services is not fully functional Concern that services are not well maintained Smoke alarms are not installed or not functioning Garden is not accessible due to clutter, or is not maintained Evidence of indoor items stored outside Evidence of light structural damage, including damp Interior doors missing or blocked open	Limited access to the property due to extreme clutter Evidence of extreme clutter in windows Evidence of extreme clutter outside the property Garden not accessible and extensively overgrown Services not connected and not functioning properly Smoke alarms not fitted or functioning Property lacks ventilation due to clutter Evidence of structural damage or outstanding repairs, including damp Interior doors missing or blocked open Evidence of indoor items stored outside

Level of risk	Low risk	Moderate risk	High/critical risk
Hoarding – household functions	No excessive clutter, all rooms can be safely used for their intended purpose All rooms are rated 0–3 on the clutter rating scale No additional unused household appliances appear in unusual locations around the property Property is maintained within terms of any lease or tenancy agreements where appropriate Property is not at risk of action by Environmental Health	Clutter is causing congestion in the living spaces and is impacting on the use of the rooms of their intended purpose Clutter is causing congestion between the rooms and entrances Rooms score 4–5 on the clutter rating scale Inconsistent levels of housekeeping throughout the property Some household appliances are not functioning properly and there may be additional units in unusual places Property is not maintained within the terms of the lease or tenancy agreement where applicable Evidence of outdoor items being stored inside	Clutter is obstructing the living spaces and preventing the use of the rooms of their intended purpose Rooms score 7–9 on the clutter rating scale Beds are inaccessible or unusable due to clutter or infestation Entrances, hallways and stairs are blocked or difficult to pass Toilets, sinks are not functioning or not in use The person is at risk due to the living environment Household appliances are not functioning or are inaccessible and there is no safe cooking environment The person is using candles Evidence of outdoor clutter being stored indoors No evidence of housekeeping being undertaken Broken household items not discarded, such as broken glass or plates Concern for declining mental health Property is not maintained within the terms of the lease or tenancy agreement where applicable and the person is at risk of notice being served by Environmental Health

Level of risk	Low risk	Moderate risk	High/critical risk
Hoarding – health and safety	Propery is clean with no odours (pets or other) No rotting food No concerning use of candles No concern over flies Person is managing personal care No writing on the walls Quantities of medication are within appropriate limits, in date and stored appropriately Personal protective equipment is not required	Kitchen and bathroom are not kept clean Offensive odour in the property Person is not maintaining a safe cooking environment Some concern with the quantity of medication or its storage or expiry dates No rotting food No concerning use of candles No writing on the walls Person is trying to maintain person care but is struggling Light insect infestations (bedbugs, lice, fleas, cockroaches, ants etc.) Latex gloves, boots, needle stick safe shoes, face mask, hand sanitiser and insect repelllent required	Human urine or excrement may be present Excessive odour in the property, may also be evident from outside Rotting food may be present Evidence of unclean, unused or buried plates and dishes Broken household items discarded, such as broken glass or plates Inappropriate quantities of storage of medication Concern with the integrity of the electrics Inappropriate use of electrical extension cords or evidence of unqualified work to the electrics Concern for declining mental health Heavy insect infestation (bedbugs, lice, fleas, cockroaches, ants, silverfish etc.) Visible rodent infestation Protetctive equipment required
Hoarding – safeguarding of children, family members and animals	No concern for household family members	Hoarding on clutter scale 4–7 constitutes a safeguarding alert. Enquiries need to be made Please note all additional concerns for householders Properties with children or vulnerable residents with additional support needs may trigger a safeguarding alert	Hoarding on clutter scale 7–9 constitutes a safeguarding alert Please note all additional concerns for householders

Level of risk	Low risk	Moderate risk	High/critical risk
Responsibility	All workers to enage with the person, develop a rapport, supporting them to address concerns, engage with community activities and develop/repair relationships, gain access to health care and counselling and improve wellbeing – preventative measures	Workers to follow the processes identified by local procedures for safeguarding and use the resources in the toolkit. Consult with local authority safeguarding adults services for advice and guidances. Inform the social worker or nurse if they are involved with the person	Referral to social services and follow local authority safeguarding procedures. Use the resources in the toolkit

Figure 6.1: Self-neglect and hoarding and defensible decision-making tool

Please remember that safeguarding is everyone's business. For cases of self-neglect and hoarding a multi-agency response is required even if your local authority safeguarding team decides that it is not going to invoke safeguarding procedures. Remember that the Mental Capacity Act requires agencies to determine whether the person has the capacity to consent to actions, tenancies, repairs, services, assessments and so on. It is likely that a number of agencies will be required to conduct capacity assessments, or support someone to undertake capacity assessments with the person self-neglecting. Other forms of abuse or neglect must be ruled out. See the ten steps to information sharing and the assessment processes.

1 Background
- Background information
- Environmental risk
- Other abuse/neglect
- Health and Safety assessment
- Level of squalour
- Level of engagement
- Barriers

2 Risks and assessments
- Risk assess situation, person and carers
- Consider any dependents
- Mental health issues
- Substance misuse issues
- Mental capacity assessments (including the capacity to understand tenancy agreement)

3 Multi-agency response
- Consider the need for a lead and who is best to lead enquiries
- Consider capacity assessments to be coordinated, risks to be considered, assessment coordination and legislative considerations
- Consider fire risks
- Financial considerations
- Previous action taken and outcomes
- Previous safeguarding issues

4 Resources available
- Fire service
- Vulnerability meeting or similar
- Housing or landlord
- Environmental health issues
- Access to community and services
- Family and friends
- Links with others in the community or potential to regain links
- RSPCA
- Access to mental health services (as appropriate)
- Think creatively and support access to community

5 Therapeutic services
- Access to therapeutic services; psychology, counselling, therapeutic assessment process, independent and voluntary sector support for therapeutic work
- Access to GP and nursing services
- Drug and alcohol services
- Bereavement services

6 Legal processes
- All agencies have legislation that may apply, this will require consideration and coordination
- Consider whether the person is at risk of eviction
- Consider any prosecutions
- Consider any debt issues affecting the person
- Consider any potential child protection issues

Figure 6.2: A journey of support

Assessing capacity

The Mental Capacity Act 2005 provides a statutory framework for people who lack capacity to make decisions for themselves. The Act has five statutory principles and these are the values that underpin the legal requirements of the Act:

1. A person must be assumed to have capacity unless it is established that they lack capacity.

2. A person is not to be treated as unable to make a decision unless all practical steps have been taken without success.

3. A person is not to be treated as unable to make a decision merely because he or she makes an unwise decision.

4. An act done or decision made, under this act for or on behalf of a person who lacks capacity must be done, or made in his or her best interests.

5. Before the act is done, or the decision is made, regard must be had to whether the purpose for which it is needed can be as effectively achieved in a way that is less restrictive of the person's rights and freedom of action.

When a person's hoarding behaviour poses a serious risk to their health and safety, intervention will be required. With the exception of statutory requirements, any intervention or action proposed that affects the individual must be with the person's consent. In extreme cases of hoarding behaviour, the very nature of the environment *should* lead professionals to question whether the person has capacity to consent to the proposed action or intervention and trigger a capacity assessment. This is confirmed by The Mental Capacity Act Code of Practice, which states that one of the reasons why people may question a person's capacity to make a specific decision is 'the person's behaviour or circumstances cause doubt as to whether they have capacity to make a decision' (Mental Capacity Act Code of Practice, p.52). Arguably, extreme hoarding behaviour meets this criterion and an assessment should take place. Consideration must be given where there is dialogue or situations that suggest a person's capacity to make a decision with regard to their place of residence or care provision may be in doubt.

Any capacity assessment carried out in relation to self-neglect or hoarding behaviour must be time-specific and relate to a specific intervention or action. The professional responsible for undertaking the capacity assessment will be the person who is proposing the specific intervention or action, and is referred to as the decision maker. Although the decision maker may need to seek support from other professionals in the multi-disciplinary team, they are responsible for making the final decision about a person's capacity.

If the person lacks capacity to consent to the specific action or intervention, then the decision maker must demonstrate that they have met the requirements of the best interests 'checklist':

- ☐ Do not discriminate. Do not make assumptions about someone's best interests merely on the basis of the person's age or appearance, condition or any aspect their behaviour.

- ☐ Take into account all relevant circumstances.

- ☐ If faced with a particularly difficult or contentious decision it is recommended that practitioners adopt a 'balance sheet' approach.

- ☐ Will the person regain capacity? If so, can the decision wait?

- ☐ Involve the individual as fully as possible.

- ☐ Take into account the individual's past and present wishes and feelings, and any beliefs and values likely to have a bearing on the decision.

- ☐ Consult as far and as widely as possible.

Due to the complexity of such cases, multi-agency meetings to coordinate capacity assessments may be required. Where the person denies access to professionals, the individual who has developed a rapport with the person self-neglecting will need to be supported by the relevant agencies to conduct capacity assessments.

In particularly challenging and complex cases, it may be necessary for the local authority to refer to the Court of Protection to make the best interest decision. Any referral to the Court of Protection should be discussed with legal services and the relevant service manager.

Practitioners will need to assure themselves that they recognise the difference between a test of competency such as the mini mental state test and a capacity assessment. The two assessments are very different and a competency test should not be used instead of a capacity assessment. It may be used to determine whether a person has an impairment of the brain or mind and will have to be conducted by a suitably qualified person but does not cover the functional element of the capacity assessment.

Competency

To be competent means that the overall function of the brain is working effectively to enable a person to make choices, decisions and carry out functions. In many people who have, for example, dementia, Parkinson's or Huntington's disease, the first aspect of brain function affected is the executive function and unfortunately this is not tested very effectively using the standard mini mental state test. The competency testing may be used to meet the diagnostic element of the capacity test and in cases of self-neglect the executive functioning of the brain may also need to be determined.

The executive function of the brain is a set of cognitive or understanding and processing skills that are needed to plan, order, construct and monitor information to set goals or tasks. Executive function deficits can lead to problems in safety, routine behaviours, voluntary movements and emotional wellbeing – all associated with self-neglect and hoarding behaviours.

Capacity is decision-making ability and a person may have quite a lack of competency but be able to make a specific decision. The decision-making ability means that a person must be able to link the functional demands – the ability to undertake the tasks, the ability to weigh up the risks and the ability to process the information and maintain the information to make the decision. In some way, shape or form the person has to be able to let the assessor then know that they are doing this. Many competent people make what others would consider to be bad decisions, but are not prevented from taking risks and making bad decisions. This is *not* a sign that a person lacks capacity to make the decision, just that they have weighed everything up, considered the factors and determined that for them this would be what they wanted. The main issue in the evaluation of decision-making capacity is the process of making the decision, not the decision itself.

This is important because the first part of the capacity assessment attempts to establish whether there is impairment of the brain function or mind. Someone who hoards or self-neglects can take huge risks with their own health and often professionals assess the person as having capacity, as they are deemed competent. The person is therefore deemed to not meet criteria for a capacity assessment and is said to be making poor decisions that are autonomous and therefore they are able to make this choice without professional intervention. If you are concerned, then an assessment of the executive functions of the mind would support the capacity assessment in the functional aspect.

The second part of the test should be directly related to the first part. This means that a person can only be said to lack capacity if the reason for the inability – for example to understand the decision to be made, weigh up the risks and positives of a situation, retain and communicate the decision – directly links to the functional aspect of the test or the impairment of the brain function or mind. If the first element of the test is not accurately assessed then this creates difficulty in understanding whether the person can undertake these decision-making skills.

Decisions should not be broad decisions about care, services or treatment, they should be specific to a course of action. If a practitioner requires the consent, agreement, signature or understanding of the individual, then they should determine the capacity of the person to consent to that action using the assessment process defined in the Mental Capacity Act 2005. This may be for tenancy, individual treatment options, aspects of care offered, equipment required, access to services, information sharing or any intervention. If you understand the course of action being proposed and offered to the person, then you will be required to assess their capacity to consent to the proposed care, service or treatment. If there is only one agency able to gain access to the person, all agencies are responsible for developing questions for that agency to ask to determine their capacity as far as is practicably possible. The following examples illustrate these points.

Housing – the housing officer understands the tenancy agreement, therefore it is appropriate for them to determine whether the person understands the tenancy agreement. The housing officer will need to conduct (and record) a capacity assessment where there is doubt about the person's ability to provide consent. If the person is deemed to lack capacity to make that decision, a best interest decision must be made.

A third party cannot sign a tenancy agreement on behalf of another person unless they have court-appointed deputyship or a lasting power of attorney that specifies such actions under 'finance'.

Health – if a health professional is proposing a course of treatment, medication or intervention, they understand the intervention proposed, therefore it is appropriate for them to determine whether the person self-neglecting understands the intervention. If the health professional doubts the person's ability to understand they must conduct (and record) a capacity assessment. If the person is deemed to lack capacity to make that decision, a best interest decision must be made. A third party cannot give consent on behalf of another person unless they have court-appointed deputyship or a lasting power of attorney that specifies such actions under 'welfare'.

Occupational therapy – the occupational therapist understands the rehabilitative process and the equipment required by the person to meet their needs. If the person does not appear to understand then the occupational therapist must assess the person's capacity to make a decision about the proposed equipment.

If a person is deemed as lacking capacity to make a particular decision, the decision maker will need to make a decision in their best interests. The best interest decision maker may consult with family and friends, but unless someone has a lasting power of attorney or court-appointed deputyship, the decision maker will have to make an informed decision. This requires the person to consider the identity, wishes, values and feelings of the person, weigh this up against the actual risks and balance the decision without being risk averse. If a family member or identified person has a lasting power of attorney or court-appointed deputyship that specifies the decision to be made, then they will become the decision maker, but must make this decision in the best interests of the person concerned. The decision maker should not be influenced by their own values or opinions, but solely those of the person concerned.

In a severe case of self-neglect there may be a number of agencies involved with the person (and others) concerned. The safeguarding enquiry will not only require the coordination of risks to the person and others, depicted in Figure 6.3 by the 'A' sign for 'alerts', but also the coordination of the required capacity assessments, depicted by the 'C' signs.

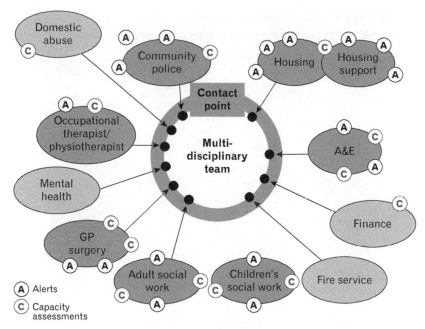

Figure 6.3: The safeguarding response

The person coordinating the safeguarding response will need to ensure that the safeguarding plan includes actions for each agency to assess the person's capacity to make specific decisions. These actions should be time-specific and indicate exactly what is required.

The risks will be considered in relation to the capacity of the person and potential impact on others. Risks to the person will be addressed or minimised with the person's consent where they lack capacity.

In addition to coordinating all agencies' concerns and capacity assessments it is useful for the multi-disciplinary team (MDT) to share relevant legislation, how and why it applies this and address any conflicting aspects of legislation using the Human Rights Act as a multi-agency basis for decision making.

Comprehensive assessment

In assessing someone who self-neglects and/or hoards, the social worker must go beyond basic assessment. It is often the wish to respond to the impact on the person's physical wellbeing that overrides other aspects of assessment, but this can be to the detriment of developing a full understanding of the situation and putting together an effective care and support plan. Figure 6.4 is based on Maslow's Hierarchy and demonstrates the layers of assessment to be considered.

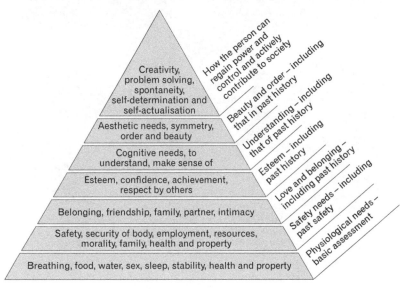

Figure 6.4: Layers of assessment

Physiological needs – basic assessment

Most social workers will assess the basic needs of an individual. Assessments will cover whether the person can eat, sleep and is warm enough. Assessments will also, in general, cover the physical and mental health needs of the individual concerned and whether they have access to the community. The social work assessment should involve all relevant agencies to ensure that the assessment identifies whether the person has the capacity to make specific decisions about each identified need. If the person will not engage with other agencies the person who has developed a rapport with them should seek support from agencies to undertake relevant capacity assessments (see the previous chapter).

If the person has a diagnosis, disability, learning disability, mental health problem or sensory impairment this must be assessed in context with the environment and how this impacts on them.

- Can the person use any rooms for their intended purpose?

- Can the person prepare food and cook?

- Is the fridge/freezer useable?

- Can the person clean areas?

- Can the person access the bath, toilet, sink, shower and use them for their intended pupose?

- Can the person sleep in a bed?

- Does the person sleep?

- Can the person wash their clothing?

- Are there mains services (gas, electric, water)?

- Is the person able to stay warm?

Safety needs – including historical safety

Assessments must consider the safety of the person concerned. In assessing safety, the social worker must assess not only the individual's safety, or perceived safety, but also the safety of others potentially affected.

- Are there any children, other adults with care and support needs, carers residing at the property?

- Are carers supportive, do they report concerns, are others in the house identifying themselves as carers, are carers obstructive?

- Is there a potential fire risk to others?

- How severe is the fire hazard?

- Is there structural damage to the property?

- Are there public or environmental health issues that could impact on others, for example vermin, flies, and cockroaches?

- Is there mould, rotten food, vomit, faecal matter or urine (human or animal)?

- Is there bathroom waste such as toilet paper, sanitary products, dirty tissues, hair lying around?

- Could there be dangerous materials at the property, for example toxic substances, oxygen, near someone who smokes?

- How clean is clothing, towels, bedding?

- Is the person at risk of falling?

- Is there access for emergency services?

- Can the person find bills and pay them?

- Can the person manage their finances?

- How safe does the person feel?

- Is there any historical abuse or neglect?

- Is the person subject to anti-social behaviour, other crimes or domestic abuse?

- Has the person been served with eviction orders, or do they have debt affecting the stability of their home?

- Does the person have financial security?

- Has the person had children removed from their care in the past or are they subject to child protection proceedings?

Love and belonging

- Does the person have family, friends, and access to community activities?

- Does the person belong to any groups, attend education or work?

- What was/is the person's relationship like with their parents?

- What was/is the person's relationship like with their children/grandchildren?

- Has the person suffered any bereavements?

- Does the person have regular contact with anyone?

- How does the person feel about social services, health services, fire services and their GP? Do they have anyone professionally that they have regular contact with?

Esteem – including past history

- How does the person feel about themselves?

- Has the person ever felt depressed, anxious or upset?

- How did the person feel growing up?

- When did the person start self-neglecting/hoarding and what was happening for them when this began?

- How did the person feel as a child growing up?

- Did the person consider themselves popular at school, or were they socially isolated?

- Does the person have set routines, and how set are they?

- Does the person consider themselves to like cleanliness?

- Has the person ever had a diagnosis of a disability/mental illness and how did this affect them?

- Can the person identify any traumatic events in their life and how did this make them feel?

- How much does the person drink or take drugs (illicit or non-illicit)?

- When did the person begin drinking?

- Does the person ever harm themselves?

- Does the person have religious beliefs, cultural beliefs, political beliefs or environmental beliefs that affect their decision making?

- How does the person describe the way they perceive others to regard them and how different do they think this is to their own perception of their identity?

- What does the person see as major achievements in their life?

- What have they celebrated in the past?

- When does the person feel most confident about?

- What is the best time of day, day of the week, part of the month or part of the year for the person and why?

- What was the best time in the person's life and why?

Understanding – including past history

- How does the person cope with difficult situations?

- How did the person cope with things in childhood?

- Did the person understand the responses of their parents/ other professionals growing up?

- What kind of things did parents/partners say that caused a reaction in them that they can remember?

- What was the reaction?

- What helps the person to cope with things now?

- What is the person afraid of and what do they do when they are afraid (consider fight, flight, freeze or flop responses)?

- Has the person ever returned to a dangerous or frightening situation?

- What is the person's understanding of their current situation?

- If the person could change this situation, what would they want to see/feel/be?

- If the person were to begin a project, what would it be and where would they start?

- What is important to the person past and present?

- Does the person consider themselves to have a good memory?

- What kind of things does the person find difficult?

- When thinking or getting rid of something, how does the person feel and what do they think about? What does the person think might happen and what do they feel is bad about this?

- When does the person feel the need to go out and collect more and what kinds of situation might trigger this?

Beauty and order – including that in past history

- How did the person order things in the past?

- How does the person organise the things that they have now?

- Are items on view or are some items stored?

- Does the person feel able to organise things into appropriate places, such as clothes in drawers/wardrobe, paperwork in the filing cabinet, books on a shelf, newspapers in a rack or stand?

- What is it that the person values in the things that they collect?

- What is of prime importance, or is this difficult to determine? For example, is it preserving the environment, sentimental value, perceived usefulness, for the person or others?

- How does the person perceive themselves?

- What do they see that is beautiful or useful in themselves and others?

- Consider spaces that the person perceives as beautiful in pictures and magazines. What does the person like about the space or object? What is preventing them from achieving this in their own home?

- Hypothetically, how does a person feel when asked to discard an object? You can try an experiment and ask the person to select something that is less valuable to them. Ask them to place this in the bin and leave it there. Find out how the person feels and what their worries are.

Person-centred assessment

A person-centred assessment should consider the strengths of the person concerned as well as the things that they might need help with. We can all find it difficult to talk about things that we are good at. If a person has not considered what they would like in their life, or how they manage things, it may be difficult for them to talk about what they would like to do or achieve.

It is helpful to get a person to determine on a scale how important things are to them and provide an explanation or rationale for this.

On a scale of 0–10, with 0 being not important at all and 10 being very important, ask the person to rate their answers and describe why. Here are some topics that you may want to consider for discussion.

- Accepting things as they are
  Not important at all 0 1 2 3 4 5 6 7 8 9 10 Very important to me

- Having traditions in my life
  Not important at all 0 1 2 3 4 5 6 7 8 9 10 Very important to me

- Fitting in
  Not important at all 0 1 2 3 4 5 6 7 8 9 10 Very important to me

- Being part of a community
  Not important at all 0 1 2 3 4 5 6 7 8 9 10 Very important to me

- Having people think well of me
  Not important at all 0 1 2 3 4 5 6 7 8 9 10 Very important to me

- Being one of a kind
  Not important at all 0 1 2 3 4 5 6 7 8 9 10 Very important to me

- Finding out what makes people tick
  Not important at all 0 1 2 3 4 5 6 7 8 9 10 Very important to me

- Having lots of interesting things to do
  Not important at all 0 1 2 3 4 5 6 7 8 9 10 Very important to me

- Having a comfortable home
  Not important at all 0 1 2 3 4 5 6 7 8 9 10 Very important to me

- Being really good at something
  Not important at all 0 1 2 3 4 5 6 7 8 9 10 Very important to me

- Having a close family
  Not important at all 0 1 2 3 4 5 6 7 8 9 10 Very important to me

- Making a contribution
  Not important at all 0 1 2 3 4 5 6 7 8 9 10 Very important to me

- Feeling peaceful
  Not important at all 0 1 2 3 4 5 6 7 8 9 10 Very important to me

- Being part of a team
  Not important at all 0 1 2 3 4 5 6 7 8 9 10 Very important to me

- Allowing others to be themselves
  Not important at all 0 1 2 3 4 5 6 7 8 9 10 Very important to me

- Having a place where I belong
  Not important at all 0 1 2 3 4 5 6 7 8 9 10 Very important to me

- Exploring new ideas
  Not important at all 0 1 2 3 4 5 6 7 8 9 10 Very important to me

- Taking risks
  Not important at all 0 1 2 3 4 5 6 7 8 9 10 Very important to me

- Having enough money
  Not important at all 0 1 2 3 4 5 6 7 8 9 10 Very important to me

- Being in charge of my own life
  Not important at all 0 1 2 3 4 5 6 7 8 9 10 Very important to me

- Making people laugh
  Not important at all 0 1 2 3 4 5 6 7 8 9 10 Very important to me

- Managing money well
  Not important at all 0 1 2 3 4 5 6 7 8 9 10 Very important to me

- Sharing
  Not important at all 0 1 2 3 4 5 6 7 8 9 10 Very important to me

- Being honest
  Not important at all 0 1 2 3 4 5 6 7 8 9 10 Very important to me

- Helping others
  Not important at all 0 1 2 3 4 5 6 7 8 9 10 Very important to me

- Being emotionally strong
  Not important at all 0 1 2 3 4 5 6 7 8 9 10 Very important to me

- Keeping busy
  Not important at all 0 1 2 3 4 5 6 7 8 9 10 Very important to me

- Being caring
  Not important at all 0 1 2 3 4 5 6 7 8 9 10 Very important to me

- Having intelligence
  Not important at all 0 1 2 3 4 5 6 7 8 9 10 Very important to me

- Being successful
  Not important at all 0 1 2 3 4 5 6 7 8 9 10 Very important to me

- Having things organised
  Not important at all 0 1 2 3 4 5 6 7 8 9 10 Very important to me

- Having friends and getting on with others
  Not important at all 0 1 2 3 4 5 6 7 8 9 10 Very important to me

- Having enough time
  Not important at all 0 1 2 3 4 5 6 7 8 9 10 Very important to me

- Being competitive
  Not important at all 0 1 2 3 4 5 6 7 8 9 10 Very important to me

- Exploring old ideas
  Not important at all 0 1 2 3 4 5 6 7 8 9 10 Very important to me

- Having beautiful things around me
  Not important at all 0 1 2 3 4 5 6 7 8 9 10 Very important to me

- Being appreciated
  Not important at all 0 1 2 3 4 5 6 7 8 9 10 Very important to me

- Being strong
  Not important at all 0 1 2 3 4 5 6 7 8 9 10 Very important to me

- Ensuring cleanliness
  Not important at all 0 1 2 3 4 5 6 7 8 9 10 Very important to me

- Having things
  Not important at all 0 1 2 3 4 5 6 7 8 9 10 Very important to me

- Having money
  Not important at all 0 1 2 3 4 5 6 7 8 9 10 Very important to me

- Being in control
  Not important at all 0 1 2 3 4 5 6 7 8 9 10 Very important to me

- Things being predictable
  Not important at all 0 1 2 3 4 5 6 7 8 9 10 Very important to me

- Having a social life
  Not important at all 0 1 2 3 4 5 6 7 8 9 10 Very important to me

- Being understood
  Not important at all 0 1 2 3 4 5 6 7 8 9 10 Very important to me

- Learning and growing
  Not important at all 0 1 2 3 4 5 6 7 8 9 10 Very important to me

- Change
  Not important at all 0 1 2 3 4 5 6 7 8 9 10 Very important to me

- Having fun
  Not important at all 0 1 2 3 4 5 6 7 8 9 10 Very important to me

- Having a good friend and someone to trust
  Not important at all 0 1 2 3 4 5 6 7 8 9 10 Very important to me

- Having a relationship
  Not important at all 0 1 2 3 4 5 6 7 8 9 10 Very important to me

- Being the best I can be
  Not important at all 0 1 2 3 4 5 6 7 8 9 10 Very important to me

- Caring what people think of me
  Not important at all 0 1 2 3 4 5 6 7 8 9 10 Very important to me

- Religion
  Not important at all 0 1 2 3 4 5 6 7 8 9 10 Very important to me

- Culture
  Not important at all 0 1 2 3 4 5 6 7 8 9 10 Very important to me

You can ensure that you are focusing on the priorities that the person has identified rather than your own perceived priorities. In the same way, it may be helpful to get the person to consider what is important to them and complete the sheet in Figure 6.5.

What is important to me	
At home	
Just for fun/hobbies	
Places I go	
Music	
Food	
Drink	
TV or radio programmes	
Getting around/transport	
Money	
Health care/fitness	
Cultural/religious	
People around me	
What I really do not like/want	
At home	
For fun/hobbies	
Places to go	
Music	
Food	
Drink	
TV or radio programmes	
Getting around/transport	
Money	
Health care/fitness	
Cultural/religious	
People around me	

Figure 6.5: What is important to me?

The questions (about important things) are not as important as the discussion invoked by the question. Do not try to ask all the questions in one go. It is often surprising the things that people say in response to the questions.

Discovering what the person perceives as the best part of their day or week can be very insightful.

....

is the best part of my day because

....

....

....

....

....

....

....

is the best part of my week because

....

....

....

....

....

....

is the best part of my evening or weekend because

....

....

....

....

....

....

is the best time I ever had because

....

....

....

....

....

I like to spend time with ....

....

....

I don't like to spend time with ....

....

....

....

I have always wanted to ....

....

....

I would never want to ....

....

....

....

Figure 6.6: The best part of my...

Family			
Friends, colleagues, neighbours			
Professionals			
Other, including assistive technology			

Figure 6.7: My circles of support

Ask the person to consider activities, hobbies, education or work pursuits that interest them and complete:

I used to like . . . .
I currently like . . . .
I would like to . . . .
What stops me from doing these things is . . . .

Or

To do these things I would need . . . .
I can achieve . . . .
What you need to know to help me is . . . .

Sport, recreation and leisure

Break down the information into types of sport and leisure and then break this information down again.

On a scale of 1–10: 1 = dislike and 10 = really enjoy.

Rate how you would find these activities, or simply tick things that you like. You can make similar lists for anything such as jobs, music, or food, to help a person break down information.

- Sport and physical recreation

    - Solo activities – gym or swimming
    - Group activities – team games

- Arts and entertainment

    - Theatre
    - Gigs and concerts
    - Comedy clubs
    - Films

- Countryside recreation

    - Hiking
    - Camping
    - Picnics
    - Cycling
    - Youth hostelling
    - Horse riding

- Home-based leisure

    - Reading
    - Make-overs
    - Gardening
    - TV, videos and DVDs
    - Playgrounds

- Visitor attractions

    - Theme and leisure parks
    - Museums
    - Historic building
    - Catering

      Fast food restaurants
- Cafes
- Pub restaurants
- Top restaurants

- Computer games and the internet

  - Technology
  - Games
  - Internet
  - Social media

Strengths

- Who have you cared about?

- Who would you go to talk to when you needed to talk about something important?

- Who helps you out when you need it?

- What do you like about the area that you live in?

- What about where you live feels safe?

- What about where you live feels pleasing?

- What is of great value to you?

- What makes you feel stronger?

- What makes your home a good place to be?

- What do you like about your appearance?

- What about your character is good and strong?

- What foods do you enjoy that are healthy?

- How do you get around?

- When did you feel strongest and why?

- What skills do you have that you are proud of?

- What do you care about?

- What strengths do others see in you?

- What do you see as a personal achievement?

- When do you have the best sleep?

- What have been your educational strengths?

- What do you do to feel safe?

- What makes you feel proud?

- What would you describe your best qualities to be?

These questions should be approached with sensitivity and the practitioner should not push for answers, but return to the difficult question on another occasion. The questions that evoke emotion are often the ones that hold the key to a person's difficulties and barriers.

The self-esteem issues can significantly debilitate a person and prevent them from moving on. Figure 6.8 is a model adapted from Anderson (2011).

Figure 6.8: Managing the challenging child

In exploring the remit of the care and support plan it can be helpful to explore the person's own narratives.

- Ask the person to consider what they would like to do and write these goals in the person column

- Next ask the person to identify how they plan this and write this in the Ida column.

- Then ask the person to tell us what Egor the devil on their shoulder says about these plans.

- Tell the person to consider the devil on their shoulder as being a naughty child, a challenging, troublesome child that is easily offended, easily hurt and is prone to tantrums. What would they say to this child and how would they help this child? Write this in the final column. See the example below.

Person	Ida (Angel)	Egor (Devil)	If Egor was a child who was saying this, how would you manage the child?
I want to have an organised house.	I will begin in the morning sorting out the shelves.	There is too much to do you will never achieve it. You have tried before and failed.	Let's just begin with this little bit. It will prove that something can be achieved.
I want to go out and join that club.	I shall go to the reception and ask for more information on Tuesday.	Don't bother, you won't like going in on your own, they won't be your kind of people and you will just feel more lonely.	You don't have to feel lonely, you can just go out to the club. Let's get the information off the internet and see what you could get involved in and go to on Tuesdays.
I would like to eat a good meal.	I shall do some food shopping when I get some money on Thursday.	You will never clear the space to cook it. Get the snacks out of the cupboard, its easier.	Let's clear the cooking area now. Make the area around the cooker safe and clean the cooker. Then you can cook whenever you want to.

Person	Ida (Angel)	Egor (Devil)	If Egor was a child who was saying this, how would you manage the child?
I want to pay my bills on time.	I shall get the pile of bills and sort through them tonight.	You will have to find them first and they won't all be in the same pile. You know that this will make you more anxious because you won't have the money to pay them all.	Let's make a list of the main service providers and find contact numbers. We can ring them and find out what money is owed. We can make arrangements to pay an affordable amount.
I want to talk to someone. I feel lonely.	I shall answer the door the next time the social worker comes.	Don't bother, they won't understand, they will just let you down and you will feel worse after telling them all the bad things.	Let's talk about the easy things until you know that you can trust them. Try a little bit of difficult information at a time.

After engaging with the person and gathering all of the information about them, we must put this information into an assessment and develop a care and support plan. The Care Act 2014 identifies strengths-based assessment that places the person at the centre of their own care and the guidance tells us to use the 'I' statements of the person wherever possible. In practice and consultancy work, I have had the opportunity to read many social work assessments about people who self-neglect/hoard. The assessments largely focus on the risks presented as a result of hoarding and it is rare that the identity and history of the person can be seen within the assessment. Doel and Shardlow (2006) in their book *Modern Social Work Practice* suggest an exercise called 'Hold the Front Page' in which the practitioner is asked to interview the person and write a front-page newspaper article from the person's views and perspectives, supported by interviewer narrative. This will shift the focus away from the interviewer and place emphasis on the person's own perspective of their life. I have adapted this suggestion slightly to create more emphasis on the strengths of the person. The methodology will be described via the case study below.

James is a 60-year-old ex-police officer who retired due to ill health 15 years ago. James worked interviewing child sex offenders in prison and as a result of the horrific stories and images that he witnessed, he began drinking heavily. James' relationship with his wife broke down. He became overprotective with his children and eventually these relationships broke down too. He eventually lost contact with his wife and children. James moved in with his elderly mother and cared for her until she died two years ago. James describes happy times in the police force, working with colleagues in a variety of services, but feels that he could never achieve enough. James now drinks heavily and his liver is beginning to fail.

An interest in police vehicles began when his relationship broke down and he began collecting boxed toy police cars. This interest expanded into fire and rescue vehicles and James began collecting newspaper and magazine articles about the vehicles. James then began making model cars and collected packs to build; however, most of these packs have never been taken out of their boxes. James initially filled his bedroom with these objects but as his collection expanded he moved into all other areas of the house. James can no longer access his bed, his kitchen or his bathroom. A water pipe leads around from an outside tap to the living room where he fills a kettle to cook on a gas camping stove and washes in a bucket. James sleeps on the sofa and uses another bucket as a toilet. James is ashamed of his current situation but is very proud of his collection and knowledge. James goes out most days taking photographs of the countryside, animals and old vehicles. James recently won an award for one of his photographs which was published in a national magazine.

On asking James what the title of his journal should be he said, 'Peace and Acceptance Found in a Frame'. To James, someone seeing beauty in his photography work meant that he had achieved something which he felt he had never achieved with the police. James described the torment in his head over and over again, day and night for years, yet when he got out into the countryside and took his photographs he found solitude and he produced something others appreciated. Expanding on this, James described the chaos in the house as reflective of the chaos in his head.

James described how he could no longer engage with people, as the 'bad' people wanted to engage with him and tell him about their horrendous crimes and the 'good' people all left him. Eventually he had found good people who accepted him and he was ready to begin engaging with the world. James's story was much more emotive than the one that I might have produced about his bravery as a police officer, the clutter in the house and the loss in his life. The strengths that James had were the key to his change and engaging with others allowed a healing process to begin.

Once James began engaging with the local photography class, he began clearing space within his house, joined a counselling group held for ex-police who suffer from post-trauma and reduced his drinking. James described the assessment process as helpful in enabling him to focus on what was important to him.

Consider what you would put as the headline title and sub-titles?

THE FRONT PAGE	
Headline:	
The story:	The story continued: James says:
Sub-story: James's strengths	Also: Interviewer's perspective (justified)
More news:	
And finally:	

Figure 6.9: Front page news

Clutter rating scale

One person's cluttered and dirty is another person's average home condition and so determining clutter and risk can be very subjective. To ensure that all agencies have a clear idea about the level and clutter and can discuss the level of concern, I have devised the clutter rating tool, adapted from the Clutter Image Rating (Frost *et al.* 2008) to be used alongside the tool.

Level 1

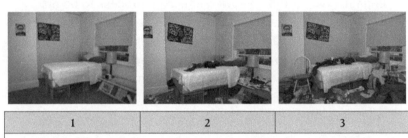

1	2	3

Low-level clutter – develop a rapport with the person concerned. Consider the person's ability to understand the tenancy agreement. Support person to engage with topics of interest and meet with others who have similar interest in local community – develop relationships.

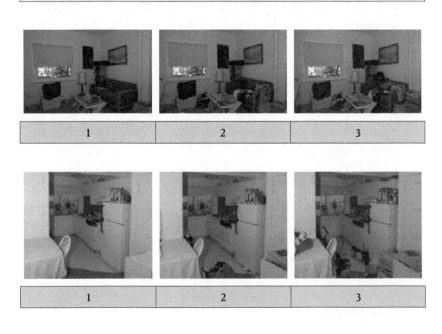

1	2	3

1	2	3

Level 1 *Clutter image rating 1–3*	Household environment is considered standard No specialised assistance is needed
1 Property structure, services and garden area	• All entrances and exits, stairways, roof space and windows are accessible • Smoke alarms are fitted and functional or referrals made to fire brigade to visit and install • All services are functional and maintained in good working order • Garden is accessible, tidy and maintained
2 Household functions	• No excessive clutter; all rooms can be safely used for their intended purpose • All rooms are rated 0–3 on the clutter rating scale • No additional unused household appliances appear in unusual locations around the property • Property is maintained within terms of any lease or tenancy agreements where appropriate • Property is not at risk of action by Environmental Health
3 Health and safety	• Property is clean with no odours (pet or other) • No rotting food • No concerning use of candles • No concern over flies • Person manages personal care • No writing on the walls • Quantities of medication are within appropriate limits, in date and stored appropriately
4 Safeguard of children and family members	• No concerns for household members
5 Animals and pests	• Any pets at the property are well cared for • No pests or infestations at the property
6 Personal protective equipment (PPE)	• No PPE required • No visit in pairs required

Lovol 2

4	5	6

Moderate clutter – make a safeguarding referral. Identify the most suitable person to engage with the person. Enquiries to consider why and when this began, capacity of person to make each relevant decision, including capacity to understand tenancy agreement. Multi-agency response may be headed by the most suitable agency. Risk assessment required. Work with the person concerned at their pace. Do not discuss removing any goods until a rapport is developed and full assessment of the person's needs, values and wishes has been conducted. Safeguarding duties and responsibilities apply.

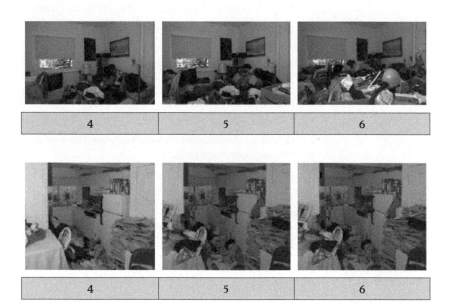

4	5	6

4	5	6

Level 2 *Clutter image rating 4–6*	Household environment requires professional assistance to resolve the clutter and the maintenance issues in the property
1 Property structure, services and garden area	• Only major exit is blocked • Only one of the services is not fully functional • Concern that services are not well maintained • Smoke alarms are not installed or not functioning • Garden is not accessible due to clutter, or is not maintained • Evidence of indoor items stored outside • Evidence of light structural damage, including damp • Interior doors missing or blocked open
2 Household functions	• Clutter is causing congestion in the living spaces and is impacting on the use of the rooms for their intended purpose • Clutter is causing congestion between the rooms and entrances • Rooms score 4–5 on the clutter scale • Inconsistent levels of housekeeping throughout the property • Some household appliances are not functioning properly and there may be additional units in unusual places • Property is not maintained within terms of lease or tenancy agreement where applicable • Evidence of outdoor items being stored inside
3 Health and safety	• Kitchen and bathroom are not kept clean • Offensive odour in the property • Person is not maintaining a safe cooking environment • Some concern with the quantity of medication, or its storage or expiry dates • No rotting food • No concerning use of candles • Person is trying to manage personal care but is struggling • No writing on the walls
4 Safeguard of children and family members	• Hoarding on clutter scale 4–7 doesn't automatically constitute a safeguarding alert • Please note all additional concerns for householders • Properties with children or vulnerable residents with additional support needs may trigger a safeguarding alert under a different risk
5 Animals and pests	• Pets at the property are not well cared for • Person is not unable to control the animals • Animals' living area is not maintained and smells • Animals appear to be undernourished or overfed • Sound of mice heard at the property • Spiderwebs in house • Light insect infestation (bedbugs, lice, fleas, cockroaches, ants etc.)

6 Personal protective equipment (PPE)	• Latex gloves, boots or needle stick safe shoes, face mask, hand sanitiser, insect repellent • PPE required

Level 3

7	8	9

High-level clutter – a safeguarding referral will be required. Where there is a risk to the person's physical and mental wellbeing, safeguarding processes should be followed and a full multi-agency meeting held to plan the enquiry and assessment process.

7	8	9

7	8	9

Level 3 *Clutter image rating 7–9*	Household environment will require intervention with a collaborative multi-agency approach with the involvement from a wide range of professionals. This level of hoarding constitutes a Safeguarding referral due to the significant risk to health of the householders, surrounding properties and residents.
1 Property structure, services and garden area	• Limited access to the property due to extreme clutter • Evidence may be seen of extreme clutter seen at windows • Evidence may be seen of extreme clutter outside the property • Garden not accessible and extensively overgrown • Services not connected or not functioning properly • Smoke alarms not fitted or not functioning • Property lacks ventilation due to clutter • Evidence of structural damage or outstanding repairs including damp • Interior doors missing or blocked open • Evidence of indoor items stored outside
2 Household functions	• Clutter is obstructing the living spaces and is preventing the use of the rooms for their intended purpose • Rooms score 7–9 on the clutter image scale • Rooms not used for intended purposes • Beds inaccessible or unusable due to clutter or infestation • Entrances, hallways and stairs blocked or difficult to pass • Toilets and sinks not functioning or not in use • Resident at risk due to living environment • Household appliances are not functioning or inaccessible • Person has no safe cooking environment • Person is using candles • Evidence of outdoor clutter being stored indoors • No evidence of housekeeping being undertaken • Broken household items not discarded, for example broken glass or plates • Concern for declining mental health • Property is not maintained within terms of lease or tenancy agreement where applicable • Property is at risk of notice being served by Environmental Health

3 Health and safety	• Human urine and or excrement may be present
	• Excessive odour in the property, may also be evident from the outside
	• Rotting food may be present
	• Evidence of unclean, unused and or buried plates and dishes
	• Broken household items not discarded, for example broken glass or plates
	• Inappropriate quantities or storage of medication
	• Pungent odour can be smelt inside the property and possibly from outside
	• Concern with the integrity of the electrics
	• Inappropriate use of electrical extension cords or evidence of unqualified work to the electrics
	• Concern for declining mental health
4 Safeguard of children and family members	• Hoarding on clutter scale 7–9 constitutes a safeguarding alert
	• Please note all additional concerns for householders
5 Animals and pests	• Animals at the property at risk due to the level of clutter in the property
	• Resident may not be able to control the animals at the property
6 Personal protective equipment (PPE)	• Animals' living area is not maintained and smells
	• Animals appear to be undernourished or overfed
	• Hoarding of animals at the property
	• Heavy insect infestation (bed bugs, lice, fleas, cockroaches, ants, silverfish etc.)
	• Visible rodent infestation

Listed below are examples of questions to ask where you are concerned about someone's safety in their own home, and where you suspect a risk of self-neglect and hoarding?

The information gained from these questions will inform a hoarding assessment and provide the information needed to alert other agencies. Many people with a hoarding problem will be embarrassed about their surroundings, so adapt the question to suit your people.

- How do you get in and out of your property? Do you feel safe living here?

- Have you ever had an accident, slipped, tripped up or fallen? How did it happen?

- How have you made your home safer to prevent this (above) from happening again?

- How do you move safely around your home (where the floor is uneven or covered, or there are exposed wires, damp, rot, or other hazards)?

- Has a fire ever started by accident?

- How do you get hot water, lighting, heating? Do these services work properly? Have they ever been tested?

- Do you ever use candles or an open flame to heat and light here or cook with camping gas?

- How do you manage to keep yourself warm, especially in winter?

- When did you last go out in your garden? Do you feel safe to go out there?

- Are you worried about other people getting into your garden to try and break in? Has this ever happened?

- Are you worried about mice, rats, foxes or other pests? Do you leave food out for them?

- Have you ever seen mice or rats in your home? Have they eaten any of your food? Could they be nesting anywhere?

- Can you prepare food, cook and wash up in your kitchen?

- Do you use your fridge? Can I have a look in it? How do you keep things cold in the hot weather?

- How do you keep yourself clean? Can I see your bathroom? Are you able to use your bathroom and use the toilet OK? Have a wash, bath, shower?

- Can you show me where you sleep and let me see your upstairs rooms? Are the stairs safe to walk up (if there are any)?

- What do you do with your dirty washing?

- Where do you sleep? Are you able to change your bed linen regularly? When did you last change it?

- How do you keep yourself warm at night? Have you got extra coverings to put on your bed if you are cold?

- Are there any broken windows in your home? Do any repairs need to be done?

- Because of the number of posessions you have, do you find it difficult to use some of your rooms? If so, which ones?

- Do you struggle with discarding things? To what extent do you have difficulty discarding, recycling, selling or giving away things?

An example of a safeguarding adult referral and assessment

Gina Collins is a 42-year-old woman who has been diagnosed with anxiety and depression. A referral was made to children's services two years ago regarding housing conditions and potential neglect. Both teenage children spend much of their time at boarding school and therefore concerns for children were lessened. Gina is described as warm, sensitive and loving towards both children.

On this occasion, a safeguarding adult referral under the category of self-neglect was made after Gina had a fall at home. The district nurse made the referral after expressing concern at the condition of the property. An assessment of need has been requested from the safeguarding team. Information gathered is to be shared with children's services.

Note: Work to develop a good working relationship with Gina began three weeks prior to the assessment. Regular visits were made to see Gina after her working day had ended.

Assessment overview (this can be a chronology of events or the key issues that have affected a person's life)

Gina is a 42-year-old woman with two teenage children: John who is 15 years old and Constance who is 13 years old. Gina's children attend Primrose Valley Boarding School, returning in the summer holidays to spend six weeks with their mother. Education is paid for by Gina's father. Gina lives in a small detached house set on the outskirts of a small rural village.

Gina and her husband (Fred) separated three years ago with him citing 'irreconcilable differences' in the divorce. Gina identifies the irreconcilable differences being her collecting behaviour. Fred visits the children regularly and has a good relationship with them.

Gina was raised by her parents in a fairly affluent middle-class urban environment. The family moved out into the countryside when Gina was ten years old. Gina's grandparents emigrated from Eastern Europe at this time and the family required a larger home to accommodate the elderly family members.

Gina's father was an accountant for a large global company before retiring four years ago. Gina's mother was an English teacher and worked in a local comprehensive school. Gina has lost contact with her father, her mother died two years ago and she has no siblings.

Gina describes her relationship with her father as poor, saying that he did not pay her very much attention, and when he did he was verbally and occasionally physically aggressive and often put her down, ridiculing her. Gina can recall some good times with her father, particularly when he returned from his travels and talked to her of the people he met, places he had explored, history and art that he had seen and the food that he had eaten. Gina describes being very close to her mother and sought reassurance and comfort from her whenever things became stressful.

Fred met Gina while studying at university and proved an additional source of support. Both Fred and Gina studied the history of art and Gina describes a common love in understanding the world through the objects that people leave behind. Throughout her school years Gina had been an exceptional student; however, during her time at university she became concerned with the detail and often got distracted by additional exploration of the things that she was learning, to the point that deadlines loomed and Gina was nowhere near completing her work. Gina describes wanting to die. She states that she felt that death was a better option than failure. This was when Gina's depression began and she identifies that she has struggled with low mood and anxiety since university, although she no longer feels that she would want to die.

Gina presents as a friendly, bright and engaging person, who is quick witted with a good sense of humour. Gina is very well read and can talk about almost any subject raised with her. Within the definition of the Mental Capacity Act there are no identified concerns with Gina's ability to make decisions of any kind for herself. In 2010, a referral was made to mental health services and Gina engaged in the assessment but refused anti-depressant medication. With little change occurring, Gina was discharged from services in 2011.

Gina describes herself as a comfort eater and states that she has used food as a source of comfort since childhood. Gina has reflected on her time at university and feels that she may have suffered from anorexia during this time, but this was not formally diagnosed.

Gina currently works three days per week (Mondays, Tuesdays and Thursdays) in a local library and meets up with friends occasionally after work. Gina describes how much she enjoys her work and her friendships.

Assessment – physiological and safety needs (eating, drinking, personal care/hygiene, sleep, physical care, home environment)

Home environment
Are you able to manage things for yourself around your home?

I manage fine, but it takes a long time. My collection keeps growing and growing and I never seem able to sort things out. The last letter that my father wrote to me said that I had failed in my duty to look after the children and my home. My father helped to buy the property and has now threatened to stop helping with the mortgage payments if I do not get it cleared. I can find it difficult to find bills and pay them on time, but I try to keep the bills on the top of the important papers pile. The trouble is that everything seems so important.

I can get to the bathroom but it takes me around an hour to get there and clear everything to get a bath every day. The sink is also difficult because there are so many things stored there. I have difficulty getting to the toilet on time because of all the things in my way and I sometimes have an accident. This is very embarrassing and frustrating. It takes so long to clean everything afterwards and to put everything back.

I like to buy gifts for people and I collect toiletries and towels as these can be good gifts. I use the cheaper toiletries myself sometimes because I would not wish to offend anyone. I don't use the new towels, I make do with the old tatty ones. I don't like taking medication, but keep it in stock just in case one of the children becomes ill. Some medication gets out of date, so I buy more, but I keep the older tablets and creams as a backup in case we run out. They always put dates on things to make you buy more.

I try to keep everything as clean as possible. I have clean and less clean piles and I try to keep the dust down as my daughter is allergic to dust. This can be very difficult with so many things to keep clean. I feel that this is more than a full-time job. I never fully manage to stay on top of things and it is very difficult to clean the kitchen properly.

I can no longer cook in my kitchen because there are so many boxes and papers there. I sometimes use the microwave but have trouble clearing up afterwards so prefer to eat out on work days and bring home takeaways on the days in between.

There is also a problem with the gas and the gas man said that this could not be resolved until an area to work in safely was made. It can get quite cold during the winter as I only have a couple of electric heaters that I use in the bedroom.

I sleep in my bed, but this also takes me time to move my books and papers to get in and out of bed. I don't sleep very well, or very long, usually about five hours per night. I am always thinking about the jobs that need doing to prepare myself for work, to eat, get washed and dressed. Working in a library, I need to be clean. I would hate people to think that I was smelly. My grandparents used to live with me when I was young. They never bathed, never wore perfume or deodorant. I could smell when they had been in the room. I couldn't sit on a chair after they had sat in it because I worried that it would make me smell too. I felt that everything was made dirty by them.

I wash my clothes in the washing machine but struggle to get things dry properly. I have a clothes horse in front of the electric fire in the bedroom. I used to have a tumble dryer but that broke a few years ago and has so many papers on top that I have not found time to reorganise them and replace it.

I use the garage door to get in and out of my house as this is the easiest way to get around my things. I fell in the bathroom a little while ago and hurt my leg. I was not able to get to the phone because I could not get around the house with my leg injured. I was very upset as I could not get to work the next day. They called around and you can imagine my embarrassment when they were looking through the windows. I had to shout and ask them to get the nurse. Worried about me, my colleague contacted the local GP, and the district nurse called around, but could not get in, even though I told her that the garage was free. I can't understand how other people seem to manage this and I cannot. It all seems so simple for other people.

IDENTIFIED NEEDS/RISKS

Gina's house is excessively cluttered. Using the clutter rating scale, Gina would be on the most severe end of the scale at an 8 or a 9. There is little to no access for emergency services and an inability to use most areas for their intended purpose. This has a significant effect on her emotional and physical wellbeing.

Moving through the property is difficult, with little to no floor space clear except for narrow trails through piles of collected items, boxes, magazines and newspapers that are between three and six feet high. When asked on a scale of 0–10 how difficult she finds it to get rid of things, Gina was very insightful and identified her problem as being 10 (maximum). When asked using the same scale how much of a problem she felt she had collecting things or buying new things, Gina identified this as a 9. When asked about the emotional distress suffered as a result of the clutter, Gina became quite tearful saying that she feels she is a disgrace and cannot even clean herself properly because of the things that she collects and said if there were a number on my scale greater than 10 she would say that that was how she felt. We discussed:

- Access for emergency services

- Fire risks

- Gas risk

- Falls risk

- Personal hygiene requirements

- Adequate diet

And worked out strategies to minimise harm and/or risk.

IDENTIFIED STRENGTHS

Gina:

- has insight into her collecting behaviour and the difficulties that this presents her in her life

- wants to do something about her collecting and to reorganise/declutter

- has organisation skills that she uses daily at work

- identifies herself as sensitive and caring

- has friends who may offer emotional support

- has, despite a lot of loss and grief, managed to prevent her depression from regressing back to the level it was at when she was at university

- makes every effort to reduce the dust and keep items clean.

BARRIERS

Gina:

- describes getting comfort from her belongings

- feels that acquiring things makes her happier

- is overwhelmed by the amount of considerations to be made

- is worried about the possibility of her children being taken away from her

- is worried about her ability to pay her mortgage should her father stop paying

- describes feeling tired, isolated and alone

- describes an emotional attachment to the objects and feels responsible for their wellbeing

- feels that possessions play a role in her identity

- has a strong connection to preserving things for historical value and also sees her history in the things that she collects

- sees the objects that she collects as an opportunity or chance that she needs to preserve.

Identified goals/solutions

Gina:

- identified that she would feel uncomfortable having the fire service in her home, but as long as they did not touch any of her belongings she would be OK for them to fit fire alarms. The fire service is visiting to give advice about the location of fitting fire alarms, and to return in two weeks' time to fit alarms in hall, bedroom, lounge and kitchen

- agreed to move some belongings from the kitchen ready for the fire service and to have the gas man return to make sure that the gas is safe

- would like to begin by looking at the collected items in the kitchen and bathroom

- has said that she would like to spend more time with her friends and has set herself a target to achieve this once the fire service and the gas issues have been addressed

- would like to make sure that emergency services have access through the main door but feels that this would take a long time to achieve.

Physiological care and friendship

How do you feel about your job, family, friends and the things that you do in your local community?

I sometimes think that I should give up my job as I could then concentrate on the house and my family. I need the money to pay the bills and I also find it good to get out of the house some days. It lifts my mood being at work and doing the things that other people do. I can organise things well at work because I am not attached to them, but as soon as someone says that I have to sort the books, magazines and papers to get rid of them I see them as my belongings, unwanted by anyone else. I want to give them a home and a use. I bring the unwanted books back here, as you never know when that information might come in useful.

I was very frightened of my father and tended to keep out of his way. I stayed in my room most of the time. When we moved to the village I moved away from all my friends, I hated school and I hated the man on the bus. I became so frightened of the angry and aggressive people. I think it was because I always expected them to hurt my feelings, or harm me like my dad did, just as I learned to trust him again. We could have such lovely conversations about his travelling experiences but then as soon as the conversation was finished there was always something that he was not happy about, wanted doing or changing, and I was never good enough. My father never respected me or my things; he even threw out my favourite toy as a child. I learned to find the things that he had thrown out and used to hide them. I often lost things, but now I have more control and I can keep everything where I can see it, so I don't forget it is there.

I buried my head in books, studied and learned about things, hoping that he might talk to me about them. I thought that if someone spoke to me and found me interesting then I might connect with them. No one spoke to me back then; people rarely speak with me now. I want to be more interesting and so much more than a boring child, or a boring librarian. I want to make people laugh, feel things, experience things and be important. I can do that with my friends so there are some good people who do not make me anxious. We met at work and they have similar interests. We discuss all sorts of things, including the things that we have read about.

I think that the books became a barrier between me and my father, me and the world. The things that I collected, like the gifts to give people, offered potential friendship and recognition that I was a nice and good person. The information I collected made me clever and engaging and the links between people meant that I could help others to get to know each other. History is very important because if we understand out past we can help each other to not make the same mistakes in the future. Some things from the past are very beautiful and I admire how people in difficult situations struggled every day but managed to see such beauty.

The things that I collect are not just an emotional barrier. I recognise that I feel safe and secure knowing that I have something of my own, just for me, but the things also create a physical barrier, like wrapping a duvet around you and covering your head so you don't need to look at the world.

When my mother died, I felt as if my world had ended, the collecting got so much worse and I ate takeaways every day. I think that I fill my body up to get comfort in the same way that I fill my house up to get comfort. My mother had provided some comfort, she was a face that I wanted to see, she was never critical or angry, she loved me unconditionally, but now she is gone there is a hole in my life that I fill with things.

I have never brought my friends home. I would be too embarrassed. I was so ashamed after my work colleagues called that I hid in the inventory of the library for weeks, claiming that I needed to get that work out of the way. I would be too ashamed to face them if they knew about me. They are very kind and generous but they don't know about how my life feels and get upset if I cancel meeting them.

As a young child, I used to love going out to play with the other children and we were always laughing and joking. I can go weeks without finding someone to laugh and joke with now. I call into the local newsagents every day and get the basic food items like milk and bread, along with the papers. Jean, who works in the newsagents, has a great sense of humour and I stop to chat with her for a while every day, but then I feel guilty that I should be back home sorting things out and cleaning things.

I sometimes get the feeling that in the end everyone either leaves or hurts you. My father left us regularly for long periods of time and when he came back he hurt me. My mother who I loved with all my heart died and left me. My husband left me and my children are never home, as they prefer to stay at school or their father's house. I am sure that my friends will get fed up with me cancelling on them and eventually give up asking me to come along. Every time I have someone important to me they leave me or hurt me. My things never leave me or hurt me, they make me feel safe and secure. I like to see things so that I do not forget them, or where they are so that I can use things.

IDENTIFIED NEEDS/RISKS
Gina:

- has identified feelings of loss, bereavement and lack of control over her environment. She describes having little love or sense of belonging to a place. Gina attaches her emotions to her belongings. These things are identified as a result of difficult past relationships.

- describes feeling low in mood and how her collection has an impact on this but she also describes the benefits of her collection.

Her collecting and mood are impacting on her relationships, causing her to lose her husband and have less contact with her children and friends.

IDENTIFIED STRENGTHS

Gina:

- maintained her relationship for a long time

- still has contact with her children

- has friendships that she has sustained

- does use some community resources

- has maintained work

- has emotionally managed some difficult and challenging times

- has faced the embarrassment of work colleagues seeing her home environment and managed this when returning to work

- has goals and targets with regard to friendships and relationships that need further exploration.

BARRIERS

Gina:

- describes guilt associated with not sorting out her house, a negative emotion that is preventing her from engaging effectively with others

- has negative experiences of relationships as a child

- had an experience of being isolated from people as a child, which is replicated in the present

- finds knowing where to begin, prioritising and sorting difficult.

IDENTIFIED GOALS/SOLUTIONS

Gina:

- would like to establish small-scale goals and targets because she feels it is important that people understand why she has kept something and her attachment to it. Gina has identified that it is easier to let go of something once she has talked about why she kept the object. She identifies that if the item would not be wasted, could go to a good home, or that it could be proven that the opportunity it represents is no longer available, then it is easier to let it go

- has agreed to meet with a psychologist to talk about her attachment to objects, her relationship with her family and friends, her feelings of lack of control and that she might forget something

- would like to work with someone in her home who will not judge her or be negative with her. A local person is to be commissioned using a direct payment to listen to Gina while she explains the meaning behind her objects, and a plan of support to help her sort and discard objects at her own pace has been put into place. Key access routes for emergency services are Gina's first target

- all services will be coordinated with psychology-leading safeguarding response.

Mental wellbeing and self-esteem
How do you feel about yourself now and how do you manage this?

Every day I wake up feeling afraid. I seem to be afraid of everything: afraid of what people think, afraid of people's responses and reactions to me, afraid of the prospect of managing all the stuff in the house, afraid of being seen as dirty or smelly. When I stop and think about it, I am not really sure what I am frightened of, and why I feel anxious all the time. I should be able to cope, I am an intelligent woman who seems to struggle with the things that people do every day, why is that? Sometimes the local children run in the garden and I can hear them calling me names. At university, they used to call me the bag lady because I carried so much information with me and now they call me worse things.

I feel upset with myself. I try so hard but I constantly seem to let my family down. Sometimes I feel so bad I just want to hide and not face anything. When I think about myself and my situation I feel disgusted at what I have become. I want to walk in here and have a clean, tidy house. I want to see nice things, art and creative things around me. I want my house to reflect who I am. Then I look around and think but this is who I have become. My father being so critical did not help me. When I was young I used to talk to him about his travels and use his experiences to describe how I felt. My father seemed much more interested in his travels than in me, but it was a way to get him to listen to me and begin to understand. I want my father to love me.

I want cleanliness and cannot stand the dirt. If someone touches me I feel contaminated. I cannot even hug my own children. How would that make you feel? I try to clean things and sort things into clean and less clean piles. The things on the furniture are clean and the things on the floor are dirty. I carry antibacterial wipes with me and clean things all the time. If someone touches something, I have to clean it.

I feel most dirty when trying to sort things out, but how do you sort things? Look at this magazine I kept this because there is an advert for a holiday that I thought Constance would like to go on when she is older. I kept this phone number because I met a wonderful woman from America who was my age about ten years ago and I thought that I would like to keep in touch and perhaps go to America to meet her. Here are my children's nursery school photographs. I remember those times when they were so young, bright and bubbly. Here is some money I set aside for Fred when he needed a new car, but now it might be useful for John learning to drive. I look around the room and every pile of things has useful information, useful connections, everything seems important to me. I want to see it so that I don't forget it.

I am not a religious woman but I wish that I was. I would like to have faith in something. I sometimes think about drinking to take away the pain, but it just makes me want to use the toilet more and if I get a hangover and feel sick it becomes intolerable. I could not even be a good drunk because of my stuff. I don't like drugs of any kind, even the ones prescribed by the doctor. I feel that I do not deserve to be given the medical help, if I cannot try to help myself first.

I feel most confident when I am out shopping. I love shopping for presents for people, I like a bargain. I feel as if I am in my own little world and that all the stress has disappeared, I feel free. I love Christmas when I get to give gifts to people. I can collect all year round to create the best Christmas present. I also like singing and sometimes call into the local church at Christmas time to listen to the carols being sung. I feel safe and calm in the church listening to them sing. I love the bright colours in the shop windows, the bright fires in the pubs and the happy chatter. The best time of my life was before we moved to the countryside, when I had friends and we played outside and sang songs. I remember when my dad was away my mother would let me have my friends round. We would light the fire in the Aga and sit cosy and warm around the table playing board games, drawing or planning a stage performance for my mum. I can't invite friends here and I cannot remember the last time I was able to see the fireplace.

The most traumatic times in my life include leaving my home as a child to move to the countryside, feeling like a failure at university, my father hitting me for being messy, my mother dying, my children leaving for boarding school and my husband leaving me. I would say that I feel quite traumatised now. I know that I have to change but I feel like a failure before I begin, it is just who I am.

My greatest achievement is a little more difficult. What have I really achieved? I once cleared a space in the dining room so that I could use the desk. I began to paint and also wrote an article about Eastern European art. My painting was sold in the local art gallery and the article was published. People appreciated the effort put into the painting and the effort to write the article, but the greatest effort was to clear the space to do these things. Nobody recognised the greatest achievement and that made me feel that it wasn't an achievement at all.

I get stuck in a rut and just seem to be going around in circles with a never-ending task list. This gets me down and when I feel depressed I despair at what is going to become of me and my children. I worry about what others think and feel about me all the time. I try to make connections between me and the children. I show them pictures, save articles, buy gifts, save their drawings and their schoolwork alongside my own school work and talk to them about how things have changed in our history. I can't believe that they do not want to look at the things I save for them, they just want to throw them out saying that they are rubbish. How can our emotions and past be rubbish? I guess I respond by not saying anything and hope that some day they will recognise how much I love them and the connections that I try to make. I take myself off to my room, which I find clean and I hide behind my stuff. I read my books and they are not allowed in there so I do not hear their criticisms. If I get really down I go out shopping for gifts, thinking that if I could find something to light up their world then perhaps they will understand and forgive me.

IDENTIFIED NEEDS/RISKS

Gina:

- identifies that her anxiety and depression may be getting worse, as she realises that something must change

- feels the affects of loss and bereavement very strongly

- describes feeling out of control

- finds cleaning problematic but she does not worry about illness or germs, it appears to be more about a perception of cleanliness and a method of ordering things

- has an inability to organise and sort objects in terms of importance.

IDENTIFIED STRENGTHS

Gina:

- is good at writing and painting

- identified an exception to the usual routine when she found the ability to clear the dining table to write and paint

- enjoys friendships and family time and identifies this as a strength in her past and something that she would like to create in her future

- sees having a clear space as an achievement

- aims to find solutions to her interactions with her father and children.

BARRIERS

Gina:

- has a current inability to discard

- lacks control over decisions regarding her children, her home environment and to some degree her finances. Many of these things are controlled by her father, with whom she has little contact with and is afraid of

- struggles to manage the cleaning routines

- lacks engagement with medical professionals and has low self-esteem, which impacts on decision making.

IDENTIFIED GOALS/SOLUTIONS

Gina:

- has described an ideal environment, in other words a long-term goal. She would like a kitchen with a fire, a place to write and draw, the ability to have friends round and to make better connections with her children and perhaps her father

- has identified an exception to the rule, a time when she was able to clear the clutter. She identifies the barrier as people not recognising the efforts that she made in preparing to draw and write. This could be a starting point to build self-esteem and begin clearing and achieve praise for the clearing of the space as well as the writing and painting. It is also a potential source of income that Gina might enjoy

- has made some connection with singing and while she is not religious, she has used the church to offer a social outlet, a place of calm and safety

- likes to talk to people and is happy to go to bereavement counselling as she recognises that she needs to talk about her feelings of loss

- is beginning to consider relationships with her father and children and wants to talk about how she might achieve closer relationships with people.

This assessment helped Gina to recognise the scale of the difficulties in access within her home. She could then identify the important starting points and was reassured that she would remain in control. There are lots of key therapeutic leads, such as bereavement, attachment and childhood difficulties in Gina's story. Gina has lots of interests and is keen to engage with others more often. The assessment process has supported Gina in contemplating change and what that might look like. This would be a good time to ask the miracle question about waking up in the morning and the house looking like you wanted it to look – what would you be hearing, seeing, doing and how would it feel?

Self-assessment

After I conducted a thematic review of safeguarding adults reviews, domestic homicide reviews and mental health homicide reviews over the past five years, key themes began to emerge. These themes have been collated into a self-assessment document. Begin with the questions in the middle section and, reflecting on the work that you are doing with the person self-neglecting, consider each question. You can use the left-hand column as guidance and the right-hand column to consider the potential barriers and the efforts to break down these barriers.

This tool may prove useful for supervision sessions in cases of self-neglect, self-reflection or as a structure for those conducting safeguarding adults reviews. All themes relating to self-neglect are not covered here, but all repetitive patterns or aspects of poor practice are identified.

Self-neglect practitioner self-assessment		
Guidance	Criteria	Barriers
1 Identifying self-neglect		
Self-neglect covers a wide range of behaviours including: • neglecting to care for personal hygiene • neglecting to care for health • neglecting to care for surroundings • behaviours such as hoarding. A safeguarding referral should be made in cases of self-neglect where the three-part test is met and the person: • has needs for care and support • is experiencing or at risk of abuse or neglect (including self-neglect) • as a result of those care and support needs is unable to protect themselves from either risk of, or the experience of abuse and neglect. You do not need consent to make a safeguarding referral: • Checking out the person's consent is part of local authority S42 duties, therefore a referral can be made without consent. • Enquiries can be made about the issues affecting the person/others, including whether the person consents or not. • If they do not consent, this simply means that the local authority does not have their cooperation, but does not prevent agencies from taking any steps that they can. The purpose of the enquiry is to establish a person's capacity to make certain decisions, determine the level of risk to the person and others, coordinate personalised responses to abuse and neglect, and explore potential crime.	Self-neglect has been appropriately identified and a safeguarding referral has been made to the local authority. (See ten steps to information sharing, clutter rating scale guidance, risk-assessment tool and safeguarding referral procedures.)	Barriers can include: • Not recognising or identifying the issue as self-neglect or neglect. • Not recognising appropriate threshold criteria for safeguarding or applying additional thresholds. • Where a person's self-neglect is impacting on their emotional or physical wellbeing, then it is no longer questionable whether they have needs for care and support – they meet the three-part test. • You do not need consent to make a safeguarding referral to the local authority. Lack of consent for safeguarding purposes should not be a barrier.

2 Section 42 enquiries

The purpose of an enquiry is to: • get a picture of the abuse/neglect/self-neglect • make sure that the person is safe (consider the Mental Capacity Act and personalised response) • consider capacity assessments required and by whom • rule out additional or historical abuse/neglect • explore potential crime • identify any coercive or controlling behaviours • explore any mental health or substance misuse concerns • consider risks to others • determine the care and support needs of the individual • consider advocacy and methods of communication • determine whether a multi-agency response is required. The local authority must have oversight of safeguarding procedures, but can request another agency to make enquiries on their behalf, or chair multi-agency meetings for safeguarding purposes. Information and outcomes must be shared with the local authority. The benefit of invoking safeguarding procedures (risk assessment and clutter rating scale 4-6) is: Safeguarding duties and responsibilities apply: • Duty to share information for enquiry purposes. • Duty to cooperate with the local authority and the local authority to cooperate with other agencies for safeguarding purposes. • Duty to assess where there is an identified need. • Duty to determine consent. • Duty to provide appropriate advocacy. • Duty to assess carers' needs. In most cases where hoarding reaches scales 7–9 on the clutter rating scale, or self-neglect is having a significant impact on the person's physical or emotional wellbeing, the local authority will make safeguarding arrangements, unless there is an agency more appropriate to do so. In cases where there is a potential crime, the police will lead the investigation process.	Have S42 enquiries been implemented appropriately? (See clutter rating scale guidance. Where there are issues with hoarding, see tool and safeguarding referral procedures.)	Barriers can include: • Lack of understanding about what an S42 enquiry is. • Reluctance to coordinate a multi-agency response to prevent further neglect/self-neglect. • A lack of confidence in coordinating, delegating and utilising all partnership agencies to make enquiries and respond to abuse or neglect. • Local authority doesn't just have oversight but wants to maintain control, rather than a multi-agency response, or is overwhelmed with safeguarding referrals and refers back to single agency to deal with the case without multi-agency support or coordination.

3 Risk to others

Risks to others can include: • Fire risk • Rats, vermin, flies • Faecal matter, vomit or other bodily fluids • Toxic substances • Open wires, unsafe gas, structural issues • Oxygen tanks where someone smokes, or other medical equipment • Drugs paraphernalia (uses needles, spoons, knives) • Weapons • People using the property who may target other vulnerable people • Anti-social behaviour • People who may have needs for care and support also residing at the property • Children residing or spending time at the property • Animals at the property.	Has the risk to others been considered?	Barriers can include: • A strong focus on individual rights and needs without consideration of the needs and rights of others to be safe. • Not reporting, or poor response to potentially criminal activity. • Other forms of abuse are explored without consideration of self-neglect.

4 Risk assessment		
Risk assessments should include: • Historical abuse and past knowledge of the person. • Previous safeguarding referrals. • Cumulative risk. • The vulnerability of the person (capacity, mental ill health, physical disability, learning disability, autism spectrum disorder, age and frailty of the person, social isolation and support the person has, acceptance of care and support, insight the person has into their problems and difficulties). • Type and seriousness of self-neglect/hoarding. • Level of self-neglect/hoarding (clutter rating scale). • Background to self-neglect/hoarding (does the person have a disability/mental health problems that prevent self-care? Has this been a long-standing problem? When did it begin and was there a trigger? Does the person engage with services and was there a time when this was different? Is social isolation a concern?). • Impact on others. • Reasonable suspicion of abuse (could self-neglect be an indicator of abuse/neglect, is the person targeted for abuse/anti-social behaviour/mate crime, is the person neglected by someone responsible for their care?). • Legal frameworks (is the person at risk of eviction? Are there pressing environmental concerns or public health concerns, debt issues that may lead to prosecution, other criminal convictions, child protection proceedings?). • Is there anyone obstructing or preventing work with the person (family members, other people at the property)?	Has the appropriate risk assessment been completed? (See clutter rating scale guidance, tool and safeguarding procedures.) Has the reason for the refusal of care, services or treatment been explored in relation to risk?	Barriers include: • Services identifying risk but not identifying the risk-management plan. • Services recognising level of risk but not implementing defensible decision making e.g. evidence of capacity assessments and outcomes, use of Human Rights Act, recognition of someone being deprived of their liberty in the community. • Cases being closed with escalating risks identified. • Is the person being moved from service to service without a safeguarding oversight and coordination of services?
5 Carers' assessment		
Carers' assessments to consider: • Carers' needs in continuing to support the person. • Capacity issues relating to carer and ability to provide care. • People residing at the property who may not consider themselves carers, but may still have a duty to care. • Obstructive or aggressive carers/family member. Note: If there is an identified carer, then this may be a case of neglect rather than self-neglect. Wilful neglect is a potential crime.	Have carers' needs been considered and a carers' assessment completed? Have carers been identified on care and support plans where they are meeting an identified need of the person for whom they care? Are carers aware of their duties and responsibilities and the potential consequences of these?	Barriers include: • Carers not identifying as carers. • Carers not being identified on care and support plan as meeting a need. • Not recognising carers who self-neglect – eligible for safeguarding.

6 Mental health and substance misuse

In assessing mental health and substance misuse consider:
- Does the person require a mental health assessment?
- Has a referral been made?
- Are there barriers to assessment?
- Does the person misuse substances?
- Would they engage with substance misuse services?
- What is the impact of substance misuse on physical and mental wellbeing and on daily functioning and increased risks?
- Is assessment needed, including that of executive functions of the brain?

When someone self-neglects there may be a range of psychological issues impacting on them, for example attachment issues, issues of neglect in childhood, executive function difficulties, trauma and loss issues, agoraphobia. Mental health services should consider access to psychology support even if there is not a defined medical treatment route. Access should be defined as accessible to the person i.e. someone with agoraphobia is not going to make it to a clinic appointment and someone self-neglecting is unlikely to respond to appointment letters.

Have referrals for mental health and substance misuse services been considered and recorded?

Have all legal duties under the Mental Health Act been considered (S117 aftercare, community treatment orders, guardianships etc.)?

Barriers can include:
- Sending appointment letters to someone who is not engaging (not an appropriate form of communication).
- Maintaining that someone with agoraphobia needs to attend a clinic appointment (not accessible to the person).
- Unclear pathways between services.
- Case closure – no risk/capacity assessments.

7 Capacity and consent

You assume capacity unless there is reason to believe otherwise. The Mental Capacity Act Code of Practice states that one of the reasons why people may question a person's capacity to make a specific decision is 'the person's behaviour or circumstances cause doubt as to whether they have capacity to make a decision' (Mental Capacity Act Code of Practice, p.52). Arguably, extreme self-neglect or hoarding behaviour meets this criterion and assessments should take place.

In determining who assesses capacity, or who is accountable for assessing capacity you should consider:
- If you are the person who requires consent, agreement, understanding or a signature from the person self-neglecting for a proposed treatment, care provision, course of action or tenancy agreement/compliance, then you need to assess whether the person is capable of consenting by undertaking a capacity assessment.
- Any capacity assessment carried out in relation to self-neglect must be time-specific, and relate to a specific intervention or action. The professional responsible for undertaking the capacity assessment will be the person who is proposing the specific intervention or action (wherever possible), and is referred to as the 'decision maker'.
- The decision maker may need to seek support from other professionals in the multi-disciplinary team, they are responsible for making the final decision about a person's capacity.
- When the person is assessed as lacking capacity the decision maker is responsible for the best interest decision.
- If the person is deemed to have capacity, this should be clearly recorded along with the things that the person did/said that made the decision maker think that the person had capacity, and the information and advice given.
- If the person self-neglecting is refusing to engage with certain professionals, anyone who has access and has developed a rapport with the person self-neglecting should be supported by the actual decision maker to carry out the capacity assessment and best interest decision.

Are all relevant capacity assessments up to date and recorded within one support plan for monitoring?

List capacity assessments required, e.g.:
- Tenancy agreement
- Tenancy support
- Tenancy review
- Medication offered
- Treatment offered
- Safeguarding referral
- Assessment and support planning
- Services offered (identified individually)
- Aids and adaptations
- Finance

Barriers include:
- Capacity assessments being too generic, not issue-specific enough and not undertaken by the appropriate agency.
- The person/agency requiring consent to provide an aspect of care or a treatment, or a service has not taken responsibility for that capacity assessment.
- Lack of understanding where a person has capacity and is making an unwise decision – entitled to do this (consider ten steps to information sharing).
- Confusion about what 'duty of care' means. A duty of care does not mean that we prevent risk and protect the person no matter what. It means respecting the wishes, expectations, values and outcomes of a capacitated individual, including their right to make what others might consider 'unwise decisions'. If the person has capacity to make a particular decision and this is not criminal, or posing a risk to others, they are not being coerced or intimidated into making this decision and they are not detainable under the Mental Health Act, we have no right to intervene in that decision, but can offer support advice, guidance, therapy to enable that person to understand more and perhaps reconsider their decision.

Safeguarding principles should be considered throughout all safeguarding interventions, including capacity assessments: • Empower the person to understand and make decisions. • Establish their desired expectations and outcomes. • Take action before harm occurs and prevent further abuse/neglect. • Use proportionate responses that are least intrusive and in the person's best interests. • Consider support/advocacy and identify someone to help the person engage in the process and provide feedback to the person. • Solve difficulties by working together across agencies. • Utilise community resources. • Ensure that agencies are accountable for their actions, knowledge, application of legal frameworks (including the ability to conduct capacity assessments and record appropriately). • Ensure that the person self-neglecting understands the roles of all agencies involved in their care and support. List all the aspects of care, treatment, service provision or intervention that requires the person's consent. Identify the person/agency that requires consent as the decision maker. Safeguarding plans should detail the capacity assessments required and the person/agency responsible with timescales for completion and follow-up monitoring. Once the capacity assessments are complete then agencies are looking to see whether there may be a change in the person's ability to consent.	Are proportionate and least restrictive interventions being considered? Where a person lacks capacity to make a decision are we balancing their rights, wishes and expectations with the actual level of risk, or are we being too risk averse?	• Lack of defensible recording when a person has capacity and their decision could have a significant impact on wellbeing. • Mini mental state tests and diagnostic tests being used instead of a capacity assessment. • Lack of coordination of capacity assessments in the safeguarding process. • Lack of access to the person – record what is known and share knowledge across agencies.

8 Advocacy and representation

The local authority has a duty to arrange for an independent advocate to be available to represent and support the person self-neglecting, to facilitate their involvement in the process. This duty applies when the person has substantial difficulty in being involved in any part of the safeguarding process. Substantial difficulty is defined as the person having difficulty in: • understanding the relevant information • retaining that information • using or weighing up that information • communicating their views, wishes and feelings. This duty does not apply if the local authority is satisfied that there is a person who: • could represent and support the person to facilitate their involvement (a friend or family member who is not part of any safeguarding procedures and does not have a vested interest in any potential outcomes) • is not engaged in providing care or treatment for the person in a professional capacity The duty also does not apply where the person has capacity and is competent to consent to consent to a course of action.	Does the person have suitable representation and support?	Barriers include: • Lack of understanding regarding local authority duties to find advocacy where a person has 'substantial difficulties' being involved in the process. • Utilising family members where they have a vested interest or may be implicated in the safeguarding issues.

9 Multi-agency response		
Multi-agency response to: • consider capacity issues in relation to a range of matters affecting the person and who should/can do them • rule out additional or historical abuse or neglect • explore potential crime • identify any coercive or controlling behaviours affecting the person • examine the person's mental health and how this may be affecting them • explore any risks to others • determine support needs of the individual including appropriate advocacy. Earlier intervention assists in developing a rapport, access to community, circles of support around the person, solution-focused and strengths-based rather than risk-management processes. In multi-agency meetings consider: • Police-led enquiries coordinated alongside any required assessment processes. • In criminal cases – the preservation of evidence. • Referrals to necessary services. • Involvement of services not already involved, such as domestic abuse, substance misuse, mental health services, fire service, anti-social behaviour services, MAPPA, MARAC, SARC, public health etc. • Coordination of assessment methodology. • Therapeutic assessment and intervention processes. • Who leads on information sharing, communication and involvement of the person self-neglecting. • Coordination of capacity assessments. • Identify gaps in knowledge and who will find this information. • The whole family approach – others at risk, support offered. • Animal welfare. • Perpetrator risks/vulnerabilities/support and who will provide feedback. • Barriers and how these will be overcome. • All aspects of the risk assessment.	Has a multi-agency response been coordinated early enough to prevent the deterioration of physical and mental wellbeing? Has a key person been identified to liaise with the person self-neglecting?	Barriers include: • The person being passed between agencies without oversight or coordination. • Where there are issues of severe neglect, short-term intervention services are not appropriate, e.g. case being held solely with the GP, single point of access or duty team. • Lack of consistency – developing a rapport with the person is of prime importance. An agency, or if possible a person, should be identified as the key agency to undertake the long-term work. • Barriers in sharing information, coordinating approaches, access to appropriate support and not ensuring that the duty to cooperate with the local authority and the local authority to cooperate with other agencies – when meeting a number of barriers from a particular organisation in trying to prevent abuse and neglect from occurring or protect someone from abuse or neglect, concerns should be escalated. Board members should be supportive and offer advice and guidance to ensure that safeguarding duties are being met within their organisation.

10 Comprehensive and holistic assessment

Where a person self-neglecting refuses an assessment, S11 of the Care Act identifies that the local authority has a duty to carry out that assessment if:
- the person lacks capacity to refuse that assessment and carrying out the assessment is in the person's best interests (must be recorded)
- the person is experiencing or at risk of abuse or neglect.

When assessing someone who self-neglects, do not assume that this is a lifestyle choice. Ask the miracle question: 'If you were to wake up tomorrow and your house was miraculously changed into the type of house you would like to be living in, what would it look like, what would you see, what would you be doing, what would be different?' or 'If you were to wake up tomorrow morning and you did not feel so low in mood what would you be doing, what would things look like, what would be different?'

Has the assessment covered enough detail to understand the reasons for self-neglect, when self-neglect began, any triggers, loss, bereavement, abuse? What are the goals of the person and are there any barriers? Is there a history of neglect or any problems with family contact, family relationships and motivation? See assessment information.

Has a comprehensive and holistic assessment of need been conducted with or without the consent of the individual where self-neglect is impacting on physical and mental wellbeing?

Is there a duty to assess?

Have non-commissioned services, other agencies, carers, friends and other parties meeting an identified need for the individual all been recorded as meeting that need on the care and support plan? Have all parties been informed of their duties, responsibilities and need to inform should needs change?

Have culture, values and religious beliefs been explored with the person?

Barriers include:
- Overly simplistic assessment that does not consider why a person is self-neglecting, how the self-neglect began and what the person gains from the self-neglect.
- Some cultures believe in alternative medicines and therapies, rejecting western medicine. Where a person has capacity to make decisions about medical intervention and treatment and has differing cultural beliefs from traditional western medical perspectives, this needs to be explored thoroughly and support plans established in a culturally sensitive manner.
- Family members, friends and non-commissioned services meeting the needs of the individual are not identified on the care and support plan – ensure that if a person or organisation agrees to meet a need they understand accountability for meeting that need.

11 Compliance and insight

When someone is not accepting of services, explore the reasons why. What prevents the person from accepting support? Consider: • Harm minimisation – what can be achieved and how much will this lessen the risks? • Has there been a negative experience of services? • How can negative experiences be changed: be prompt, remain engaged, be on time, communicate in ways that the person can respond to, do not send letters if this is inappropriate to the needs of the person, do not impose actions if at all possible. Work with the person and their timescales, and do not attempt clear-ups before other issues have been explored, and any clearing should be at the pace of the person (dependent on risks to others). • Is there someone who has a relationship with the person and are they willing/able to support services in providing care/support? • Can a rapport be developed with someone? • Look for solutions to this barrier. Consider the process of change (Kübler-Ross). If a person is in denial, angry or resistive, this is part of the change process and you can support the person to move on. Consider motivational interviewing techniques and the process of moving someone from pre-contemplative to contemplative stages (Prochaska and DiClemente).	Is the person accepting of care, support and services? Is there a plan to maintain engagement and contact? Does the person have insight into their behaviours? Have potential loss, trauma and grief been considered in the widest context and how can the person be supported through this?	Barriers include: • Recognition of loss and grief – this is not merely about bereavement and can include, for example, loss of childhood through neglect, loss of mobility or ability, loss of independence in older people, loss of confidence as a result of abuse. • Not recognising the process of change – if you are suggesting change then a person may experience a range of emotions and anxieties about leaving something that they feel safe with behind – do not suggest taking something away from the person without exploring what they gain from it and how they feel this emotion can be replaced.

12 Imposed sanctions, compliance or penalties

A person is unlikely to change when power and control are removed from them. In some cases, sanctions must be imposed and the effects of these must be considered by professionals intervening. Consider: • Eviction notices • Child protection proceedings • Imposed housing sanctions • Criminal proceedings • Debt and debt recovery • Other.	Are there any legal considerations or imposed compliance considerations and have these been clearly recorded?	Barriers include: • Lack of capacity assessments – sanctions cannot be imposed on someone who did not understand the requirements in the first place, unless there is a risk to others or criminal proceedings.

13 Information sharing

Relevant information can be shared with relevant agencies without consent when there is reasonable suspicion of: • risk to others • crime • public interest issues • coercive and controlling behaviours / domestic abuse • a need for the person to be assessed under the Mental Health Act. Confidentiality must not be confused with secrecy. It is inappropriate for agencies to give assurances of absolute confidentiality in cases where there are concerns about abuse, particularly those situations where vulnerable people may be at risk.	Is information being shared across all agencies to prevent deterioration of physical and mental wellbeing and safeguard the person?	• The Data Protection Act is not a barrier – it supports this form of information sharing.

14 Personalised safeguarding

Personalised safeguarding means that when a person has capacity to make a decision they are entitled to make an unwise decision. Ensure that:
- capacity assessments and whether the person is making a capacitated decision (assessed and recorded as such) have been taken into account
- it does not impact adversely on anyone else
- the reasoning behind this decision is explored
- information and advice has been offered in a format that the person understands (and has been recorded).

Where a person lacks capacity to make a decision are we sure that the course of action is the least restrictive possible and in the best interests of the person. Remember:
- A safe but miserable life is no life at all.
- We do not have to eliminate all risks, just minimise risk to the person as far as is comfortable for them.
- Obtain multi-agency support, senior management support, legal support or support from the Court of Protection if the situation is proving problematic.

We should explore the reasons why a person is refusing care, support or treatment. This needs to include possible correlation with past caring responsibilities and let-downs, cultural issues, and the interface with professionals in the past. We should not make assumptions based on our own culture and values, e.g. if a person has strong beliefs about non-traditional forms of medicine is this impacting on their acceptance of traditional western medicine?

After risk to others, potential crime, public interest issues, coercive and controlling behaviours have been ruled out, is there evidence of person-centred care and support planning?

Have the wishes, views and values of the person and their expectations and desired outcomes been identified and recorded? Has the reason why a person is refusing treatment, care and support been explored?

Have cultural, ethnic, religious and personal perspectives in relation to care, services or treatment been explored?

Have capacity assessments been conducted in relation to each treatment decision?

Have the person's relationship, cultures and values been assessed alongside family and community cultures and values?

Barriers include:
- Lack of understanding of the Mental Capacity Act.
- Anxiety about unwise decisions.
- A feeling that we are in trouble if we do not protect people when they are making capacitated, unwise decisions. We are not the decision maker, they are and are responsible for their decisions and the consequences, but we must demonstrate why we think that this is a capacitated decision (information and advice must be offered and the person's reasoning explored).

15 Management support and response		
When there are barriers from agencies, barriers from the person themselves, barriers in knowledge of legislation and potential responses and barriers in cooperation, and a person's physical and mental wellbeing is deteriorating, this implies that current interventions are not working and the barriers are too significant for practitioners to manage alone, even across agencies. It is helpful to have a layer of safeguarding sitting between safeguarding multi-agency response and Safeguarding Adult Review. This may be called an Executive Strategy/ Executive Safeguarding/overarching strategy. This may be chaired by a senior manager within the local authority who can look at the strategic elements of the safeguarding process to support the removal of any barriers, feed the outcomes and actions down to operational staff and up to the safeguarding adults board for action. Individual safeguarding meetings will still be held looking at the needs of the individual or people involved and feed information back to the senior manager.	Are escalating risks taken seriously and addressed at the appropriate level of management/ intervention? Is there clarity regarding when to escalate concerns and to whom?	Barriers include: • No clear escalation process in safeguarding where the person is continuing to deteriorate as a result of self-neglect.

16 Defensible decision making		
Defensible or justifiable decision making follows the word 'because': • I chose this course of action because… • I ruled this out because… And following 'because' should be recorded: • the legislation used to make the decision • in absence of legislation, the policy, model, method, theory or research that informed the decision balanced information on what the person did or said that made you think this was an appropriate course of action, or not attempts to enable the person to understand consequences, pros, cons, risks, alternative options and information and advice given. Intervention should be justified in recording logs: • Who is intervening? • What is the purpose of the intervention? • What actions were taken? • What were the outcomes of the action? If a professional is struggling to identify outcomes from intervention they need to raise this during supervision and consider: • Why am I going around in circles with this case? • What might possible solutions be? • Who do I need to help me with these solutions? • Is the mental and physical wellbeing of this person significantly deteriorating and does this need escalating? A summary of work, progress, barriers and how those barriers have been addressed can support defensible decision making. Consider including: • Referrals made • Appointments offered • Information and advice given • Capacity assessments • Access to advocacy • Person's wishes, choices, expectations and outcomes • Support given to help the person recognise/understand • Duty to assess and how this has been achieved • What was considered, what was ruled out and why • Legal frameworks used • Models, methods, theory and research used in practice • 'I' statements of the person or indicative responses.	Is my recording defensible (or justifiable) rather than defensive (offering reasons for failure)?	Barriers include: • Professionals stating 'I did this in my head' – a major barrier to defensible decision making. It is important to see your justification for actions taken, in other words demonstrate what you considered and why it was appropriate, what you ruled out and why.

Other		
Practitioners to consider the barriers and explore in supervision the possible solutions to barriers. Ensure that intervention is not overly intrusive and involves the person as far as possible. Consider the emotional impact of any decision and whether this may have a negative or positive impact. If a person has an emotional attachment to their actions or hoarded items then removing the items will only serve to increase the sense of loss and powerlessness. It will exacerbate the problem, not remove it. The wellbeing of others must be factored in but if we can achieve this working with the person, rather than against them, it will more likely be sustainable. The cost of clear-ups to the local authority is substantial and the problem will only begin again elsewhere and with less positive intervention.	Are we trying to impose large-scale clear-ups, and sanctions that are neither cost effective, nor support the person?	Barriers include: • Services imposing control with no recognised benefits.

Chapter 7

SUPPORTING THE PRACTITIONER

Creating social work strategies that are supportive

Within Health and Social Care, strategies change with the changing social, technical, economic and political climate. The introduction of the Care Act (2014) has seen the remit of safeguarding adults expand rapidly and with an influx of self-neglect cases local authorities are struggling to manage using the traditional structures and methods of adult protection. To support the practitioners a bottom-up and top-down approach needs to be used. Safeguarding Adults Board (SAB) strategies need to be considered to assist practitioners across agencies. The structure of the service provision and screening of access to services is a key task in making sure that people who require safeguarding have equitable access to services and tailored advice, guidance and support, as well as access to statutory services. The Health model to maintain wellbeing within the community is better understood and recognised than the Social Care model, however, the process is the same to maintain wellbeing within the community as long as possible and to triage, risk assess and evaluate the necessary, proportionate and appropriate intervention to meet need.

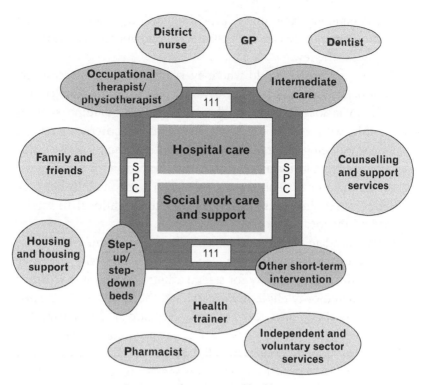

Figure 7.1: The structure of health services

The model in Figure 7.1 identifies how health services are structured. General citizen wellbeing is maintained within the community using community health resources. When these health resources are no longer sufficient to keep the person well, either a referral is made or the person accesses a triage system to determine the level of care required. This may be via the 111 system for urgent medical concerns, or similar. If the person requires some help, short-term interventions are considered; where there are concerns for the person's physical health then they receive outpatient hospital services, and where serious concerns are identified then hospital admission is considered.

The triage system is to determine the level of care and support required by the person and direct them to the most appropriate sources of support. The amount of time and variety of professional support is determined by the nature of the ailment, injury or illness. The response reflects the health need. Where a person can be redirected to appropriate community resources, this is achieved via the triage system. If the person requires short-term interventions to get them back to community care, this is provided and only those who need specialist or emergency care are admitted to outpatients, with hospital care being for the few.

Can you imagine a world where everyone was able to access any aspect of health care and the time given to patients did not reflect the need? In some local authorities the access to safeguarding services reflects this, with everyone who meets eligibility criteria under the three-part test being referred to the safeguarding team. However, this is unmanageable and local authorities then want to create additional thresholds themselves. This creates risk when someone falls between legislative thresholds for safeguarding and the additional threshold imposed by the local authority.

Referrals relate to prevention as well as protection from abuse (three-part test). Previously under *No Secrets eligibility* criteria, everyone referred to the local authority for safeguarding purposes was screened against local authority eligibility criteria and those who were deemed eligible for local authority services were safeguarded. This meant that the local authority was responsible for the planning of care for all safeguarding cases as they were eligible for social services. Under the Care Act 2014, not everyone who meets eligibility criteria for safeguarding is eligible for local authority services and many do not require them. Care may be better placed with health, housing, or other community services. The local authority must provide oversight, guidance and signposting, but does not need to do everything, as all agencies are responsible for safeguarding responses. Low-level cases of self-neglect may be signposted to community services, moderate cases may be addressed through multi-agency meetings and safeguarding plans chaired by a relevant involved agency such as housing or health. The answer is to make all agencies accountable for safeguarding and not just for identifying and reporting abuse and neglect. In relation to eligibility criteria for someone self-neglecting, some local authorities try to equate the first part of the three-part test (has needs for care and support) to eligibility criteria for local authorities. This is an incorrect interpretation, as care and support needs are not the same as eligibility criteria for social work assessment or intervention. Care and support needs are deliberately a much broader concept.

The Care Act developed a system for social care that reflects the health care process in order that health and social care can work together to prevent deterioration of mental and physical wellbeing, delay the need for services and maintain people within their own local communities for as long as possible. The local authority have a duty to ensure that community resources are sufficient to meet the needs of the community and that people have a choice in services. This is to assist in sustaining people within their own communities as long as possible. Where community services do not sufficiently support the person, the local authority is asked to establish a single point of contact for people making enquiries. The local authority's role is to signpost people towards suitable resources, or to triage, and to determine the appropriate response. To use the analogy, if someone were to contact the health 111 line with a bad cold, they would be redirected towards their pharmacy. If the person contacting the local authority has low-level needs the local authority would ensure that those needs are met by directing them to community resources. If the community resources no longer sustain a person, then short-term interventions are considered, including assistive technology. Where these interventions no longer support the person, or are ruled out, then occupational therapy, intermediate care, physiotherapy, therapeutic interventions and rehabilitation are considered. When these interventions no longer sustain the person, then intensive social work intervention is required.

1. Journey of support – not eligible for local authority services.

2. Person contacts the local authority.

3. Single point of contact determines eligibility.

4. If the person is not eligible for local authority services, determine whether there are any safeguarding issues including self-neglect (meets three-part eligibility criteria for safeguarding). Immediate risks are discussed and addressed.

5. Contact person determines the safeguarding risks and the relevant course of action required by the person affected by the risks: signposting, information and advice, assessment, actions and outcomes for a number of involved providers, adult protection, or a combination of these.

6. Contact person does not have enough information and therefore considers an enquiry to determine whether there are:

   • risks to others

- carer assessments required (carer capacity, risks, ability, stress)

- potential criminal issues

- public interest issues

- domestic abuse/coercive and controlling behaviours

- issues regarding mental ill health requiring assessment under the Mental Health Act

- requirements for capacity assessments

- legal issues affecting the person and their wellbeing/ conflicting legal issues

- communications that indicate a potential need for advocacy

- a number of agencies involved or that should be involved.

The contact person determines whether needs have been met and the person can be signposted to community support. Even though the person is not being eligible for local authority services, their wellbeing may deteriorate as a result of abuse and neglect and therefore the local authority can conduct an assessment of need (with the consent of the person) to prevent wellbeing from deteriorating further.

Having access to this form of triage requires a skilled worker at the single point of contact who is able to rapidly assess the situation and steer safeguarding issues in the appropriate direction. Triaging requires the person to undertake delegatory responsibilities, have confidence to manage risk effectively and give advice about managing situations where emergency services may require coordinating with care and support. The person triaging also needs to recognise that a person's wellbeing is central to care provision and if this deteriorates then costs and services are required, so early intervention to prevent deterioration is both person-centred and cost effective for the local authority. This is particularly pertinent in cases of self-neglect, where there is often pressure to redirect cases back to single-agency support. Key enquiry topics are overlooked, because (often) the person is capacitated and states that they do not want a referral. It is clear that without guidance, support and some intervention the person's wellbeing will deteriorate. The single point of contact will need to be skilled enough to make these autonomous decisions. Operational and strategic management will need to support decisions made by the workers at the single point of contact.

In some local authorities, safeguarding cases are not filtered through a single point of contact but elsewhere. This can place a burden on social workers in a busy duty system, or in completing rapidly increasing low-level assessments that detract from the complex targeted work that is required from our skilled workforce.

1. Journey of support – eligible for local authority services.

2. All the above issues will be considered and an assessment of need undertaken.

3. Consider whether there is any informal support (family/ friends) willing and assessed as able to provide care identified on the care and support plan and to meet specified needs.

4. Assistive technology, aids and adaptations are considered to meet needs.

5. Other agencies such as nurses, occupational therapists, tissue viability, falls assessors, physiotherapists and housing are identified on the care and support plan where they meet individual needs.

6. Community resources available to meet needs.

7. Therapeutic interventions available to meet needs.

8. Short-term interventions available to meet needs.

9. Low-level direct payments available to meet needs.

10. Creative solutions to commissioning care provision available.

Each step should be considered and if ruled out, records should justify why a less intrusive intervention has been ruled out in favour of a more intrusive one.

Social work intervention models

- In cases of self-neglect, like many other cases since the Care Act (2014) was introduced, practitioners try to seek a ready-made service. In training, I regularly hear:

- 'We do not have time'

- 'We do not have services'

- 'We do not have a hoarding service.'

The duty placed on local authorities to ensure that there is a sustainable market is failing in times of austerity (Carter 2015). Health community care provision is also groaning under the numbers of people wishing to access health care and the impact of this means that health and wellbeing are deteriorating. Some creative solutions may be required by practitioners.

- I try to understand service austerity by considering times when I have been less affluent. In times where I have more money I shop at the high-end shops, with easy prepared meals and good quality products. This saves time in preparation and shopping about for food. When I am less well off, the pick and mix of supermarkets comes into play. I gladly accept vegetables from my friend's allotments, go to the market for the main things, then consider the cheap supermarkets, then middle range ones and if I cannot get a product anywhere else I go to the high-end supermarket. Meals are produced from scratch, are time consuming and shopping takes longer, but I get good food and great value for money. Services in times of austerity are doing the same.

- Can a family member or friend help support the person to engage with local community services? What are the 'circles of support' around the person?

- Could we find services in the community that the person may be interested in and support the person to engage with these?

- Is there existing support from, for example, housing that could be used to deliver part of the care plan?

- Could I create a detailed care and support plan and therapeutic interventions that could be delivered by someone that the person trusts?

- Could assistive technology help the person?

- Are there therapeutic services that the person can access?

- Could a direct debit be used to employ someone to follow a devised care and support plan?

- How can I think outside the box and solve the resource dilemma?

We are in a time of transformation within services today and social work in particular is at a time when reflection and learning from times of historical austerity is required. I am old enough to recall social work during the reign of Margaret Thatcher and the severe austerity measures imposed. I enjoyed the challenges and the creativity that developed in workers. I worked then as a community social worker, connecting people within a designated community. Today you may hear talk of asset-based social work. One of the most valuable things that we can do when working with someone who self-neglects is re-engage them with people and meaningful relationships. People in the community, family and genuine friendships are of prime importance. The Care Act 2014 sought to develop community level services, where the whole community is considered for change rather than the community support of individual families or people. The key aim is community capacity building rather than individual intervention (Barnes *et al.* 2006). Community-based services and community social work seek to link individuals and families with other people and services within the community, developing community strength resilience and support.

Figure 7.2: Aspects of community practice (adapted from Banks *et al.* 2003).

- Developing community work not only benefits those who self-neglect but all sorts of people within the community. Links are created between local residents and community police, community centres and local businesses. People get to know each other and look out for one another. Community social work helps to link people and resources within communities and aims to prevent the need for statutory intervention. The ideal is that the community is developed to be largely self-sustaining and supportive of its own citizens. Below is an example of excellent community social work that I have experienced:

- Sean has autism and lives with his older brother. The brothers eat from the local takeaway as neither can cook. Used takeaway cartons of half-eaten food are mounting around the house. Both brothers find organising and sorting things difficult and have not had much experience of cleaning. Their mother did all the cleaning until she died two years ago. Both brothers love technology and are particularly good with computers and mobile phones. The garden is beautiful, as their father had been a local gardener and had taught them how to look after and maintain gardens.

Figure 7.2 Community practice

Sarah is 75 and has arthritis in both her legs, causing pain when she walks. Sarah is an excellent cook and enjoys baking; however, she struggles to get to the shops. Sarah uses a wheelchair when she gets out of the house but has no family living locally and so rarely gets the opportunity to get out. Sarah can no longer manage her garden and gets upset about how messy it looks.

John is 15 and is looking to gain experience working with people and eventually wants to work in a hotel. John wants to study catering and is particularly interested in baking.

The social worker introduced Sarah to John and his brother and told them how good a cook Sarah is. Sarah now goes around to the brothers' house on a weekly basis and teaches them new meal recipes and supports them to learn the cooking methods described. The brothers are now eating healthy food.

The social worker also introduced Sarah, Sean and his brother to John. John takes Sarah out shopping once a week and in return Sarah teaches him her old baking recipes. Once a week the brothers also take Sarah out shopping and when they return they tidy her garden. John has started to teach the brothers how to organise and tidy their house and in particular the kitchen, ready for the cookery lessons. Both John and the brothers are teaching Sarah to use the internet and how to video call her relatives who live abroad. Sarah has told her neighbour Fred about how great the boys are at teaching her to use the internet. Fred suggests that the brothers could start their own business repairing computers and phones, or teaching people to use them. The brothers are testing this out and are offering a free service at the local community centre.

Working within a small community area the social worker gets to know every person in the area and helps to make connections with services and people. There is always someone there to recognise if a person has not been seen for a day or two, or if rubbish is building up, or if someone is isolated. Community social work sews communities back together to be supportive and transformative.

Where people within communities have complex needs then other aspects of social work may be required:

Individual social work

This is traditional care management-type social work, focused on the person themselves, their needs and outcomes. The task is to undertake assessment and create a care plan to meet the needs and maintain wellbeing. This type of social work is very person-centred. The person

Is safeguarded from abuse and neglect, including self-neglect. The downside to only having this type of social work is that there are never enough hours to assess the person, within the family and within the community. Family strength and resources or community strengths and resources may go unidentified. This is a costly service that largely involves the commissioning of resources to meet needs. Therapeutic social work assessment and approaches are not used.

Therapeutic social work

Therapeutic social work uses forms of therapeutic assessment and intervention designed and delivered by the social worker, or developed for someone else to deliver. Psychological approaches identified within this book are used as tools to both assist the person in ongoing change and development and determine a clearer picture of the person and their goals. In cases where abuse and neglect or serious trauma have occurred, it is advisable that a psychologist leads interventions. In the absence of access to psychology, the social worker may be able to seek psychology supervision while undertaking assessment and therapeutic intervention with someone self-neglecting.

Family social work

In safeguarding adults, the Care Act identifies a whole-family approach, which means that we must consider everyone actively involved in the person's life. This may be a person providing care and support, or a family member who is struggling to cope and neglecting themselves as a result of providing care and support. The dynamics of the family will need to be explored, how the family interacts, communicates and supports each other. Barriers, obstacles and ability to provide care and support require assessment. This approach sees the person as part of a family and aims to support the family to function well. Considerations of vulnerability, children and other safeguarding matters are explored in the context of family. Any concerns regarding domestic abuse will be highlighted within the safeguarding forum, and coercive and controlling behaviours identified to enable appropriate support to be given to the person suffering domestic abuse. The importance of family and family support is recognised within this model.

- A key element of the social work process in working with people who self-neglect is to:

- empower and enable those seeking support to resolve difficulties

- break down barriers of oppression and discrimination

- increase life skills or support behaviour change to increase options

- promote independence and autonomy

- consider conflicts

- reduce or delay the need for services and maintain wellbeing

- support the person to move through a process of change towards their goals

- develop new skills or build on existing abilities

- support a person to address loss, bereavement and trauma

- balance needs, rights and responsibilities

- consider moral and ethical conflicts

- facilitate access to family and community

- maintain human rights.

To achieve this during times of austerity, an increased elderly population, increased safeguarding referrals and increased pressure on services requires creative strategies that utilise all resources available. Change must take place in the structure of services if we are to meet the outcomes and expectations of people who use our services, enable access to therapeutic interventions, and practise in an ethical manner that is justified within the law, models, methods, theories or research.

Observation, assessment, hypothesis development and exploration of potential interventions to achieve the person's desired outcomes may need to be considered and applied within a variety of social work contexts: individual/family, community and therapeutic social work. Figure 7.3 identifies the interface between the various social work models.

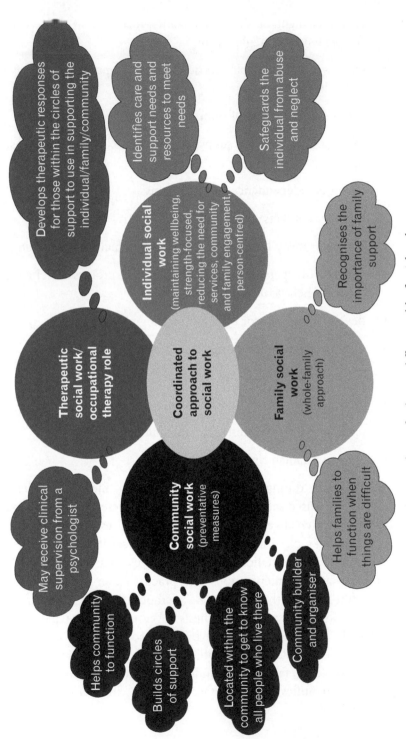

Figure 7.3: The interface between different models of social work

Governance and safeguarding adults boards

Cases of self-neglect form an increasing part of SAB work. In assessing the needs of people who self-neglect and require safeguarding within a local authority area, the difficulties, barriers to services, communication and coordination breakdowns of operational practice should be informing the purpose of the SAB to maintain wellbeing and prevent further neglect. The self-assessment process will be helpful with this. Consider the strategic and operational function identified in Figure 7.4 in relation to cases of self-neglect.

SAB core duties, goals and missions should be translated into operational outcomes, and in cases of self-neglect this may be measured by whether the strategic processes are supporting practitioners to achieve operational objectives.

If a key principle is prevention of abuse or neglect and resources are not deployed as preventative strategies (in cases of self-neglect), determine what the barrier is and how that barrier can be removed. Does the remit of prevention need to be redefined to support the practitioner operationally, for example when is prevention work prioritised? If the philosophy is making safeguarding personal and the practitioners are afraid, or feel unable to support autonomous decisions made by a capacitated person, how can the SAB support practitioners to achieve this across all agencies? If the philosophy is zero tolerance of abuse and neglect across the SAB, how can partners ensure that services are accessible to ensure this? For example, if a person self-neglecting has no defined mental health treatment pathway but diagnosis would still be useful for capacity assessment purposes and access to therapeutic services, how can the barrier of access be supported strategically? If the person is drinking and capacity is fluctuating and mental health deteriorating, how can services be more accessible to the person and work together?

In defining performance and indicators of operational performance, how often are practitioners working with cases of self-neglect feeling stuck? Practitioners and managers who are going around the same cycle of anxiety and concern for the deteriorating wellbeing of the person self-neglecting and the strategic barriers to providing consistent care provision are beyond their operational function or ability to change things. In defining indicators of operational performance, senior managers may need to consider chairing strategy meetings for self-neglect cases where risks are escalating and there are strategic barriers to services, coordination, information sharing and the passing of leadership.

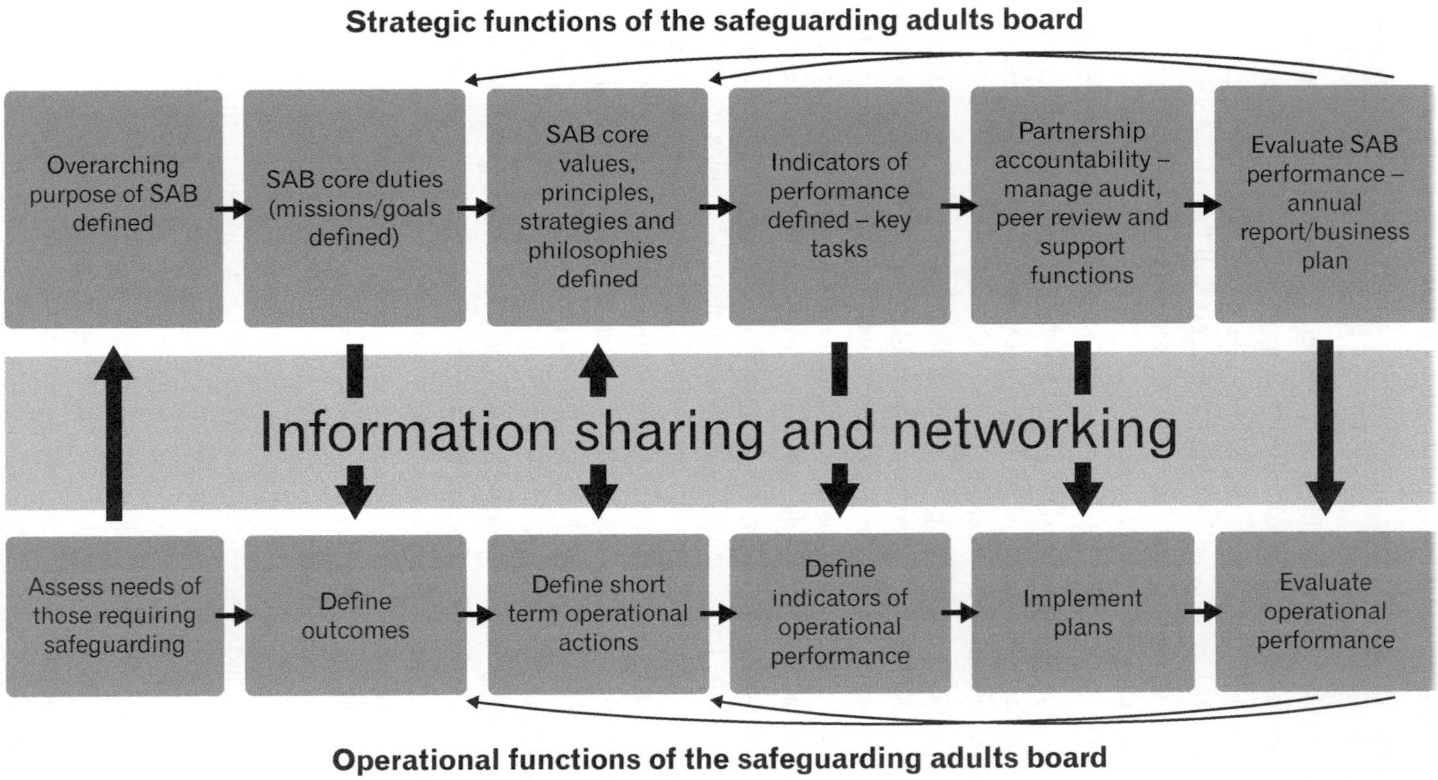

Strategic functions of the safeguarding adults board

Overarching purpose of SAB defined →

SAB core duties (missions/goals defined) →

SAB core values, principles, strategies and philosophies defined →

Indicators of performance defined – key tasks →

Partnership accountability – manage audit, peer review and support functions →

Evaluate SAB performance – annual report/business plan

Information sharing and networking

Assess needs of those requiring safeguarding →

Define outcomes →

Define short term operational actions →

Define indicators of operational performance →

Implement plans →

Evaluate operational performance

Operational functions of the safeguarding adults board

Figure 7.4: How the safeguarding adults board (SAB) works

Safeguarding adults boards will need to review, audit and support partners to understand and apply key safeguarding tools such as risk assessment and capacity assessments. Agencies and organisations should be held accountable for refusing to share appropriate and relevant information for safeguarding purposes, refusing to conduct capacity assessments or support someone conducting capacity assessments and not using effective risk-assessment processes. Processes will need to be audited, including a multi-agency audit process to collectively look at standards across safeguarding adults boards and implement plans to provide guidance and support. The operational performance and confidence in working with people who self-neglect will be determined when the operational practice is evaluated and practitioners identify improved confidence in safeguarding decision making and support for these vulnerable people.

Case loads and austerity

Managers and supervisors supporting practitioners will need to consider the appropriate and proportionate redeployment of resources relative to risks.

On a scale of 0–10, consider risks involved if resources are not directed towards those people self-neglecting and most in need, as a result of deteriorating mental and/or physical wellbeing:

- Risk to the person self-neglecting
  No risks identified 0 1 2 3 4 5 6 7 8 9 10 Significant risks identified

- Risk to the practitioner and manager if the person's mental and physical wellbeing significantly deteriorate and/or the person dies without thorough assessment and planned intervention
  No risks 0 1 2 3 4 5 6 7 8 9 10 Significant risks

- Housing risks, including, structure, fire, vermin
  No risks 0 1 2 3 4 5 6 7 8 9 10 Significant risks

- Risks to others
  No risks 0 1 2 3 4 5 6 7 8 9 10 Significant risks

- Credibility of safeguarding procedures
  No risks 0 1 2 3 4 5 6 7 8 9 10 Significant risks

- Credibility of local authority
  No risks 0 1 2 3 4 5 6 7 8 9 10 Significant risks

- Credibility of safeguarding adults board
  No risks 0 1 2 3 4 5 6 7 8 9 10 Significant risks

Consider this against other cases on the practitioner's case load and prioritise.

In times of austerity it is cost effective to direct resources towards early intervention and prevention. Supporting the practitioner during supervision and providing guidance, recording guidance given and escalating concerns when necessary are important aspects of a management role. Practitioners can feel isolated and alone when struggling to work with someone self-neglecting. Use the self-assessment process to assist in determining whether everything that should be considered has been considered and coordinated.

Training and professional development is important to practitioners. Cases of self-neglect can be some of the most complex cases and require experienced practitioners to coordinate safeguarding responses. Ongoing professional development should include time spent discussing cases of self-neglect within supervision sessions and learning on reflection. Training should be delivered in a way that practitioners can apply their learning to practice and make defensible decisions.

Chapter 8

CONCLUSION

You know the cases of self-neglect that everyone is afraid of, the ones where the person appears to be capacitated to make all their own decisions, refuses access or intervention from professionals and their health and mental wellbeing are deteriorating rapidly. The risks are increasing and no one knows what to do. These are the people that I am going to talk about to sum up self-neglect. If something is not going well in safeguarding, or in social work processes, these are the cases that will demonstrate the lessons that a local authority must learn and the challenges that must be addressed. These are the cases that will bring you face to face with your own social integrity, the integrity of your working environment and your partnerships.

I do not believe that anyone with capacity to make decisions about their own life, who would otherwise have a healthy and potentially good life, would choose to end their life in such a terrible state of self-neglect. I believe that there must be something permeating the person, invading their thoughts and dreams and affecting their self-esteem. It is as if an infection is affecting their thoughts and responses and preventing them from seeing the good in their own life. The practitioner must act like a social surgeon to find the origin of the infection, any complications since then and how the person has dealt with it in the past. Seeking the root of the problem could potentially save the person's life. Consider the role of a surgeon in saving someone's life:

Surgeon	Social surgeon (self-neglect)
Everyone must be clear about who the surgeon is and who is supporting them, with what jobs.	Everyone must be clear about who the lead person is and who is supporting the lead person, with what jobs.
You must develop an excellent rapport with the person for them to trust you with their life.	You must develop an excellent rapport with the person for them to trust you with their life.
You must introduce them to a small team of people important in providing the main care around them.	You must introduce them to a small team of people important in providing the main care around them.
Everyone within that team must be clear about their roles and responsibilities and dedicate the necessary time to saving a person's life.	Everyone within that team must be clear about their roles and responsibilities and dedicate the necessary time to saving a person's life.
The whole team must be clear about who the surgeon is and take guidance and instruction from the surgeon. No one must operate alone or outside the team. No one should be left with sole responsibility for the person's care until every lifesaving effort has been lawfully and ethically tried.	The whole team must be clear about who the lead is and take guidance and instruction from the lead. No one must operate alone or outside the team. No one should be left with sole responsibility for the person's care until every lifesaving effort has been lawfully and ethically tried.
The surgeon and team must develop an excellent rapport with the person, for them to trust you with their life. The person will be offered support by loved ones or someone who can speak up for them.	The lead and team must develop an excellent rapport with the person, for them to trust you with their life. The person will be offered support by loved ones or someone who can speak up for them.
You must present news in a clear, effective and sensitive manner, while being open and honest.	You must present news in a clear, effective and sensitive manner, while being open and honest.
You would not begin by removing things from the person before identifying what would replace those things. If a person's kidneys are failing then you need to seek out new kidneys, or an alternative option.	You would not begin by removing things from the person before identifying what would replace those things. Removing a person's belongings, or coping mechanisms before finding something to replace them with will not help the person.
Intervention will be proportionate to the risks presented.	Intervention will be proportionate to the risks presented.
If you do not understand something you seek out information or a professional to inform your decision and bring their specialist knowledge into the team.	If you do not understand something you seek out information or a professional to inform your decision and bring their specialist knowledge into the team.

Surgeon	Social surgeon (self-neglect)
If the condition poses a risk to professionals and other people this must be contained in a proportionate and sensitive manner.	If the condition poses a risk to professionals and other people this must be contained in a proportionate and sensitive manner.
Many trauma surgeons talk about the 'golden hours' as the interval starting immediately after the trauma is identified, where specific intervention will save lives and lack of intervention results in life loss. Once primary stabilisation occurs then further diagnostic processes begin to identify injuries that are not life threatening but which may become life endangering, or severely disabling in the future.	The golden hours for a social surgeon are those where self-neglect is identified, but the person is willing to accept help and support. You must find the root of the problem and solutions to the problem. Specific and targeted intervention is required. Once primary stabilisation occurs then further diagnostic processes begin to identify injuries that are not life threatening but which may become life endangering, or severely disabling in the future. What else is affecting the person and who can help?
Therapy and rehabilitation must be considered after such life-changing surgery.	Therapy and rehabilitation must be considered after such lifesaving intervention.
The lifesaving team must be reassured that they have exhausted all possibility of saving a person's life before withdrawing from care provision and moving on to make a person comfortable in preparation for their death.	The lifesaving team must be reassured that they have exhausted all possibility of saving a person's life before withdrawing from care provision and moving on to making a person as comfortable as possible in preparation for their death.
The lifesaving team must justify that they have exhausted all possible options, record who they have contacted, what they have ruled out and why. They must identify the decision maker in each decision – the patient themselves or the professional responsible for the decision.	The lifesaving team must justify that they have exhausted all possible options, record who they have contacted, what they have ruled out and why. They must identify the decision maker in each decision – the patient themselves, or the professional responsible for the decision (capacity assessments and outcomes).
The lifesaving team must identify that they have acted lawfully and considered their legal position, and recorded this. Is there a law that enables me to do this and is it ethical? The foundation law will be the Human Rights Act.	The lifesaving team must identify that they have acted lawfully and considered their legal position, and recorded this. Is there a law that enables me to do this and is it ethical? The foundation law will be the Human Rights Act.
Once everyone is satisfied that everything possible has been tried without success, exploration for new possible solutions will continue, while providing care and support in a dignified and person-centred manner.	Once everyone is satisfied that everything possible has been tried without success, exploration for new possible solutions will continue, while providing care and support in a dignified and person-centred manner.

Surgeon	Social surgeon (self-neglect)
Contact will be maintained with the person but will not be overly intrusive. Dignity for the person is always considered.	Contact will be maintained with the person but will not be overly intrusive. Dignity for the person is always considered.
The surgeon can withdraw from lifesaving treatment when the appropriate care and support for the situation have been identified.	The lead can withdraw from lifesaving treatment, when the appropriate care and support for the situation have been identified.
In any potential lifesaving treatment, the possibility of death and an inquiry into death must be considered. All legal, ethical and practice decisions will be scrutinised across services and those who did not cooperate or provide necessary care and support will be identified. If the person survives then there is excellent recording and a clue about what worked, should the problem reoccur.	In any potential lifesaving treatment, the possibility of death and an inquiry into death must be considered. All legal, ethical and practice decisions will be scrutinised across services and those who did not cooperate or provide necessary care and support will be identified. If the person survives then there is excellent recording and a clue about what worked, should the problem reoccur.
Surgery is based on research and development.	Research and development is limited. You are a pioneering social surgeon who must improvise and adapt to make things work.
You cannot expect a junior doctor or a nurse to lead lifesaving surgery. Senior staff must manage a surgeon's time effectively in order that they can operate to save lives. Respect must be given to those who operate in the most complex and difficult circumstances and it must be acknowledged that not everyone who is dying can be saved. No one should give up, but consideration to the person's own comfort and dignity must be considered.	A lead must break down barriers in access to services and break down the person's defence barriers so that they accept care and support and begin to trust. A lead coordinates a team of people to save lives. A lead who seeks therapy and rehabilitation for the person is someone who operates in the most complex and difficult circumstances. They must be given the ability and credibility to achieve the task. Safeguarding under the Care Act enables the lead to use the law to get people to share information, respond to communication and take action. Where this begins to fail, the lead must hold people accountable and challenge at a more senior level. The complexity of this role must be appreciated, respected and acknowledged. They have an important lead in the decisions made that could be life or death decisions.

A surgeon has empirical evidence, in other words data recorded and analysed by scientists and determined as ethically and medically suitable to treat certain conditions. A social surgeon is often not given this evidence, as the research has not been conducted yet and the access to psychology and exploration of the person's therapeutic needs are often denied due to lack of empirical evidence for a source of treatment. This becomes a vicious circle caused by a lack of understanding and respect for the difficult job that is required to save a person's life when they are self-neglecting. A surgeon would not be able to operate if refused the access to lifesaving treatments and therapies and in the same way the social surgeon must be empowered and enabled to operate. Further research is required to understand therapeutic interventions and enable access to psychological interventions and potential medical support and treatment in order that we can save the lives of those people whose self-neglect is critical.

When it comes to life and death situations, like medical consultants we must have open, honest and frank conversations with people, clarify what they are trying to achieve and where necessary seek legal advice. This book takes account of and is consistent with current law across the UK, including laws on decision making for people who lack capacity to make their own decisions (Mental Capacity Act 2005), the law prohibiting killing and assisted suicide, and the requirements of the Human Rights Act 1998. Nothing described within this book is intended as a legal statement or substitute for legal advice. All practitioners must seek further legal advice when there is uncertainty about how a particular decision might be viewed in the law, in the jurisdiction in which they practise. This statement and the following information is based on that which the General Medical Council (2017) uses for end-of-life treatment. I feel that this information may be pertinent to someone self-neglecting and where there are concerns that the self-neglect may be at a stage where death may be imminent. The risks and medical factors mean that the relevant people, including medical professionals, feel that the person has:

- advanced, progressive and incurable conditions

- general frailty and coexisting conditions that mean that they are likely to die within the next 12 months

- existing conditions, if they are at risk of dying from sudden acute crisis in their condition

- life-threatening acute conditions caused by sudden catastrophic events (General Medical Council 2017).

The most challenging time in working with someone who self-neglects is when they are making an autonomous decision not to accept medical or other help and support and their wellbeing is severely affected. The most challenging decision is about when to withdraw from targeted care and support and preserve the dignity of the person in making an autonomous decision to end their life in this manner. It is difficult to accept that we might not have found the root of the problem, a way that might open up life to the person again, something that will make a difference. Sometimes the issues that have affected the person are too painful to discuss or face, sometimes the person is so tired that they do not want to fight anymore and to treat this person's views with respect and provide them with a dignified end to life becomes more important.

Many years ago, I worked with someone severely self-neglecting, drinking excessive amounts of alcohol, refusing to eat, with a very low body mass index, and refusing to engage with any medical treatment. Engagement with therapeutic interventions was tokenistic. The family of the young woman paid for expensive medical and therapeutic interventions as well as the health and local authority interventions. The multi-disciplinary team tried everything that they could to engage the woman in treatment.

My manager kept telling me to close the case, that the woman had made her choice and that clearly everything had been tried. I couldn't do this and so I continued trying to find a solution that I knew did not exist. My manager said that sometimes there is a boundary between intervening and interfering in a person's life and when someone clearly decides that they have had enough and that they do not want further intervention, then we must explicitly discuss this with them, determine whether they fully understand the consequences of their decision and stop providing the support as requested. Family must be made aware and involved but where it is the decision of a capacitated adult then family cannot make decisions for them. My manager told me that sometimes when someone's life gets as bad as it can get, they get a shock and begin seeking help and support themselves, and interference in that process can be negative. I didn't agree and kept trying and trying along with the other professionals involved.

The woman died, quietly and peacefully at home, her body no longer able to sustain itself. The enquiry ruled that there was nothing else that could have been done to save the woman's life. I asked that a note be placed within the enquiry that I disagreed to some extent with this statement, that perhaps planned and sensitive withdrawal from care and treatment at the request of the woman may have made the difference. My manager came from a theological background before arriving within social work and I read more about these life and dignity in death situations and in the end I understood why we need to respect autonomous decisions about death in the same way that we do about life. It may be very important to the person themselves.

Kerrie Wooltorten (2009) was someone who posed a similar challenge to medical professionals. Kerrie had a history of mental ill health and had tried on a number of occasions to end her own life. Kerrie sought legal advice and wrote down her decision while capacitated. Kerrie's letter said that should she arrive in hospital, after taking an overdose or any attempt on her life, that she wanted no lifesaving treatment to be given. Kerrie was clear that she was aware of the consequences of her decision and took full responsibility for it. The coroner William Armstrong reflected on a similar case, the case of St George Health Care NHS Trust versus S (1999) and it was held on appeal that 'Even when his or her life depended on receiving medical treatment, an adult of sound mind was entitled to refuse it.' The law of Tort identifies that to impose treatment against the capacitated wishes of the person constitutes assault and reflects case law pertaining to trespass to a person. Kerrie said that she would accept treatment to make her comfortable.

An open and transparent conversation needs to be had with a person about the consequences of their decisions and at what point they would accept intervention and what intervention they would choose. Legal advice will need to be sought at this point and it may be useful to have legal representation during any multi-agency meetings when people self-neglecting reach this stage. There is little written about the consequences of self-neglect and how end of life should be managed both practically and ethically and this is certainly an area for further medical and psychological research.

End-of-life guidance from the General Medical Council suggests that the evidence of the benefits of any intervention should be weighed with the burdens and the risks. In some medical cases, ongoing intervention will only prolong the dying process or cause the person unnecessary distress. The task of determining this in medical cases in hospital may be complicated, however, in cases of self-neglect where all medical treatment is refused and access to the person limited, the task of determining whether everything possible has been tried and that the person would benefit from withdrawal of intervention is even more complex. No safeguarding adults review or adult serious case review has directly addressed this matter, which is an important area for all practitioners in learning lessons and ensuring dignity and respect for autonomy.

In matters relating to end-of-life care the General Medical Council identifies the importance of the Human Rights Act 1998. Within medical law there is a presumption in favour of prolonging life. This presumption requires the practitioner to take all reasonable steps to prolong a patient's life. There is no absolute obligation to prolong life irrespective of the consequences for the patient, and irrespective of their views if they can be found out. The guidance also states that:

> You should not withdraw treatment if doing so would involve significant risk for the patient and the only justification is resource constraints. If you have good reason to think that patient safety is being compromised by inadequate resources, and it is not within your power to put the matter right, you should draw the situation to the attention of the appropriate individual or organisation and act upon your concerns. (General Medical Council 2017)

In cases of self-neglect where a practitioner thinks that services are being withdrawn due to lack of resources and finances and against the needs and wishes of the person, then this will become a safeguarding matter, defined within the remit of organisational abuse.

The issue regarding whether self-neglect meets criteria for end-of-life care, without empirical medical evidence of physical health problems, requires further discussion and research. It is a debate that all parties involved in self-neglect cases appear reluctant to have and one for which there is little specific case law. Without this discussion and research, safeguarding adults reviews continue to make recommendation after recommendation about what practitioners should be doing, but not when they must stop taking action and consider a person's human rights, discussing with the person the choices that they are making, where they see these choices taking them and whether they can weigh up the risks in making these choices, if their view is that the choices will lead to their death. The right to private life, the right not to be treated in an inhumane or degrading manner, the right to freedom of thought, conscience and religion, the right to be free from discrimination, the right to liberty, and the right to peaceful enjoyment of possessions will need to be considered in determining whether action is beneficial to the person or whether the person has the capacity to make an autonomous decision to end their life in this way without imposed support or treatment. More cases need to be considered within the Court of Protection under the inherent jurisdiction of the court before the person dies. This way some precedence can be established and developed.

FINAL CHECKLIST

Tool	Question	Achieved
ELIGIBILITY – THREE-PART TEST Safeguarding duties apply to an adult who: Has needs for care and support → Is experiencing or at risk of abuse and neglect → As a result of those care and support needs is unable to protect themselves from either the risk or experience of abuse or neglect	**Eligibility** Has self-neglect been appropriately identified by all relevant parties and are all parties in agreement that the person meets the eligibility criteria? *Record why person meets eligibility or why they were deemed not to meet eligibility.*	
Safeguarding team undertake, coordinate and manage procedures Safeguarding team request actions and outcomes and feedback Local authority provides advice, guidance and oversight In cases of self-neglect, where the neglect is impacting on the person's wellbeing, multi-agency coordination will be required	**Response** Considering the person and the potential risk, has the appropriate level of response been made? S42 enquiries will determine capacity for a variety of decisions, risks to others, historical or current abuse, escalating concerns, legal frameworks and motivation. *Record why the level of response is appropriate to the risk presented.*	

Tool	Question	Achieved
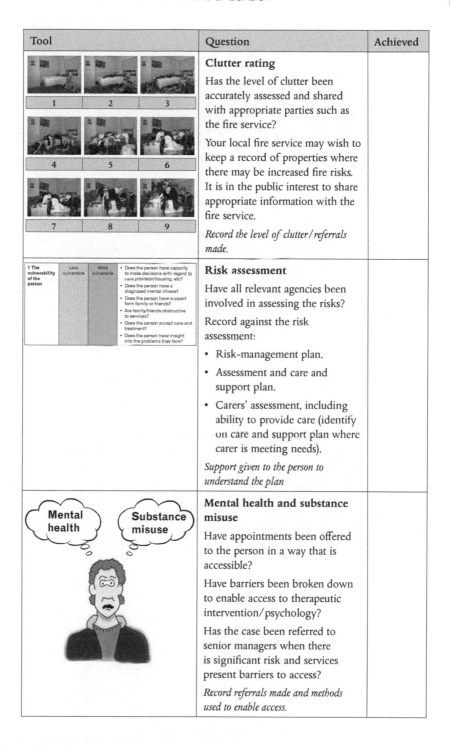	**Clutter rating** Has the level of clutter been accurately assessed and shared with appropriate parties such as the fire service? Your local fire service may wish to keep a record of properties where there may be increased fire risks. It is in the public interest to share appropriate information with the fire service. *Record the level of clutter / referrals made.*	
	Risk assessment Have all relevant agencies been involved in assessing the risks? Record against the risk assessment: • Risk-management plan. • Assessment and care and support plan. • Carers' assessment, including ability to provide care (identify on care and support plan where carer is meeting needs). *Support given to the person to understand the plan*	
	Mental health and substance misuse Have appointments been offered to the person in a way that is accessible? Have barriers been broken down to enable access to therapeutic intervention / psychology? Has the case been referred to senior managers when there is significant risk and services present barriers to access? *Record referrals made and methods used to enable access.*	

Tool	Question	Achieved
Background Risks/assessments Multi-agency response Resources available Support networks, strengths and solutions Therapuetic responses Legal processes Review JOURNEY OF SUPPORT	**Journey of support** Have you considered all aspects of the journey of support? *Record what has been ruled out and why. Justify actions taken and actions not taken. What are the gaps in your knowledge and how have you filled them?*	
1 Is there an impariment of the brain or mind? If there is not an impairment of the brain function or mind, the person has capacity to make the decision. 3 Can the person weigh up the pros, cons, consequences and risks of the situation? 2 Can the person keep up with you while you are explaining (retain)? 4 Can the person communicate their decision to you in some way? If the person can't understand or retain or weigh up or communicate (an inability to do one of these things) then they lack capacity to make that decision at that time.	**Capacity and consent** Has each agency undertaken, or supported someone to undertake capacity assessments? Have agencies been held accountable for capacity assessments? Has someone coordinated capacity assessments? *Record the outcomes of all capacity assessments and who the decision maker will be (the person or the professional). Individual agencies should maintain copies of all capacity assessments.*	

Tool	Question	Achieved
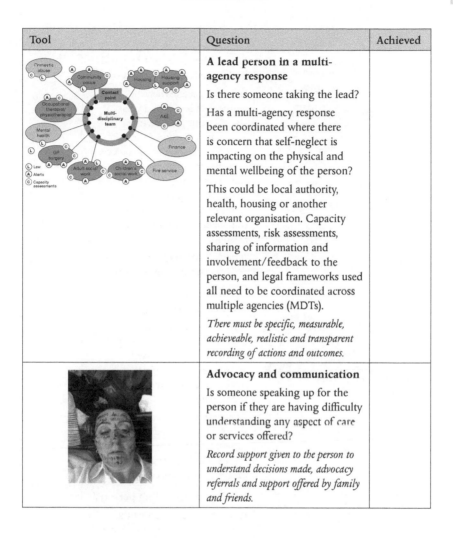	**A lead person in a multi-agency response** Is there someone taking the lead? Has a multi-agency response been coordinated where there is concern that self-neglect is impacting on the physical and mental wellbeing of the person? This could be local authority, health, housing or another relevant organisation. Capacity assessments, risk assessments, sharing of information and involvement/feedback to the person, and legal frameworks used all need to be coordinated across multiple agencies (MDTs). *There must be specific, measurable, achieveable, realistic and transparent recording of actions and outcomes.*	
	Advocacy and communication Is someone speaking up for the person if they are having difficulty understanding any aspect of care or services offered? *Record support given to the person to understand decisions made, advocacy referrals and support offered by family and friends.*	

Tool	Question	Achieved
Peeling back the layers of assessment. Adapted from Maslow's Hierarchy of Need	**Comprehensive, holistic and multi-agency assessment** Have you asked when the self-neglect began and what was happening at the time? Have you determined how the person is attached to the objects (hoarding)? Have you considered culture and background? Have you assessed carers' needs? Consider sanctions or imposed compliance issues affecting the person. *Record all aspects of the assessment and key elements of other agencies assessment.*	
	Information sharing (ten steps) Have I shared relevant information with all relevant parties? Have I addressed any barriers to information sharing and escalated concerns appropriately? *Record what information has been shared with whom and for what purpose – particularly pertinent if the information is shared without the consent of the person concerned.*	
	Making safeguarding personal Have you made sure that the principles of safeguarding have been applied within every intervention? *Record any conflicts*	
	Ethics and values Do all parties consider that decisions have been made in a manner that considers a balance of ethics and values? *Record any ethical decision-making processes, conflicts and how the conflicts were resolved.*	

Tool		Question	Achieved
Article 2 Right to life	Article 3 Right not to be tortured or treated in an inhumane or degrading way	**Management supervision and support** Have you escalated concerns to senior managers where there is a risk of severe deterioration of mental or physical wellbeing?	
Article 5 Right to liberty	Article 8 Right to a private and family life	Have the human rights of the person been considered across agencies at the appropriate level of responsibility?	
Article 14 Right to be discriminated against in relation to any of the human rights listed here	Article 9 Right to freedom of thought, conscience and religion	Where the human rights of a person have been adversely affected has this been justified in a lawful manner, or has the court made a decision regarding this matter?	
Article 1, Protocol 1 Right to peaceful enjoyment of possessions		*Record senior management decision making and rationale. Record outcome from any court ruling or recommendation.*	

Tool	Question	Achieved
Once you have completed all aspects of assessment and intervention a multi-agency meeting will need to be held to ensure that: • all possible support and action have been conducted to an appropriate standard by all agencies involved • the person has been supported to understand all decisions that they need to make • capacity assessments are in place that clearly indicate whether the person is the decision maker, or a particular professional has had to make a best interest decision on the person's behalf (with advocacy support for the person) • advocates have been made available to the person where relevant • the person has had appropriate access to any relevant therapeutic interventions and Mental Health Act and substance misuse assessments • any risks to others have been considered and addressed • assessments are comprehensive enough to consider historical loss, trauma, bereavement and abuse and the impact that this may have on the person • all agencies that could have supported the person have been involved and information has been shared • all agencies have understood their roles, responsibilities and the aspects of care and support that they are accountable for (individual agency records are sufficient to support accountability) • there has been a clear and consistent lead identified throughout the support of the person • all agencies agree that any potential actions that could be taken to prevent deterioration of physical and mental wellbeing have been taken • there is a realistic way for the person to gain care and support in the future agencies remain in contact with the person in a way that the person themselves finds the most helpful (capacitated decision regarding contact) and that would recognise deterioration of their ability to make decisions should this occur. If the multi-agency meeting has considered all these factors and public sector services have tried everything possible to prevent deterioration of mental and physical wellbeing, they have met Article 2 of the Human Rights Act by ensuring that practice has not been negligent and that all possible efforts have been made to preserve life. All parties must agree that decisions made by the person do not adversely affect anyone else, are autonomous decisions, made without coercion and that the person is not so mentally unwell that they require detaining under the Mental Health Act. Then under Article 8 of the Human Rights Act the person is entitled to a private life, where although decision making may not be seen by others as wise, the person is entitled to make these decisions that may ultimately result in their own death. We must all be reassured that the person recognises the consequences of their decision making and can get in touch for help and support at any stage.		

Epilogue: A Final Thought from the Philosophical

Consequentialism is the view that morality is all about producing the right kind of outcomes and consequences. Consider what you think morality is? Do you feel morality is about relieving suffering, spreading happiness, creating freedom, promoting survival? If you believe this then you believe in consequentialism. A consequentialist perspective on a person self-neglecting may be that we must strive to promote their survival, make endeavours to promote their happiness and relieve suffering and break down the barriers of oppression and discrimination affecting their life. The Care Act 2014 comes from a consequentialist moral perspective and encourages practitioners to obtain good outcomes as far is practicably possible.

Deontological ethics are concerned with what people do and not the outcomes or consequences of their actions. This is a duty-based ethical perspective that suggests that some things are right or wrong because of the sorts of things they are. Deontologists live in a world of moral rules where you do not need to demonstrate that an act has produced good consequences, you just have to prove that it was the right thing to do and people have a duty to act accordingly.

Human rights are based in deontological ethics:

- It is right to save a life.

- It is wrong to kill, or to not prevent death.

- It is right to promote freedom and liberty.

- It is wrong to torture, degrade, or enslave a person

- It is wrong to deprive someone of their liberty

- It is right to have a religious and cultural freedom

- It is wrong to tell someone what they must believe.

Deontological thinking focuses on giving equal respect to all human beings and forces consideration and regard to be given to a single person even though they may be at odds with the interests of a larger group. As a foundation law, this is fundamentally what any court or enquirer would consider in exploring the care provided to save someone's life and protect their human rights. So while we have excellent legislation that supports good outcomes for the person, we must consider that when we no longer appear to be achieving these positive consequences of our actions then the structure of the law in health and social care seems to suggest that the 'duty of care' comes into effect and this duty is to observe all the human rights of the individual concerned. This involves a balance of decisions using the moral hierarchy fundamental to our legal system. If I cannot achieve what in my professional opinion are the best outcomes for the person then I must observe my duties in providing care and ensure that I have considered every duty and how I have tried to achieve this. Human rights, including the right to a private life and autonomous decision making, must be clearly demonstrated in the recording of how we have met our duties and responsibilities and acted in a moral and ethical manner as a public body providing care and support. This includes the shift from one form of thinking to another (consequentialist to deontological), the decision to stop trying to save a person's life and to begin preserving their autonomy and dignity while recording and justifying this.

A collective moral and ethical stance across multiple agencies in the absence of justified research and sound empirical evidence is a very difficult task to achieve and a task that should not be considered lightly either in practice or on reflection in safeguarding adults reviews. I developed the tools within this toolkit to prompt discussion across agencies, to provide a basis for case analysis and to assist with a framework for recording. This is my method of analysis and justification and I can justify my actions in legislation, models, methods, theory and research, but there is still so much more to understand and learn.

Imagine that someone with cancer is slowly dying, upset alone and in pain. The nurse refers to the hospital and the hospital says, 'Sorry we don't have the time to offer this patient treatment; they don't come in for appointments offered.' The nurse tells the doctor that the person is not able to get into the hospital and the doctor says, 'What would you like me to do, operate on them at home?' The particular form of cancer is unusual and is taking time to diagnose and meanwhile the health of the person deteriorates. The person feels anxious and depressed but the doctor says that they cannot see the psychologist or therapist until there is a clear diagnosis and a treatment pathway. The nurse goes to see her supervisor and is told that there is not time to spend on people who are dying, they have to concentrate on those they know they can save. The nurse is told to close the case. Can you imagine the outrage that would occur if this was the way our NHS was treating people? All services help the NHS to perform these vital functions to save lives and all are held accountable for their actions and responses.

We should not forget the practitioner stood at the door of someone self-neglecting, seriously ill and yet again refusing to answer. Thoughts will be running through their head. 'Do I go away, as they are capable of making their own decisions and obviously don't want to answer? What if they are too upset to answer but need help? What if something has happened to them? What if I haven't done enough to help? Am I being too intrusive if I look through the letter box to see if they are alright? What if they have had an accident?' In their busy life, they don't record all the thoughts that went through their head, the considerations and deliberations that occurred on that doorstep. They write the appointment time and that the person did not answer. Back at the office they go in to see their overworked and stressed boss and the boss says that this is a year of little engagement and the case should be closed. Worried, the practitioner argues to keep it open a little longer to see if mental health services will engage. Mental health services send three letters yet again, none of which elicits a response from the person self-neglecting and the case is therefore closed. Housing services are seeking to evict the person, as the hoarded goods are causing a danger to others. The practitioner gets to talk to the person self-neglecting through their intercom system and the person sounds confused and upset. Another safeguarding referral is made but the safeguarding team say that they have tried and there is nothing that they can do as the person is making a capacitated decision not to engage. One person left on the doorstep trying to perform social surgery with blunt instruments or no instruments at all. No team to support with knowledge, law or decision making. No support from senior staff, no recognition of the severity of the case, and the threat that they will be held accountable if something were to happen to that person. The stress is intolerable and services ask what can be done, how we sort this situation out. 'What do I do?' is a question asked at the end of a conference session as if there is one answer that will make everything OK.

The answer lies in the structure of services and safeguarding and inclusion of all the following points:

- A single point of access that can effectively triage, signpost, give advice, oversight and guidance, offer instruction and support or request actions to be taken to safeguard individuals or refer to a specialist team to make safeguarding arrangements.

- The ability to have effective initial intervention and conduct preventative work.

- The creativity to utilise family and community resources in early intervention.

- The ability to support the person to re-engage with their community, activities and interests.

- The ability to consistently risk assess through services and discuss and record against these risk assessments as an ongoing developing process.

- Consistent understanding of the levels of self-neglect and the potential impact or outcome for the person.

- An understanding of the history of the person and the psychological impact of neglect, loss, bereavement or trauma (in the widest sense).

- All agencies recognising and being held accountable for appropriately assessing capacity.

- Understanding of the differing legislative frameworks and conflicts.

- The recognition of when to stop striving against the person to develop positive outcomes and determine when to consider the human rights as a basis of assessment to build back towards strengths-focused and outcomes-based work.

- The collective recognition and responsibility (at sufficient senior level) to determine that all potential interventions have been tried and have failed and that the person may require comfort and dignity, respect and autonomy of choice and less intrusive intervention – a considered and planned-for approach.

- The understanding of defensible decision making and recording.

- Agencies being accountable for decision making such as relevant capacity assessments and risk assessments.

- Safeguarding that recognises the safeguarding principles in every action taken.

- Safeguarding that discusses ethics, values and morals in decision-making processes.

- A process for practitioner reflection and access to senior support.

- Coordination that has the ability to break down barriers in access to services such as psychology and therapy.

- Communication that is not bureaucratic but person-centred.

- Potentially, a change in social work.

- Consideration of the different therapeutic assessment processes and use of these rather than prescriptive assessments. Re-introduction of the use of therapeutic methods of assessment in practice.

- In depth and detailed assessment that gets to the heart of the person's life story and narrative that informs their decision making.

- Time devoted to those who require time in recognition of the severity or complexity of a case.

- True multi-agency work that recognises the strengths of each agency and the knowledge that they hold.

- Detailed care and support plans that identify capacity and consent, risk and risk-management, methods of communication, culture and diversity, carers' roles and responsibilities, carers' assessments and support plans, other agencies' provision to meet need.

- Access to more senior support where there is a risk that someone may die if something does not change.

- The ability to be flexible, creative and responsive.

- Recognition of housing and support services and the work they do and the offer of multi-agency support at an earlier stage of intervention.

- Clear partnerships between health, local authority, housing and police.

Ten top tips to ensure that we safeguard people who self-neglect

1. Develop a rapport

   - Get to know the person, develop a rapport and find out when the self-neglect began.

   - Discover if there has been a time when things were different – what happened and how did this occur?

   - Do not discuss change until a rapport has been developed.

   - Remember that the earlier the intervention the easier it is for the person to consider change.

   - Find activities, work or education that the person enjoyed doing and try to help them to engage in community activities.

   - Encourage the person to get out and meet other people as this may help them to reflect on their own situation. It may identify a structure for their day/week. Meeting people and being valued by others may also help in reducing the impact of trauma, loss, bereavement, abuse or neglect.

2. Build self-esteem

   • Understand what feelings the person has about themselves, their house and why things are the way that they are.

   • Consider why the person is so attached to the current situation and if they were no longer in the situation, what would replace those feelings.

3. Adopt a strengths-based approach

   • Use a strengths-based approach to determine the positive things that a person has in their life or can achieve for themselves and how they would like to manage risk.

   • Record capacity and consent issues effectively.

   • Use scaling questions – on a scale of 0–10 how do you feel about…

4. Consider methods of motivation and communication

   • Part of the change process is to have doubt, upset, anger, resentment and finally acceptance. Plan how you can manage these changes and encourage the person to engage with appropriate counselling or therapeutic support.

   • A person may well relapse, but you can help the person to start the process over again with plenty of encouragement. Consider times when you have tried to change a behaviour or give something up – it often takes a few attempts.

   • Use the miracle question.

5. Create cognitive dissonance

   • Remember that often a person can see themselves in such a negative light that it disempowers them and prevents positive change, for example, 'I have always been untidy. I could never look as good as other people.'

   • Encourage the person to recognise their strengths and then separate who they are from their behaviours. This may free that person to address the behaviours, for example, 'I know that the house is messy and cluttered, but I am an ordered and organised person' or 'I recognise that I do not bath often, but I have always been good at making quality clothes.' Focus on the positive attributes of the person.

6. Don't rush – one small step at a time

- Take one small step at a time with lots of encouragement.

- Work together to identify the key issues in relation to safety and wellbeing.

- Work on making the person and property safe.

- Support the person in identifying what is important to them and what they would like to sort out first.

- Give lots of positive reinforcement.

- Consider the need for a multi-agency response: nursing, social work, public health, environmental services, housing, fire service, police, GP, mental health services in relation to assessing, preventing and addressing risk, support for the person and their family, communication, capacity assessments, coordinating legal frameworks and community engagement.

- Ensure that there is a coordinated response, chaired by someone who has enough seniority to delegate tasks and respond to situations. An action plan should be developed.

- Consider the assessment of any carers and the capacity of carers to provide care and support.

7. Consider wider safeguarding issues

- Consider wider safeguarding issues such as:

  - hate crime

  - domestic abuse

  - anti-social behaviour

  - safeguarding other adults

- safeguarding children

- historical abuse

- risk from potential perpetrator to person and others.

8. Do not force change if at all possible

- Remember that moving the person only moves the difficulties to another place, unless the underlying factors are addressed.

- If eviction is being considered, think about how to support the person to meet their needs before self-neglect escalates.

- Often the sense of loss associated with large-scale clean-ups and eviction can have a negative impact. Try to minimise this.

- Don't forget to use the least restrictive, least intrusive intervention possible – safeguarding principles apply to all actions.

9. Do not forget defensible decision making

- Consider:

    - referrals made (including safeguarding adults/ children, mental health, police, fire service, medical)

    - who was involved and who has been asked to be involved

    - appointments offered

    - capacity assessments by who and when

    - access to advocacy

    - person's choices and decisions

    - support given to help the person recognise, understand (information, advice and guidance given) and make decisions

    - duty to assess and how that has been achieved

    - agencies involved – roles and responsibilities

- what was considered, what ruled out and why

- decisions based on law, policy, methods, models, theories, research

- decisions based on 'I' statements of what the person wanted to achieve, or why this was not achieved and why choices were made.

References

American Psychiatric Association (2013) *Diagnostic and Statistical Manual of Mental Disorders (5th edn.)* Arlington, VA: American Psychiatric Publishing.

Anderson, S. (2011) *Taming Your Outer Child.* New York, NY: Ballantine Books.

Arnstein, S. (1969) 'A ladder of citizen participation.' *Journal of the American Institute of Planners,* 35(4), 216–224.

Baim, C. (2015) *Using attachment theory to work with adults.* Guides. Community Care Inform. Available at: http://adults.ccinform.co.uk/guides/guide-using-attachment-theory-work-adults accessed 30 March 2015.

Baker, S.M. and Gentry, J.W. (1996) 'Kids as collectors: a phenomenological study of first and fifth graders.' *Advances in Consumer Research,* 23, 132–137.

Banks, S., Butcher, H., Henderson, P. and Robertson, J. (2003) *Managing Community Practice: Principles, Policies and Programmes.* Bristol: Policy Press.

Barker, P. (2009) *Psychiatric and Mental Health Nursing.* London: Hodder Arnold.

Barnes, J., Katz, I., Korbin, J. and O'Brien, M. (2006) *Children and Families in Communities: Theory, Research, Policy and Practice.* Chichester: John Wiley & Sons.

Bream, V. (2013) *A New Foundation for Hoarding – Introduction to the Vicious Shamrock.* Paper presented at the annual conference of the British Association for Behavioural and Cognitive Psychotherapies, London.

Bozinovski, S. (2000) 'Older self-neglecters: interpersonal problems and the maintenance of self-continuity.' *Journal of Elder Abuse & Neglect,* 12(1), 37–56.

Braye, S., Orr, D. and Preston-Shoot, M. (2014). *Self-neglect policy and practice: building an evidence base for adult social care.* Social Care Institute for Excellence. Available at: www.scie.org.uk/publications/reports/69-self-neglect-policy-practice-building-an-evidence-base-for-adult-social-care/files/report69.pdf accessed 2 March 2017.

Braye, S., Orr, D. and Preston-Shoot, M. (2015) *Self-neglect and adult safeguarding: findings from research.* Social Care Institute for Excellence. Available at: www.scie.org.uk/publications/reports/report46.asp accessed 31 March 2015.

Burrell, G. and Morgan, G. (2014) *Sociological paradigms and organisational analysis.* 1st ed. Johanneshov: MTM.

Carter, R. (2015) *Care Act 2014: Councils struggling with 'market sustainability' duty.* Community Care. Available at: www.communitycare.co.uk/2015/08/24/care-act-2014-councils-struggling-market-sustainability-duty/?year=2015&monthnum=08&day=24 accessed 25 July 2017.

Court of Protection Guidance on Tenancy Agreements (2012) Available at: www.housinglin.org.uk/_library/Resources/Housing/Housing_advice/COP_guidance_on_tenancy_agreements_February_2012.pdf accessed 1 March 2017.

Department of Health and Social Care (2017) *Care and support statutory guidance.* Available at https://www.gov.uk/government/publications/care-act-statutory-guidance/care-and-support-statutory-guidance, accessed 10 Jan 2018.

Doel, M. and Shardlow, S. (2006) *Modern Social Work Practice.* 3rd ed. Hampshire: Ashgate Publishing Ltd.

Dong, X., Simon, M. and Evans, D. (2012) 'Elder self-neglect and hospitalization: findings from the Chicago Health and Aging Project.' *Journal of the American Geriatrics Society,* 60(2), 202–209.

Dyer, C., Pickens, S. and Burnett, J. (2007) 'Vulnerable elders: when it is no longer safe to live alone.' *Journal of the American Medical Association,* 298(12), 1448–1450.

Freidson, E. (1970) *Profession of Medicine: A Study of the Sociology of Applied Knowledge.* New York: Dodd, Mead.

Frost, R., Steketee, G., Tolin, D. and Renaud, S. (2008) 'Development and validation of the Clutter Image Rating.' *Journal of Psychopathology and Behavioral Assessment,* 32, 401–417.

Frost, R., Tolin, D., Steketee, G., Fitch, K. and Selbo-Bruns, A. (2009) 'Excessive acquisition in hoarding.' *Journal of Anxiety Disorders,* 23(5), 632–639.

Frost, R. and Steketee, G. (2011) *Stuff.* Boston, MA: Mariner Books.

Frost, R., Steketee, G. and Tolin, D. (2011) 'Comorbidity in hoarding disorder.' *Depression and Anxiety,* 28(10), 876–884.

General Medical Council (2017) *Treatment and care towards the end of life: decision making.* Available at www.gmc-uk.org/guidance/ethical_guidance/end_of_life_care.asp accessed 27 July 2017.

George, C., Kaplan, N. and Main, M. (1985/1996) The Adult Attachment Interview: Interview Protocol (unpublished manuscript). University of California, Berkeley.

Gerhardt, U. (1989) *Idea's About Illness: An Intellectual and Political History of Medical Sociology.* London: Macmillan.

Gibbons, S., Lauder, W. and Ludwick, R. (2006) 'Self-neglect: a proposed new NANDA diagnosis.' *International Journal of Nursing Terminologies and Classifications,* 17(1), 10–18.

Gunston, S. (2003) 'Risk assessment and management of patients whom self-neglect: a "grey area" for mental health workers.' *Journal of Psychiatric and Mental Health Nursing,* vol. 10, no. 3.

Hacker, L., Park, J., Timpano, K., Cavitt, M. *et al.* (2012) 'Hoarding in children with ADHD.' *Journal of Attention Disorders,* 20(7), 617–626.

Hartl, T.L., Duffany, S., Allen, G.J., Steketee, G. and Frost, R.O. (2005) 'Relationships among compulsive hoarding, trauma, and attention-deficit/hyperactivity disorder.' *Behaviour Research and Therapy,* 43(2), 269–276.

Herman, J. (1997) *Trauma and Recovery. The Aftermath of violence-from domestic abuse to political terror.* New York: Basic Books.

House of Lords, (2014) *Mental Capacity Act 2005: post legislative scrutiny.* London: The Stationery Office Limited.

Human Rights Act (1998) London: The Stationery Office.

Iris, M., Ridings, J. and Conrad, K. (2010) 'The development of a conceptual model for understanding elder self-neglect.' *The Gerontologist,* 50(3), 303–315.

Jantz, G.L, (2014) 'Hope for relationships: the psychology behind hoarding.' *Psychology Today.* 5 September.

Jarrett, C. (2013) The psychology of stuff and things. *The Psychologist,* 26(8), 560–565.

Kübler-Ross, E. (1998) *The Wheel of Life.* New York, NY: Touchstone.

Landau, D., Iervolinoa, A.C., Pertusa, A., Santoa, S., Singh, S. and Mataix-Cols, D. (2011) 'Stressful life events and material deprivation in hoarding disorder.' *Journal of Anxiety Disorders,* 25(2), 192–202.

Lauder, W. (2001) 'The utility of self-care theory as a theoretical basis for self-neglect.' *Journal of Advanced Nursing,* 34(4), 345–351, 545–551.

Lauder, W., Anderson, I. and Barclay, A. (2002). 'Sociological and psychological theories of self-neglect.' *Journal of Advanced Nursing, 40,* 3, 331–338.

Lauder, W., Anderson, I. and Barclay, A. (2005) 'A framework for good practice in interagency interventions with cases of self-neglect.' *Journal of Psychiatric and Mental Health Nursing,* 12(2), 192–198.

Main, M., Hesse, E. and Goldwyn, R.S., (2008) 'Studying Differences in Language Usage in Recounting Attachment History: An Introduction to the Adult Attachment Interview.' In H. Howard and M. Steele, M. (eds) *Clinical Applications of the Adult Attachment Interview.* New York, NY: Guilford Press.

Mataix-Cols, D., Frost, R., Pertusa, A., Clark, L. *et al.* (2010) 'Hoarding disorder: a new diagnosis for DSM-V?' *Depression and Anxiety,* 27(6), 556–572.

Mental Capacity Act: Code of Practice (2014) Office of the Public Guardian.

Milner, J. and O'Byrne, P. (2002) *Assessment in Social Work.* Basingstoke: Palgrave Macmillan.

National Data Guardian (2013) *Caldicott review: information governance in the health and care system.* Available at: https://www.gov.uk/government/publications/the-information-governance-review, accessed 10 January 2018.

Nordsletten, A.E. and Mataix-Cols, D. (2012) 'Hoarding versus collecting: where does pathology diverge from play?' *Clinical Psychology Review,* 32(3),165–176.

Orem, D.E. (1991). *Nursing: Concepts of practice* (4th ed.). St. Louis, MO: Mosby-Year Book Inc.

Osman and another v Ferguson and another CA ([1993] 4 All ER 344, Bailii, [1992] EWCA Civ 8).

Pertusa, A., Frost, R.O. and Mataix-Cols, D. (2010) 'When hoarding is a symptom of OCD: a case series and implications for DSM-V.' *Behaviour Research and Therapy,* 48, 1012–1020.

Prochaska, J. O. and Di Clemente, C. C. (1986) 'Toward a comprehensive model of change.' In W.R. Miller and N. Heather (Eds). *Treating Addictive Behaviours: Processes of change.* New York: Plenum Press.

Rathbone-McCuan, E. and Fabian, D. (1992) *Self-neglecting elders.* 1st ed. New York: Auburn House.

Scourfield, J. (2003) *Gender and Child Protection.* New York, NY: Palgrave Macmillan.

Sheppard, B., Chavira, D., Azzam, A., Grados, M., *et al.* (2010) 'ADHD prevalence and association with hoarding behaviors in childhood-onset OCD.' *Depression and Anxiety,* 27(7), 667–674.

Silverman, P.R. (1969) *The Client who Drops Out: A Study of Spoiled Helping Relationships.* Brandeis University, PhD thesis.

Smale, G. and Tuson, G. (1993) *Empowerment, Assessment, Care Management and the Skilled Worker.* London: Her Majesty's Stationery Office.

Social Care Institute for Excellence (2015) *Safeguarding adults reviews under the Care Act: implementation support.* London: Social Care Institute for Excellence.

Steele, H., Steele, M. and Murphy, A. (2009a) 'The adult attachment interview: a clinical tool for facilitating and measuring process and change in psychotherapy.' *Psychotherapy Research,* 19, 1468–4381.

Steele, H., Steele, M. and Murphy, A. (2009b) 'Use of the adult attachment interview to measure process and change in psychotherapy.' *Psychotherapy Research,* 19(6), 633–643.

Steketee, G. and Frost, R. (2014) *Treatment for Hoarding Disorder (1st edn.)*. New York, NY: Oxford University Press.

Subkowski, P. (2006) 'On the psychodynamics of collecting.' *International Journal of Psychoanalysis,* 87, 383–401.

Visser, C. (2013) 'The origin of the solution-focused approach.' *International Journal of Solution-Focused Practices,* 1(1), 11–17.

Subject Index

Author Index